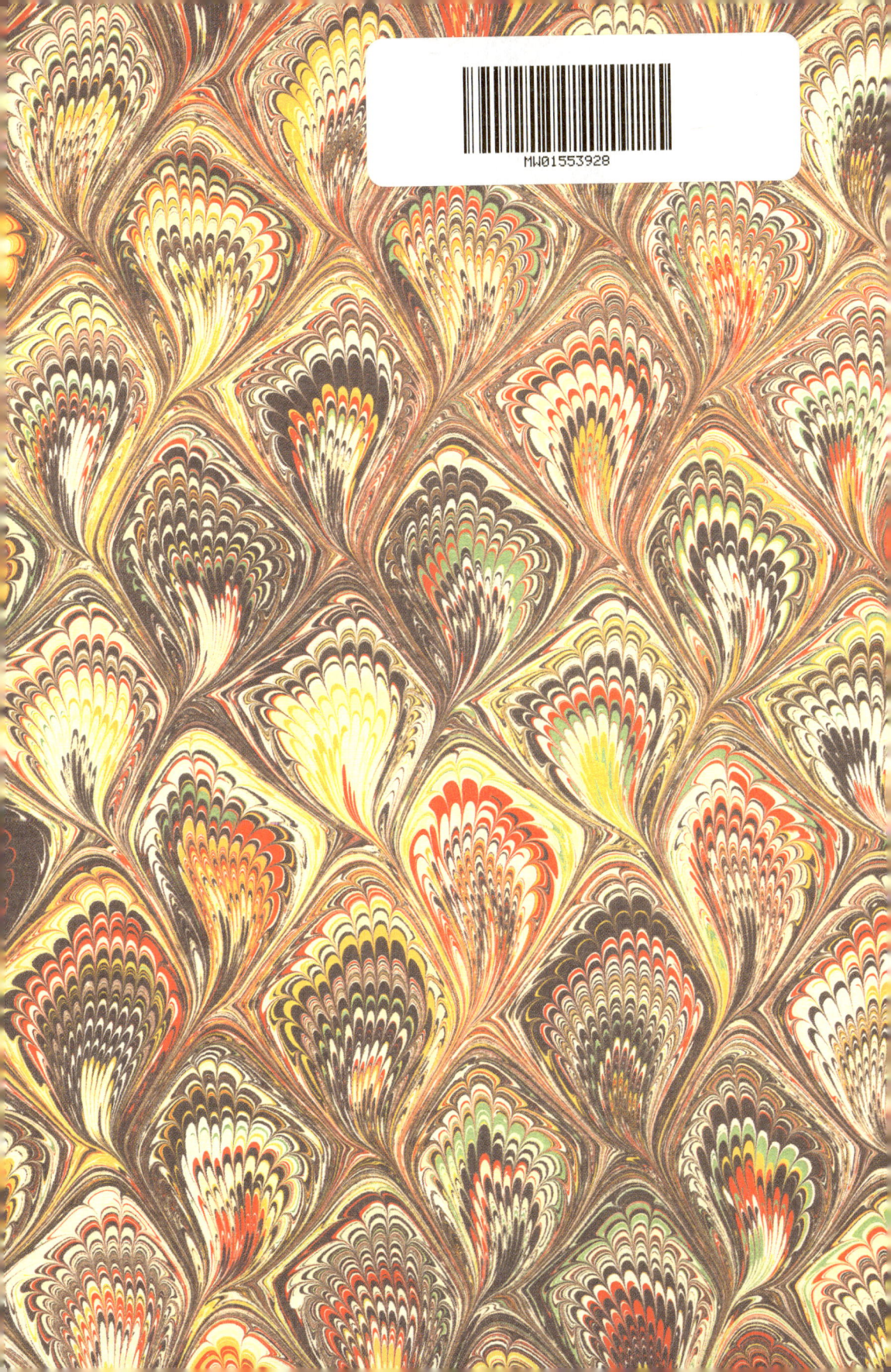

IMAGES
of America

DOWNTOWN
MINNEAPOLIS

On the Cover: Seventh Street was an extension of Minneapolis's theater row in 1916. (Courtesy of the Minnesota Historical Society.)

IMAGES
of America

Downtown Minneapolis

Iric Nathanson

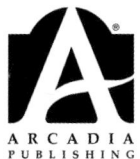

ARCADIA
PUBLISHING

Copyright © 2017 by Iric Nathanson
ISBN 978-1-4671-2437-9

Published by Arcadia Publishing
Charleston, South Carolina

Printed in the United States of America

Library of Congress Control Number: 2016941006

For all general information, please contact Arcadia Publishing:
Telephone 843-853-2070
Fax 843-853-0044
E-mail sales@arcadiapublishing.com
For customer service and orders:
Toll-Free 1-888-313-2665

Visit us on the Internet at www.arcadiapublishing.com

To Marlene.

Contents

Acknowledgments		6
Introduction		7
1.	Early Days	9
2.	Building Boom	27
3.	The New Century	47
4.	Tumultuous Decades	69
5.	Suburban Challenge	89
6.	Modern Times	107
Bibliography		127

ACKNOWLEDGMENTS

As a pictorial history, this book would not have been possible without the help of the people who shared their photographic archives with me.

They include Ted Hathaway and his staff at Hennepin County Library Special Collections, Katie Baker with the Hennepin Medical History Center, Susan Larson-Fleming with the Hennepin History Museum, Joan Mathieu with the Minneapolis Finance Department, Eric Mortenson with the Minnesota Historical Society, Mark Remme with the Minneapolis Downtown Council, Matt Liable with the Meet Minneapolis Convention and Visitors Association, Colleen Stauber with the Okabena Company, and Rodney Allen Schwartz with Westminster Presbyterian Church.

Special thanks to my editor at Arcadia Publishing, Liz Gurley, who kept me on track as this project came together over the past year.

Introduction

During Minneapolis's early years in the 1850s, the town's commercial center consisted of a few modest frame buildings clustered around the Mississippi riverfront. As Minneapolis experienced a late-19th-century economic boom, the frame structures gave way to impressive stone and brick buildings lining downtown's commercial streets. At the riverfront, a string of flour mills would soon make Minneapolis the country's milling capital.

The mills were served by a growing network of railroad lines that brought in wheat from the Midwestern prairies and shipped out flour to markets all over the world. A gracefully curving railroad bridge carried passenger trains into an imposing downtown station just up from the riverfront.

The late 19th century also brought major new civic institutions to downtown, including a public library, a city hospital, and a massive new city hall.

The early years of a new century saw new cultural and economic movements that profoundly affected life in the country's urban centers. Soon, the automobile, a hallmark of the 20th century, was a common sight on the streets of downtown Minneapolis.

Movies, another new American institution, were becoming a way of life for thousands of Minneapolitans. In the beginning, motion pictures were shown in dingy reconverted storefronts. Then, during the World War I era, theater owners started building elaborate move palaces with marble staircases and crystal chandeliers. A six-block stretch of downtown's Hennepin Avenue, lined with more than a dozen theaters, was now the city's Great White Way.

One block over from Hennepin, the city's major retail district stretched along Nicollet Avenue. The street's department stores and fashionable shops were soon attracting customers from all over Minnesota.

Just beyond Nicollet, Marquette Avenue had become the city's financial center. The large banks on Marquette extended their reach throughout the Upper Midwest with the creation of a national banking system and Minneapolis's designation as a regional center for that new system.

With the addition of several new skyscrapers, downtown started to acquire an impressive skyline. The largest of those structures, built in 1929 and modeled after the Washington Monument, dominated the city's skyline well into the post–World War II era.

The turmoil of the Great Depression brought labor strife and protests to downtown's streets. Then, with the advent of World War II, those streets were the scene of loyalty parades, bond rallies, and military recruitment campaigns

With full employment on the home front during the war years, the department stores and theaters were filled with people who had money to spend but not much that they could buy. Minneapolis emerged from the war with a thriving downtown, but there were danger signs on the horizon even as the city reached its peak 20th-century population of 521,000 in 1950.

By then, the milling industry had fallen into decline. As the mills closed, urban blight spread from the riverfront to an expanding skid row at the northern end of downtown. Known as the Lower Loop, the district was filled with sleazy bars and decrepit rooming houses. During these postwar years, a suburban boom threatened downtown's role as the region's major retail hub. Shoppers now had the option of driving to the new suburban shopping centers, with their acres of free parking, rather than contending with downtown's traffic and congestion.

Along Hennepin Avenue, the downtown theaters began losing their audiences with the advent of television. During the prewar years, moviegoers took the streetcars downtown to see the latest Hollywood hits, but soon, the streetcars themselves were gone. Now, Minnesotans were fully embracing car culture, and that culture was causing many of them to shun the inner city altogether.

Several of the theaters that did remain on Hennepin Avenue slid into decline as venues for tawdry X-rated films, casting a shadow of blight that threatened the entire downtown.

In an effort to combat this spreading urban blight, city leaders embarked on an ambitious and controversial plan to clear a large swath of the Lower Loop. Known as the Gateway Center, this urban renewal project leveled a 70-acre tract, which included several of the city's most historic sites. The Gateway succeeded in eliminating Minneapolis's skid row, but it took years for new development to occur on many of the district's empty blocks.

During the later decades of the 20th century, civic and business leaders responded to the suburban threat with several innovative development projects aimed at maintaining downtown's economic base. These included a transit mall on Nicollet Avenue and a system of enclosed second-story walkways linking downtown office buildings. During these years, local leaders rediscovered Hennepin Avenue's aging movie theaters and restored them to their original splendor as theatrical palaces, creating a new Great White Way for Minneapolis.

By the early years of the 21st century, downtown Minneapolis, now a new city neighborhood with more than 30,000 residents, had emerged as one of this country's most vibrant and forward-looking urban centers.

One

Early Days

In 1850, an early Minnesota settler named John. H. Stevens built the first permanent house in what later became downtown Minneapolis. His home on the west bank of the Mississippi River at St. Anthony Falls was built on land that was then part of the sprawling Fort Snelling military reservation. The Fort itself was located seven miles downstream at the confluence of the Mississippi and Minnesota Rivers.

St. Anthony Falls, the only true falls on the Mississippi, soon became an economic magnet for ambitious entrepreneurs from the East. With the falls as their power source, these early business leaders built a string of lumber and flour mills that sprawled along the east and west riverbanks. Separate communities sprang up on each side of the river to serve the mills. The two communities combined when Minneapolis, based on the west bank, annexed St. Anthony, its neighbor on the east bank.

The milling industry was now the engine driving Minneapolis's rapid economic expansion during the late 19th century. On the west bank, the area's largest mill was owned by an imposing Wisconsin businessman named Cadwallader Washburn. In 1873, Washburn's A Mill exploded in a fireball whose reverberations could be heard for miles around. Quickly rebuilding on the same site, Washburn used his new plant to help the city vastly expand its leading industry.

Only a few blocks from the downtown riverfront, the town's commercial center began to grow at the intersection of Minneapolis's two major streets, Hennepin and Nicollet. Initially, the area had been known as Bridge Square, because it served as an approach to an early toll bridge across the Mississippi. In 1873, Minneapolis's first city hall was built on a triangular plot of land that had originally been part of the square.

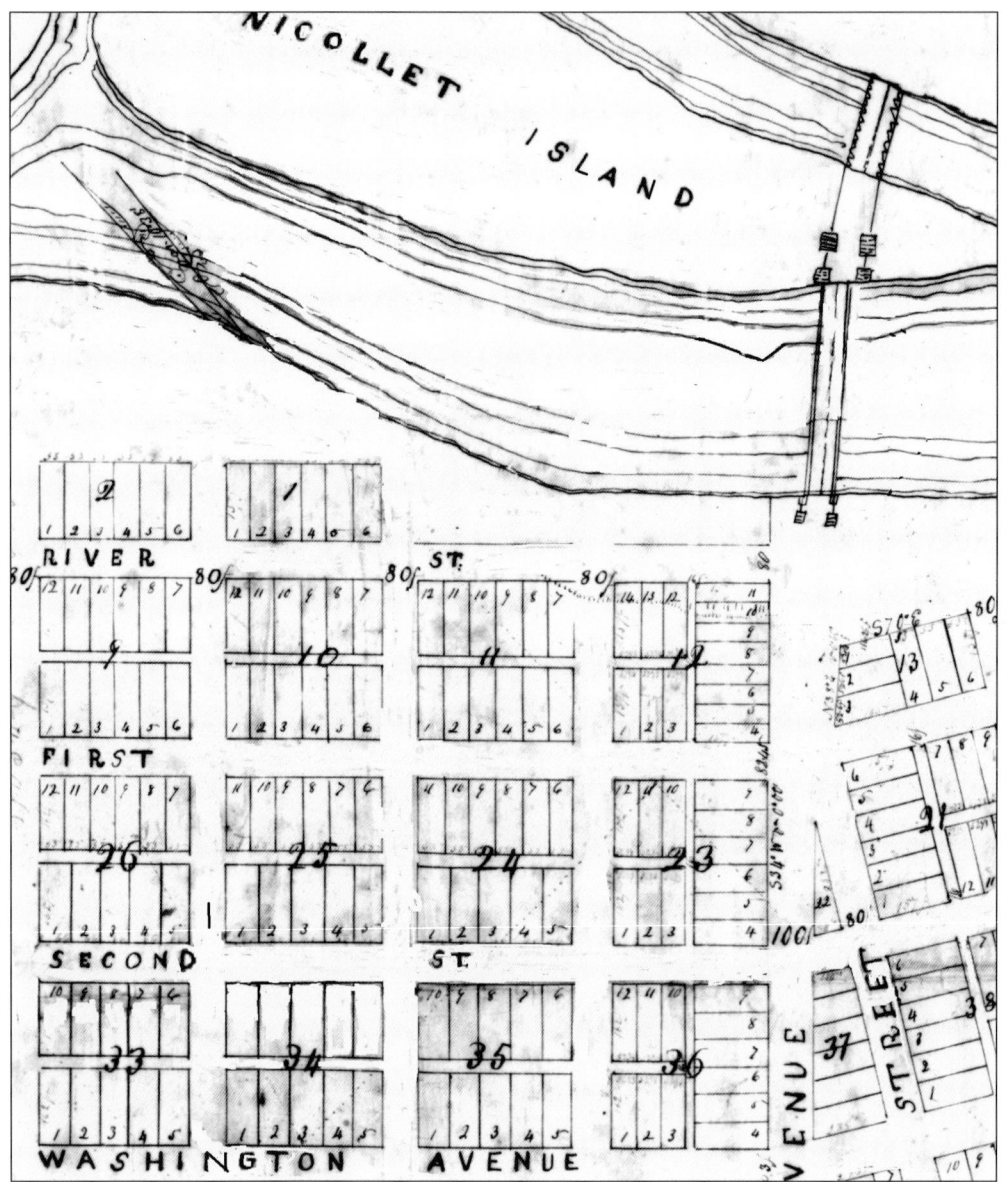

The first-known plat map of Minneapolis, created in the early 1850s, shows the street pattern for what would later become the city's central business district. While some downtown streets have been reconfigured and others have undergone name changes, Washington, Hennepin, and Nicollet Avenues, downtown's three thoroughfares, have remained at their original locations. (Courtesy of Hennepin History Museum.)

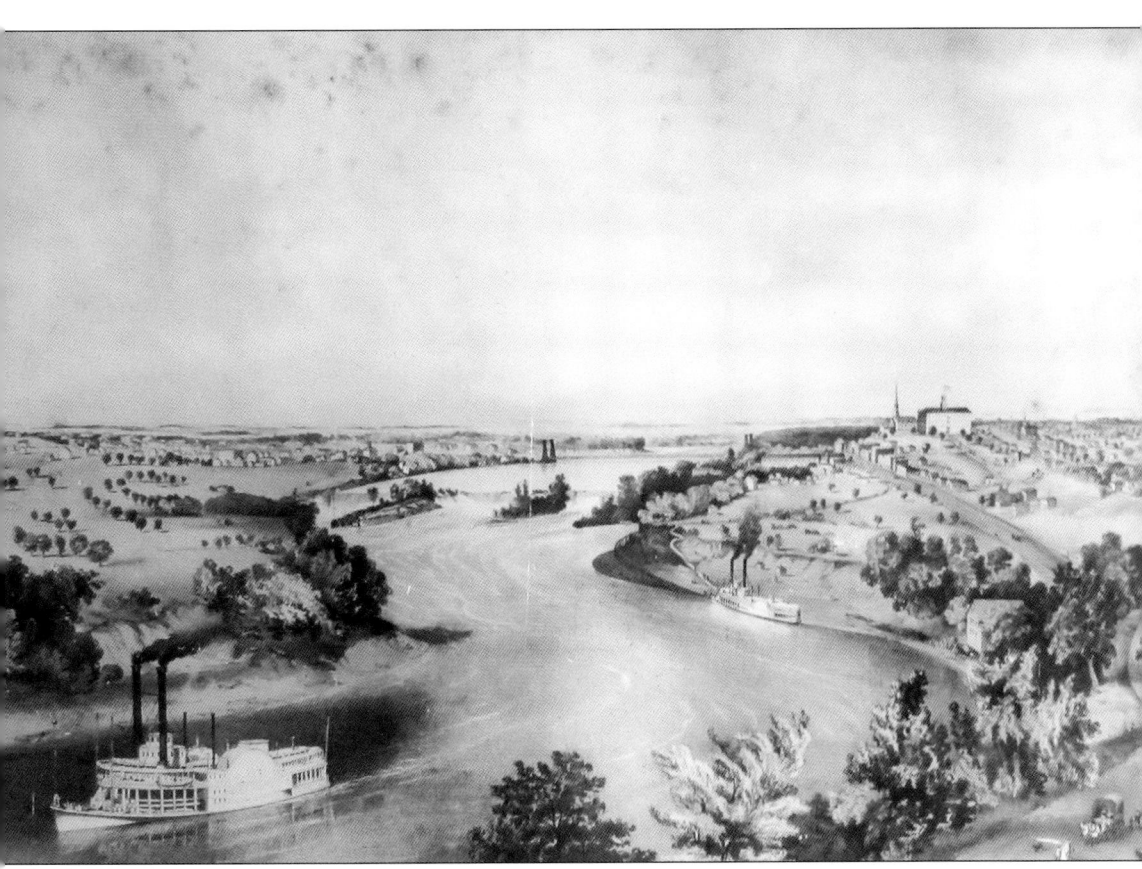

This drawing from the mid-1850s shows a steamboat traveling back downstream toward St. Paul. The boat's journey northward would have been halted at St. Anthony Falls, visible in the distance. Just beyond the falls, the first bridge spanning the Mississippi River connected the west bank settlement of Minneapolis with the east bank town of St. Anthony. (Courtesy of Hennepin History Museum.)

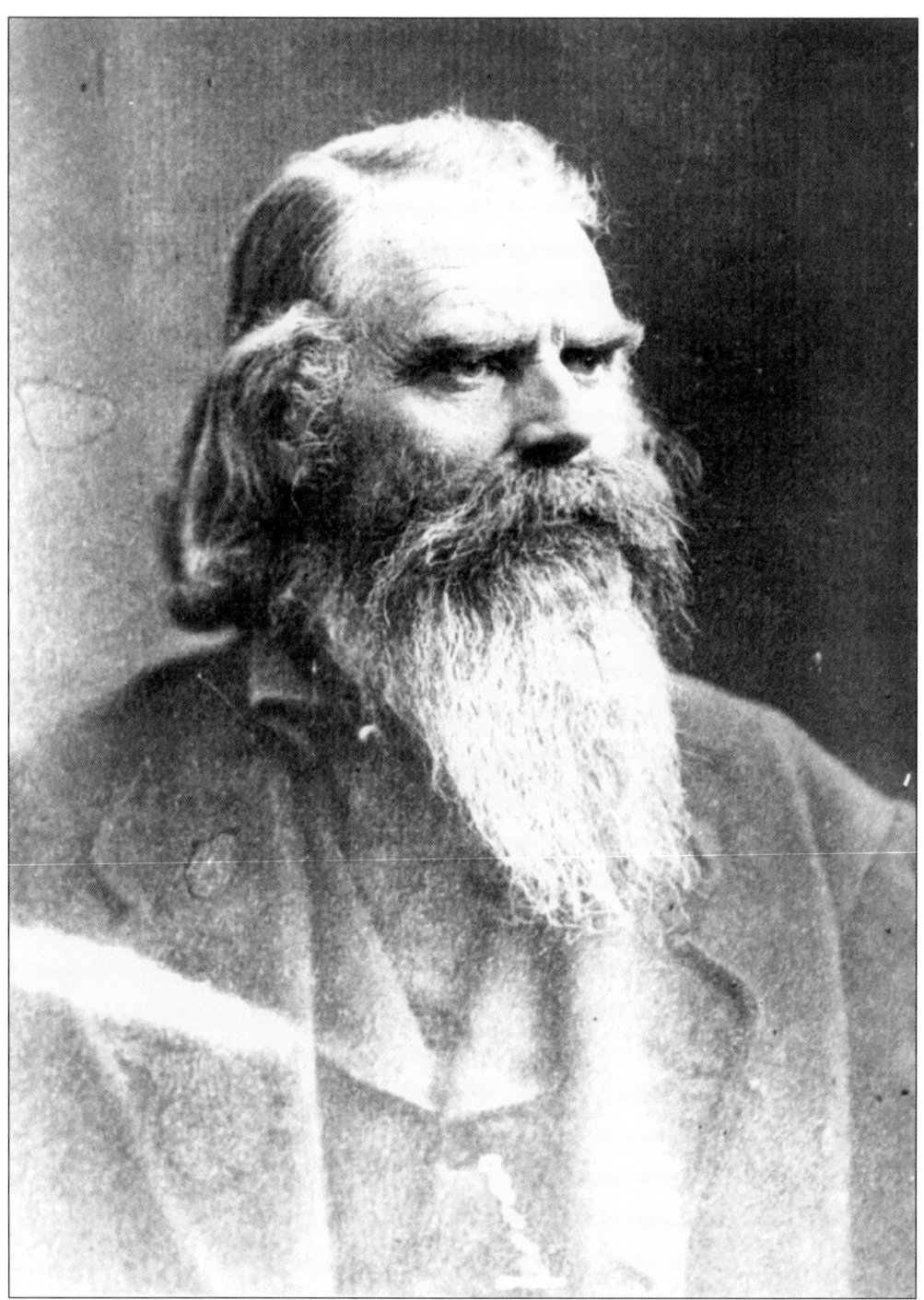
John Stevens, an early Minnesota settler, built the first permanent home in what would later become downtown Minneapolis while the area was still part of the Fort Snelling military reservation. Stevens received permission from the War Department to build a home there in exchange for providing a ferry service across the river. His home would later become a historic site, moved to a new location at Minnehaha Park. (Courtesy of Hennepin County Public Library Special Collections.)

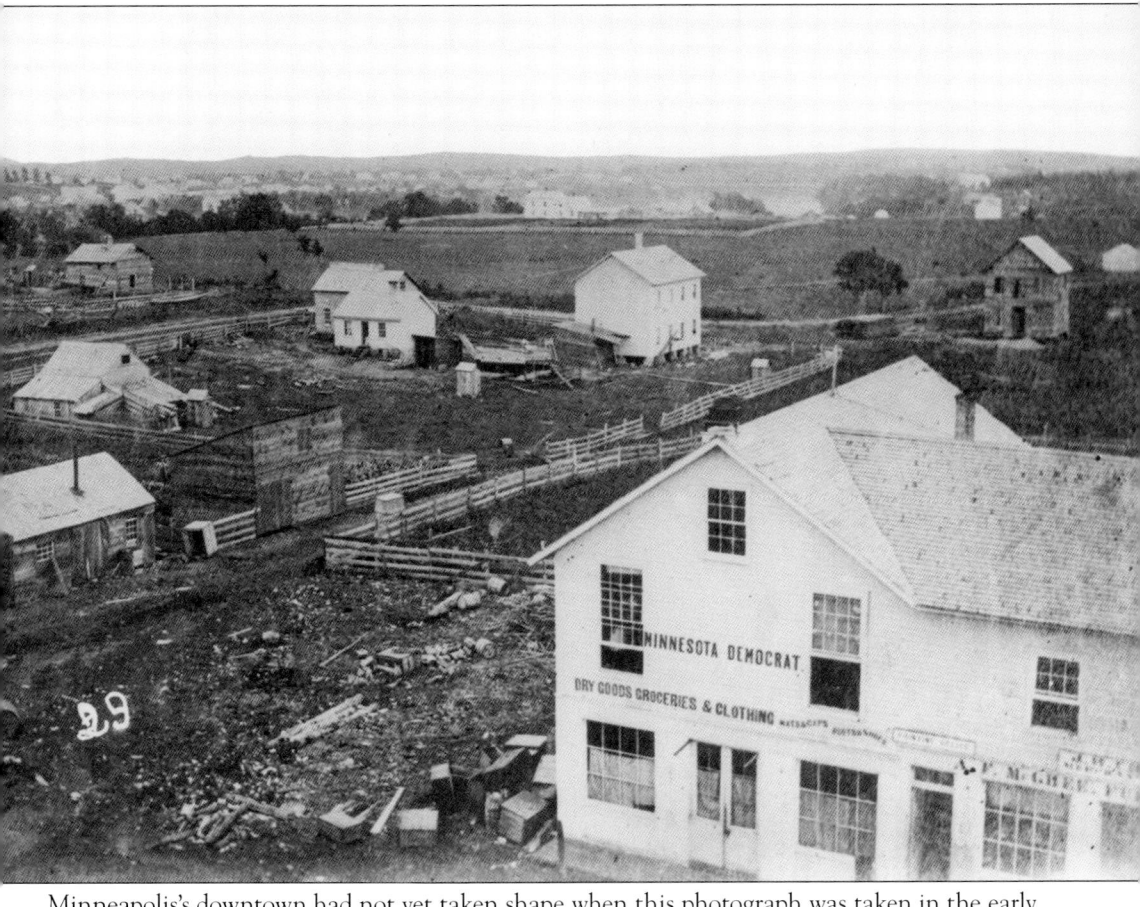

Minneapolis's downtown had not yet taken shape when this photograph was taken in the early 1850s. Then, the town site was occupied by a scattering of modest frame dwellings. The Mississippi River can be seen in distance, with the hills of St. Anthony just behind it. (Courtesy of Hennepin County Public Library Special Collections.)

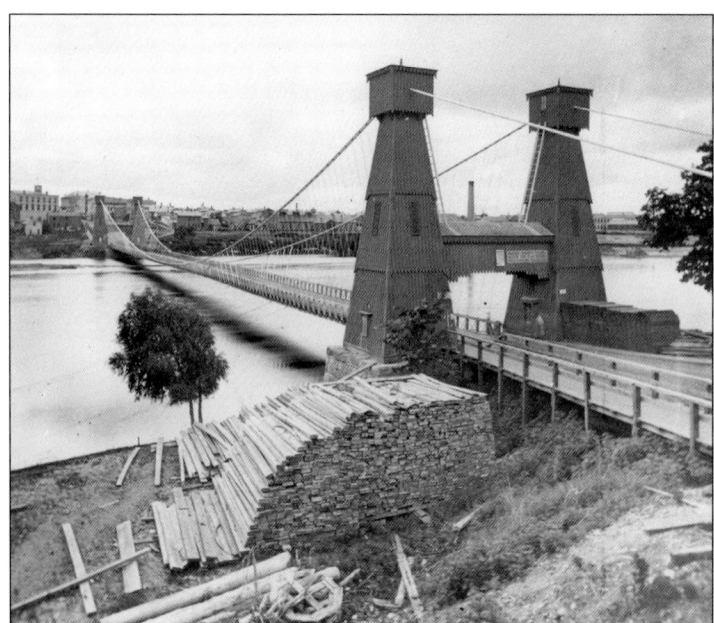

When this toll bridge opened in 1855, it was the first commercial span to cross the Mississippi River at any point along its 2,300-mile length. Travelers paid a 15¢ toll if they were on horseback but only 5¢ if they were on foot. One observer described the structure as "one of the most elegant tasteful and substantial works of art in the west." (Courtesy of Hennepin County Public Library Special Collections.)

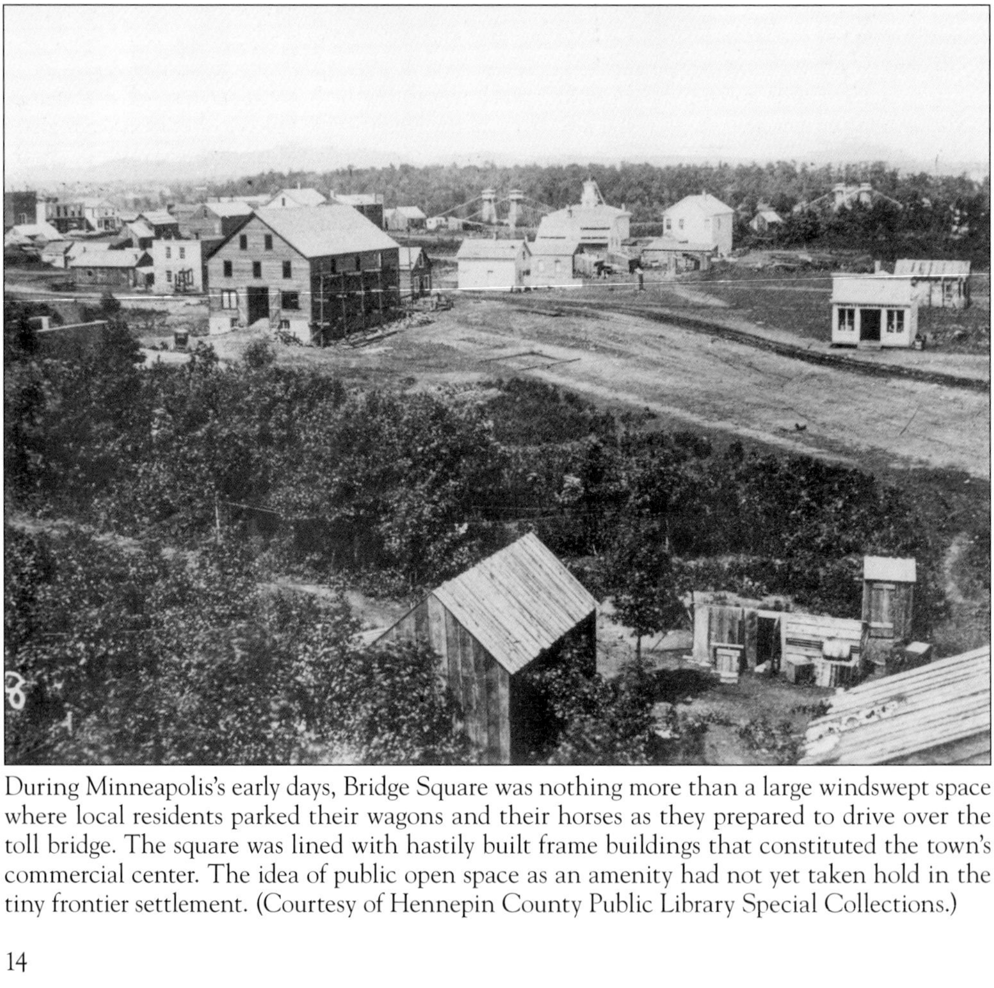

During Minneapolis's early days, Bridge Square was nothing more than a large windswept space where local residents parked their wagons and their horses as they prepared to drive over the toll bridge. The square was lined with hastily built frame buildings that constituted the town's commercial center. The idea of public open space as an amenity had not yet taken hold in the tiny frontier settlement. (Courtesy of Hennepin County Public Library Special Collections.)

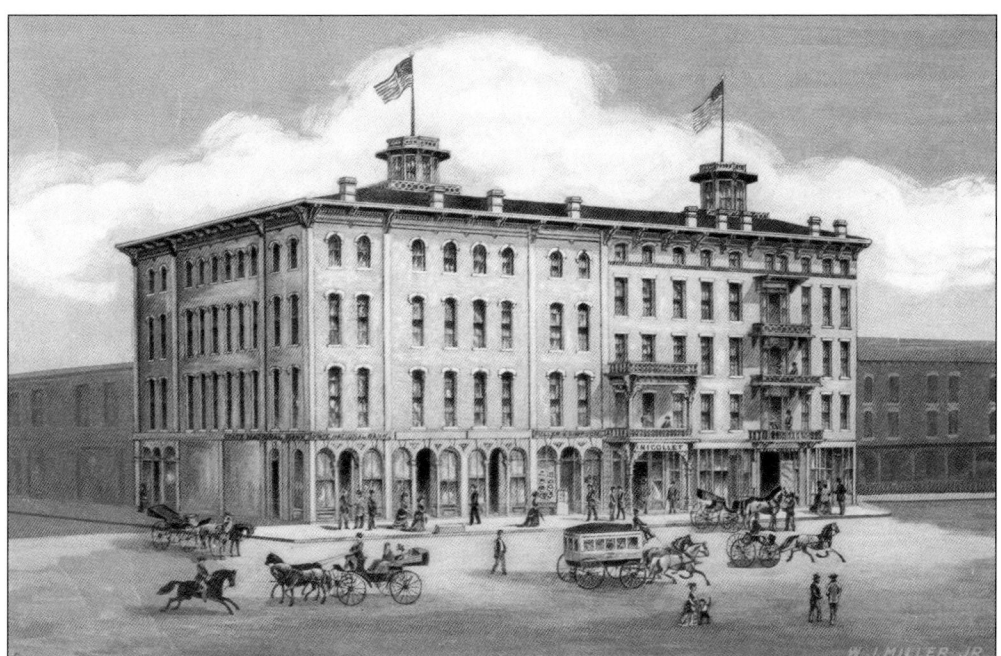

When it opened in 1858, the Nicollet House provided lodging for the town's visitors, including Southerners who traveled up to Minnesota by steamboat to escape the summer heat back home. With its lace curtains, mirrored parlors, and plush furniture, the hotel added a touch of elegance to the small frontier settlement on the west bank of the Mississippi. The Nicollet House remained at its downtown site through the 1920s, when it was replaced by a new, more modern hotel. (Both, courtesy of the Minnesota Historical Society.)

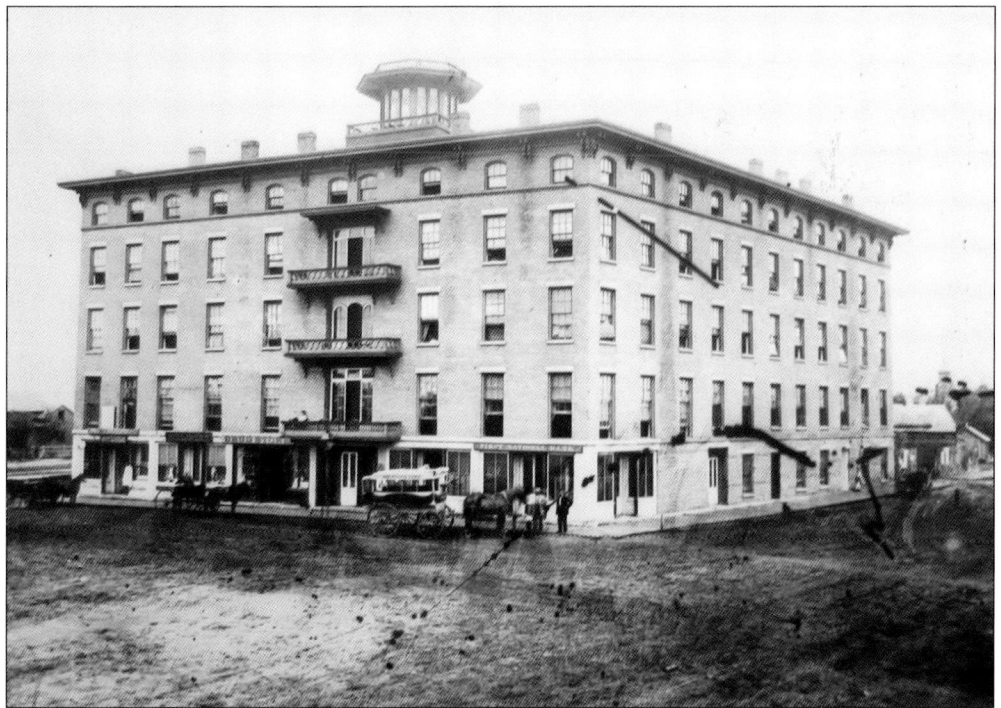

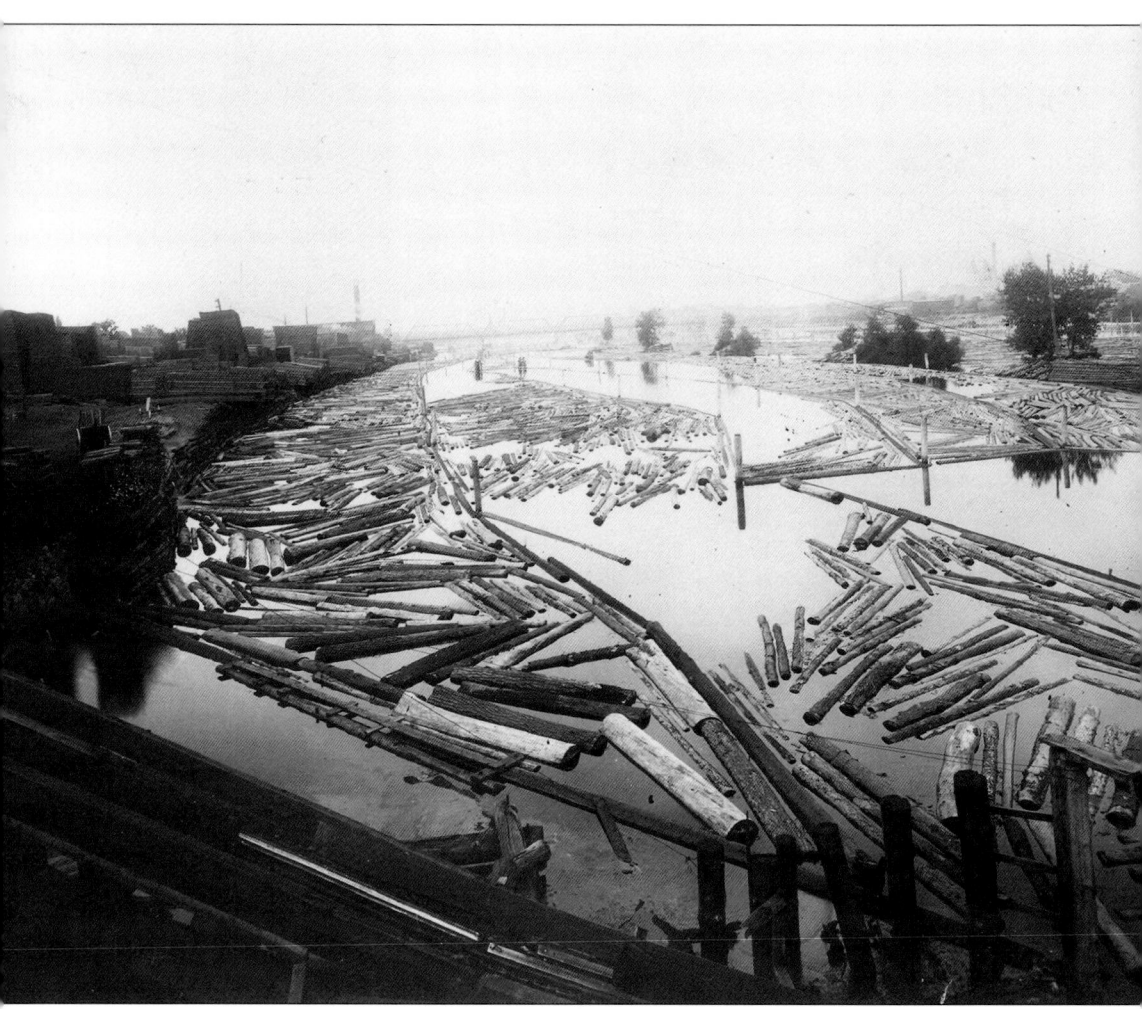

The first mill at St. Anthony Falls was established by the soldiers at Fort Snelling to provide lumber for the fort. The Falls district would later become an important lumber milling center as logs were floated down the Mississippi River to the sawmills at Boom Island just above the falls. (Courtesy of Hennepin County Public Library Special Collections.)

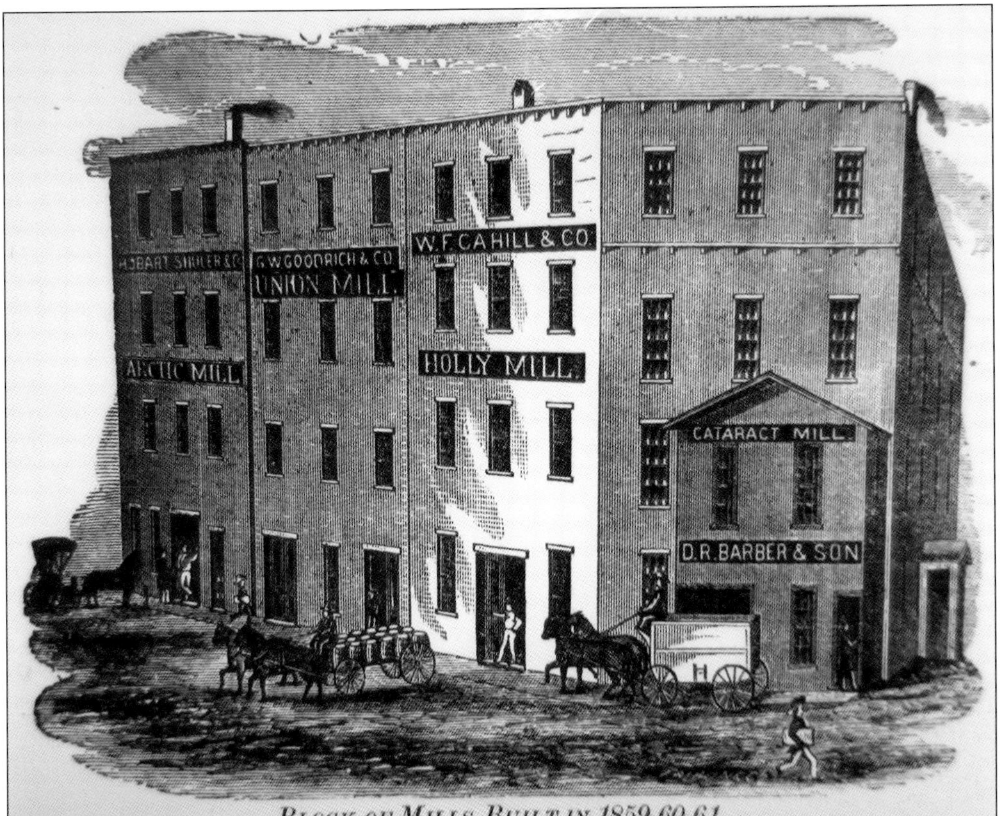

BLOCK OF MILLS BUILT IN 1859-60-61.

By the Civil War, flour had begun to replace lumber as the major product produced by the mills at St. Anthony Falls. Enterprises were formed on both sides of the river to harness the power of the falls and use it to operate the mills that lined the riverbank. On the west side, a 215-foot tunnel channeled the flow of the falls to power a series of milling machines. (Both, courtesy of the Minnesota Historical Society.)

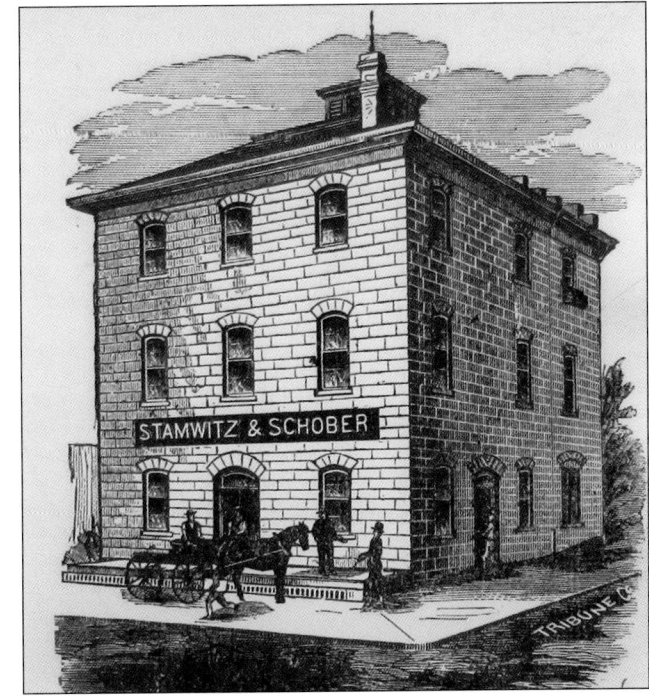

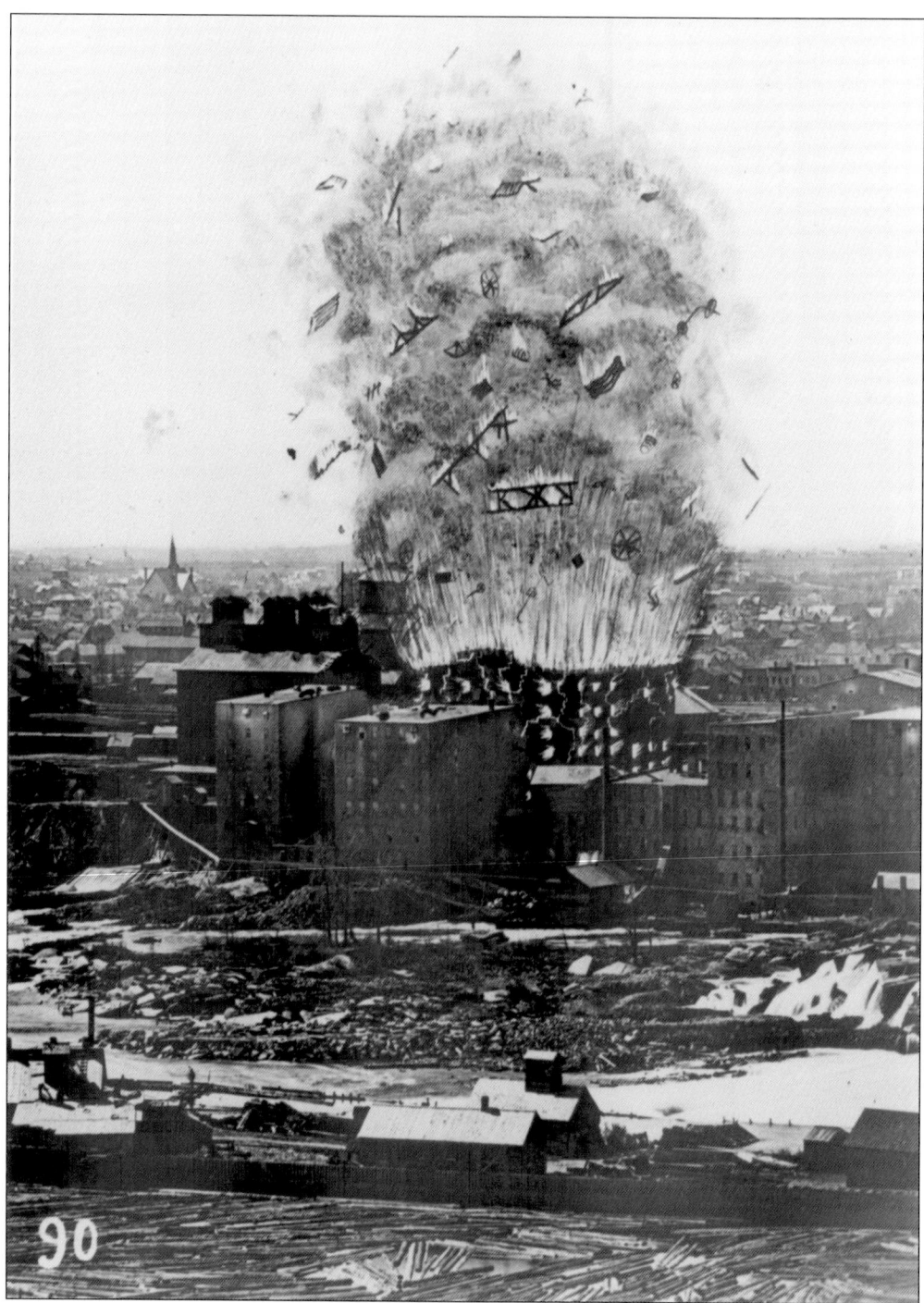

On the evening of May 2, 1878, the downtown riverfront was rocked with an explosion that could be heard as far away as St. Paul. The explosion destroyed Cadwallader Washburn's massive A Mill, killing 14 of his workers along with four workers at adjoining mills. Washburn quickly rebuilt his riverfront facility, which operated at its downtown site well into the 20th century. (Courtesy of Hennepin County Public Library Special Collections.)

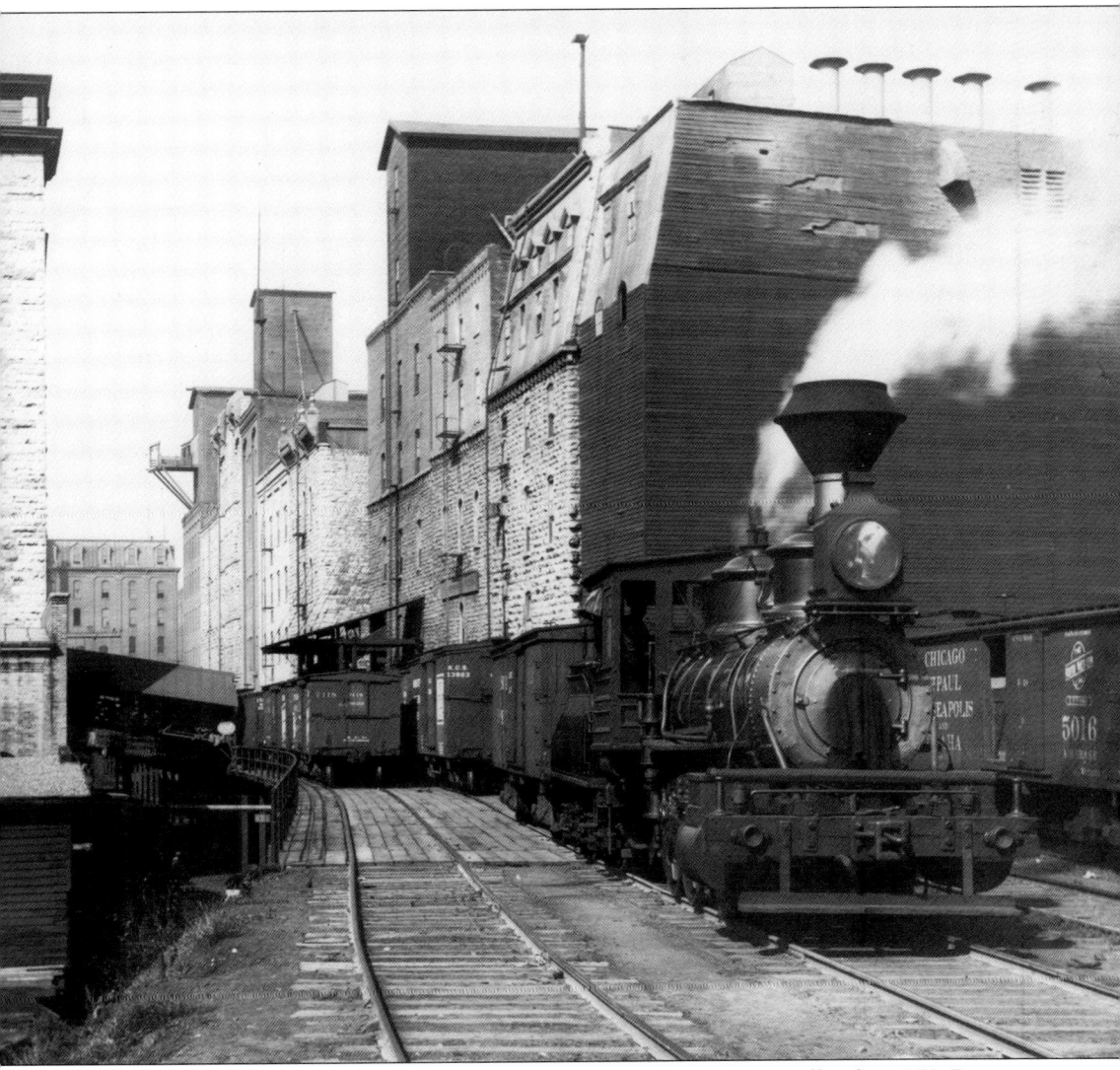
With advances in milling technology, the city's milling industry grew rapidly after 1870. During these years, an expanding network of railroad lines delivered wheat from Upper Midwest farm fields to the downtown riverfront. By the turn of the 20th century, Minneapolis had become the flour milling capital of the world. (Courtesy of the Minnesota Historical Society.)

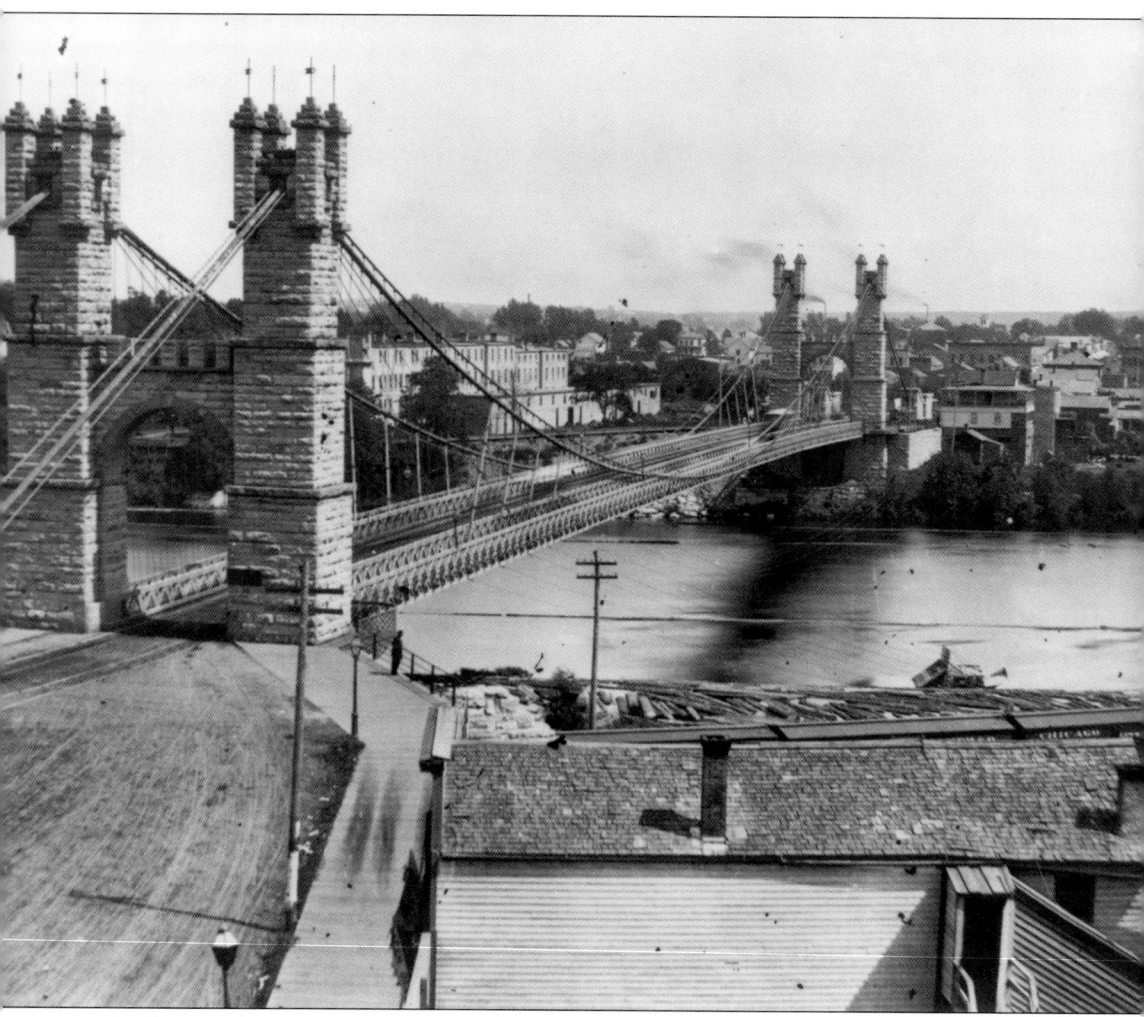

As the growth of the west bank mills outpaced those of the east bank, Minneapolis's population also outpaced that of St. Anthony across the river. Minneapolis annexed St. Anthony, and the east bank community ceased to exist as a separate municipality. In 1876, a new Hennepin Avenue bridge connected both banks of the river, now part of an expanded city of Minneapolis. (Courtesy of Hennepin County Public Library Special Collections.)

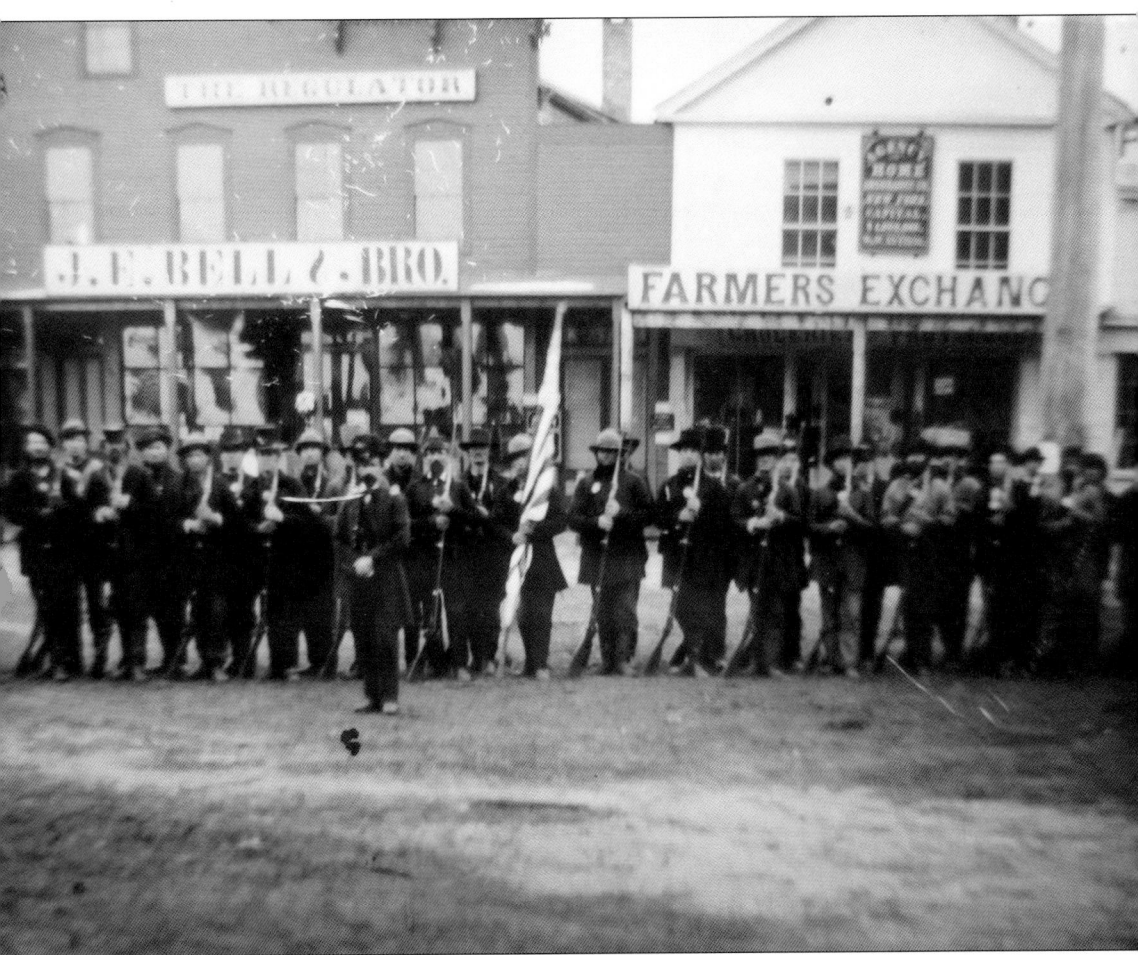

Members of the First Minnesota Volunteers gather for a photograph in downtown Minneapolis during the Civil War. The Volunteers took heavy casualties at the battles of Bull Run, Antietam, and Gettysburg. The wartime service of this Minnesota military unit has been memorialized in the 1993 book *The Last Full Measure: The Life and Death of the First Minnesota Volunteers*. (Courtesy of the Minnesota Historical Society.)

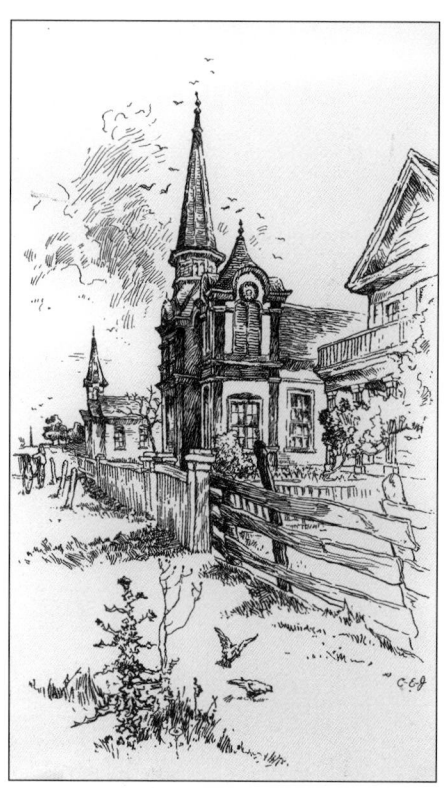

Westminster Presbyterian was one of the first Protestant congregations established in Minneapolis. At its founding in 1857, the congregation consisted of eight people of Scotch, Irish, and Welsh heritage. After raising $2,000, the founders built this church on Fourth Street in what would later become the city's downtown. (Courtesy of Westminster Presbyterian Church Archives.)

The Westminster congregation grew rapidly and later relocated to a new, larger church on Seventh Street and Nicollet Avenue in 1883. The congregation's time on Seventh Street was short lived. In 1895, a fire destroyed the new church just 12 years after it was built. George Draper Dayton purchased the burned-out site and built the department store that later carried his name. In 1897, Westminster built the congregation's current home at Twelfth Street and Nicollet Avenue. (Courtesy of Westminster Presbyterian Church Archives.)

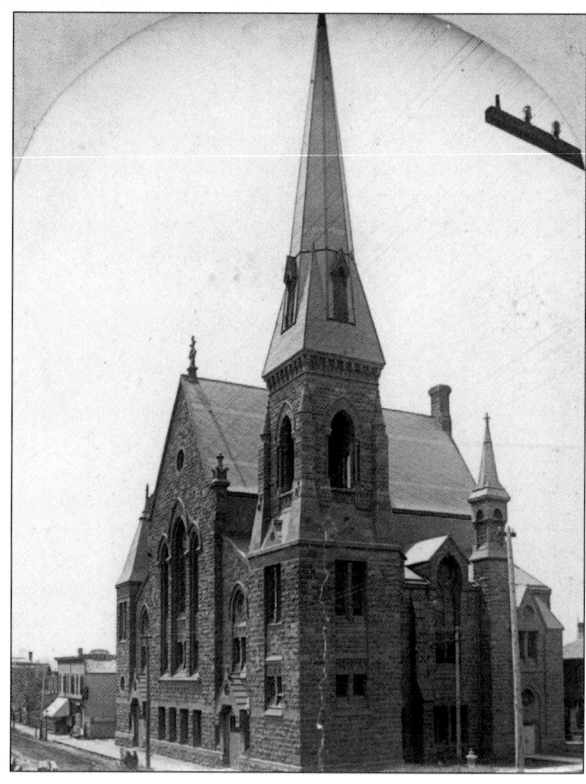

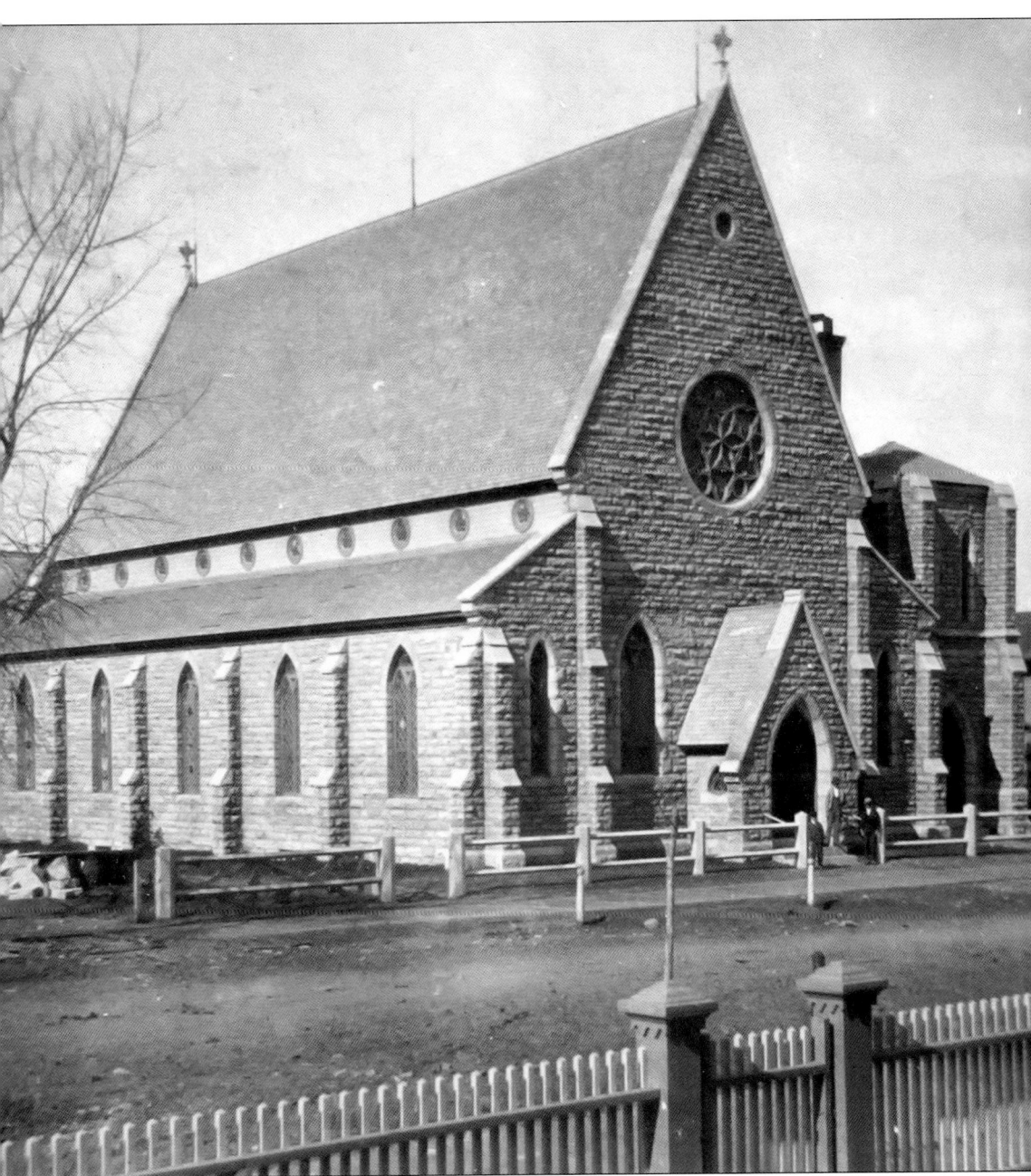

The history of St. Mark's Episcopal Church extends back to 1858 when it was established as a north Minneapolis mission of Gethsemane Church. In 1863, St. Mark's relocated to downtown Minneapolis and later moved to Loring Park, where it evolved into a cathedral and the seat of the Episcopal diocese of Minnesota. (Courtesy of the Minnesota Historical Society.)

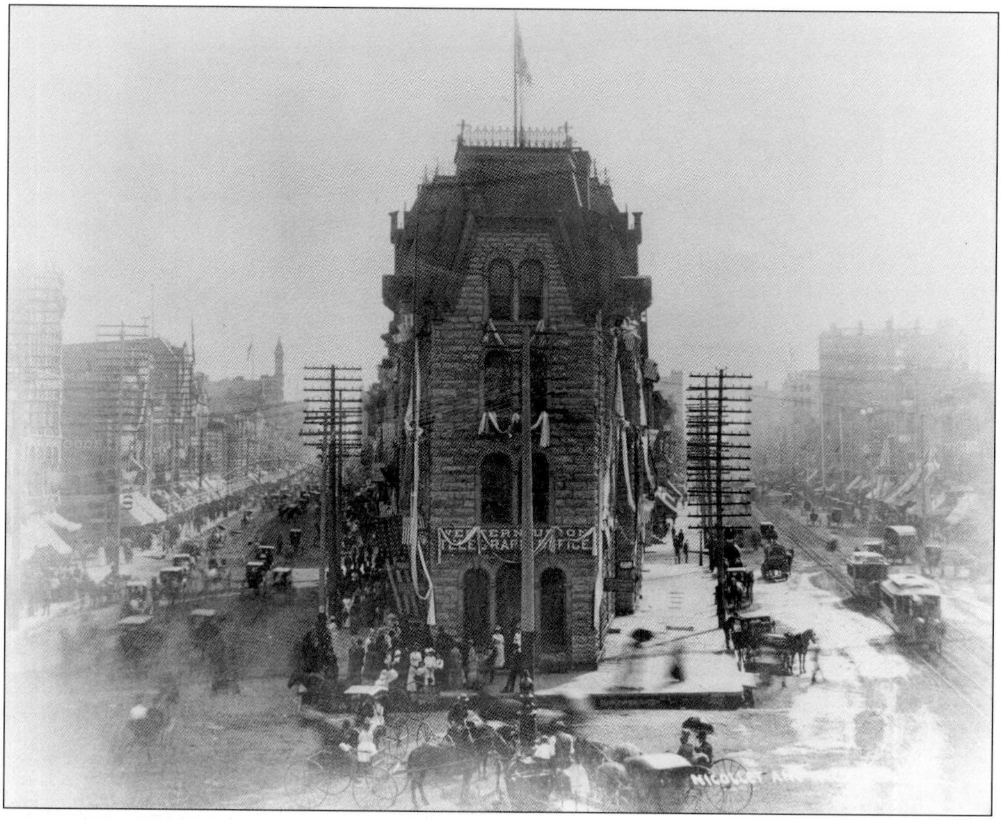

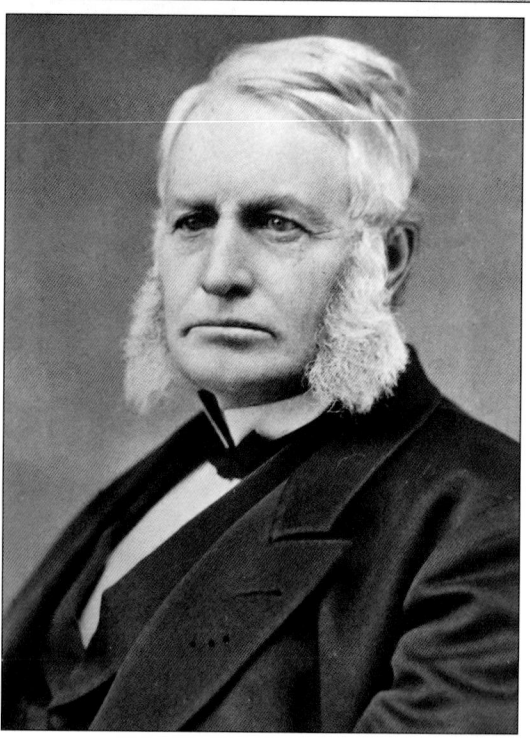

Minneapolis's first city hall was built on a triangular plot of land at Bridge Square, where Nicollet and Hennepin Avenues intersected. In the 1870s, city hall became the seat of government for an expanded municipal jurisdiction when Minneapolis annexed the town of St. Anthony across the river. (Courtesy of Hennepin County Public Library Special Collections.)

When Minneapolis was incorporated as a city in 1867, Dorilus Morrison became its first mayor. A native of Maine, Morrison moved to Minneapolis in 1854 and became an early leader of the city's milling and banking industries. His estate, Villa Rosa, later became the site of the Minneapolis Institute of Arts. (Courtesy of Minnesota Historical Society.)

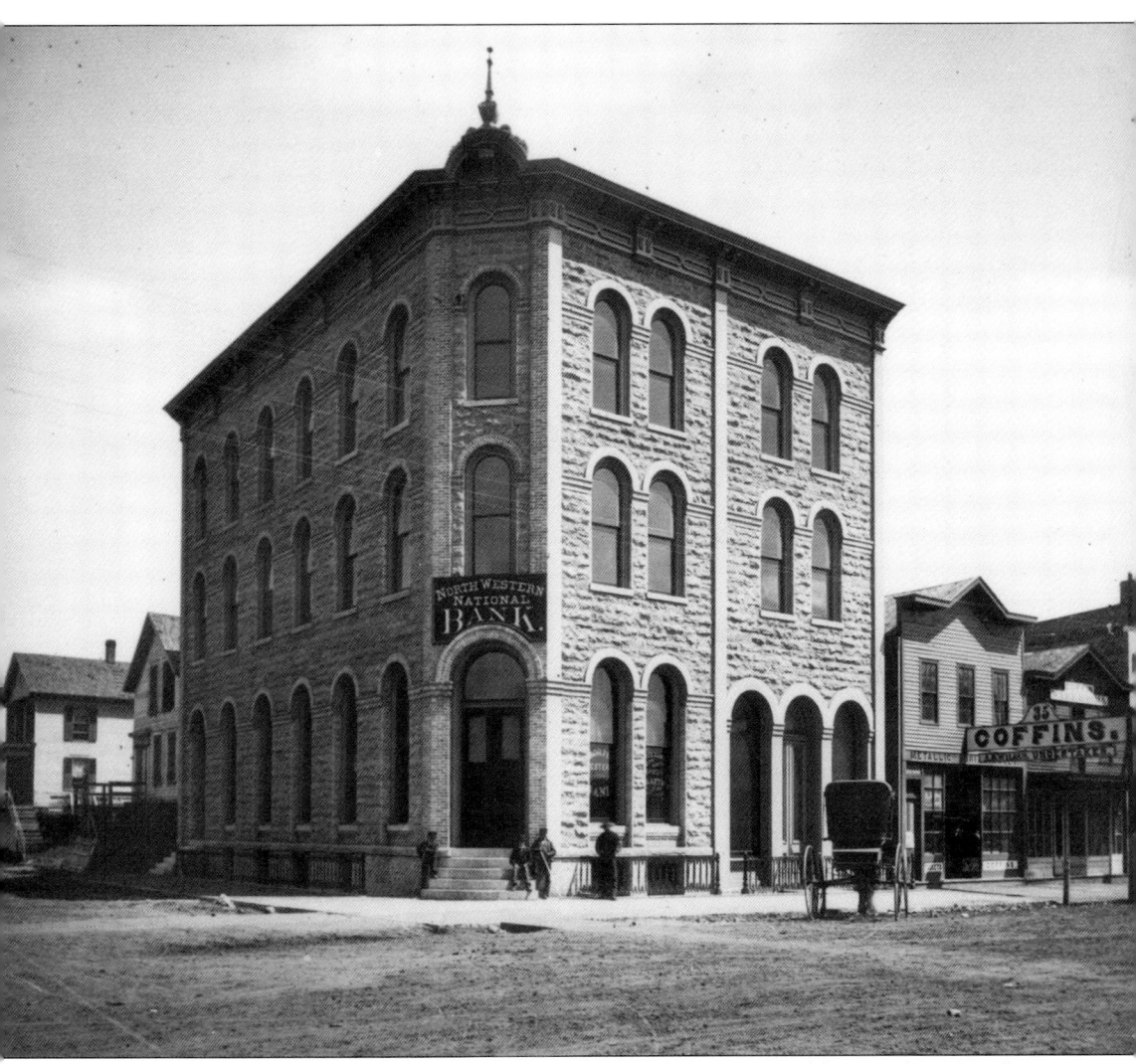

North Western Bank opened for business in 1872 to support the interests of the Northern Pacific Railroad and to serve as its banking house. As the city continued to grow in the late 19th century, the bank prospered. North Western deposits had increased from $50,000 in 1872 to $3 million by 1892. (Courtesy of Hennepin County Public Library Special Collections.)

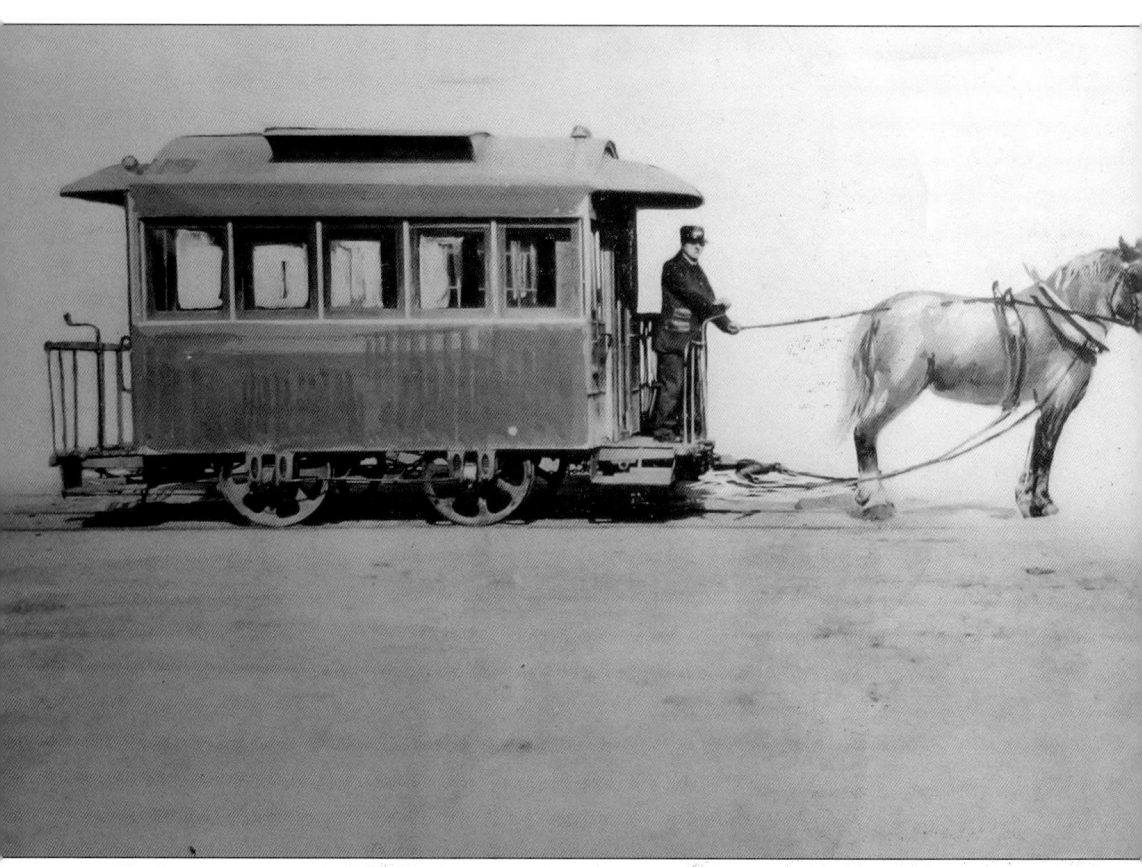

The horsecars, an early form of urban mass transportation, first appeared on the streets of downtown Minneapolis in 1869. The Minneapolis Street Railway became the first permanent company to offer this service on a regular basis in 1875. By the late 1880s, the Minneapolis company and its St. Paul counterpart were operating more than 350 horsecars on 110 miles of track. (Courtesy of Hennepin History Museum.)

Two

BUILDING BOOM

Starting in 1880, Minneapolis embarked on a period of explosive growth that transformed the young Minnesota town into a major Midwestern metropolis. During the final two decades of the 20th century, the city's population quadrupled from 50,000 to 200,000.

This economic boom permanently altered the city's commercial center. Initially little more than a collection of modest frame structures, downtown Minneapolis streets were soon lined with impressive multistory masonry buildings, several of which have survived into the 21st century.

Downtown's most prominent building from that period, the 12-story Northwestern Guaranty Insurance Building, later known as the Metropolitan Building, fell to the wrecking ball during the urban renewal era of the 1960s. Its demise helped launch an active historic preservation movement in Minneapolis.

Located several blocks to the east of the Metropolitan Building, the massive Romanesque Revival city hall was built over a 17-year period from 1889 to 1906. The city hall, officially known as the Municipal Building, remains one of downtown's most iconic structures.

The latter decades of the 19th century saw the establishment of key community institutions that continue to have a major impact on civic life in Minneapolis. The Minneapolis Public Library opened its doors for the first time in 1889 in an impressive Romanesque Revival building on Tenth Street. The facility for Minneapolis's first public medical institution, City Hospital, was anything but impressive when it opened in 1887. Initially, the hospital occupied two modest frame buildings in a quiet residential neighborhood just east of downtown.

At the downtown riverfront, a string of water-powered mills were making use of new technologies to boost the city's flour-milling production. By the turn of the 20th century, with milling serving as the city's chief economic engine, Minneapolis had become the world's flour-milling capital.

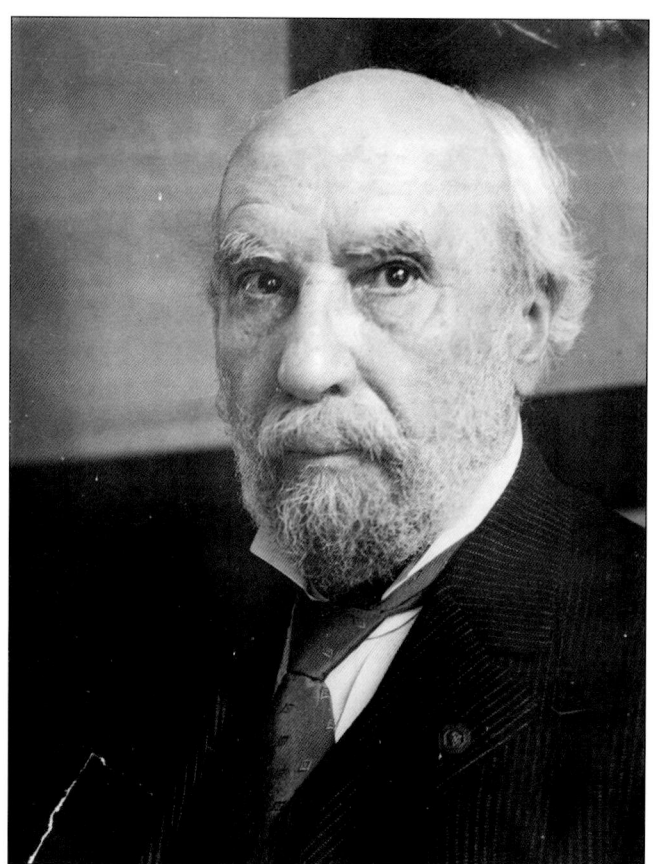

James J. Hill was a Canadian-born business tycoon who settled in St. Paul during the Civil War. Known as the "Empire Builder," Hill amassed a fortune building railroads throughout the Great Plains and the Pacific Northwest. His home on Summit Avenue in St. Paul is now one of Minnesota's major historic sites. (Courtesy of Hennepin County Public Library Special Collections.)

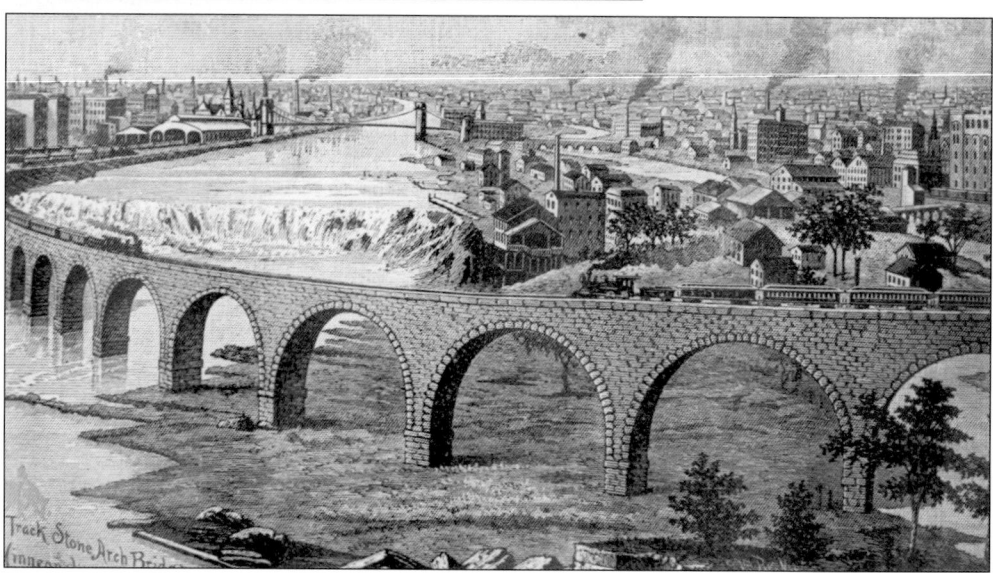

Hill's gently curving Stone Arch Bridge is considered a masterpiece of engineering and design. The railroad bridge, which opened in 1882, connected Minneapolis's east bank with the railroad yards on the west bank. The Stone Arch continued to carry rail traffic until it was closed in 1978. (Courtesy of Hennepin County Public Library Special Collections.)

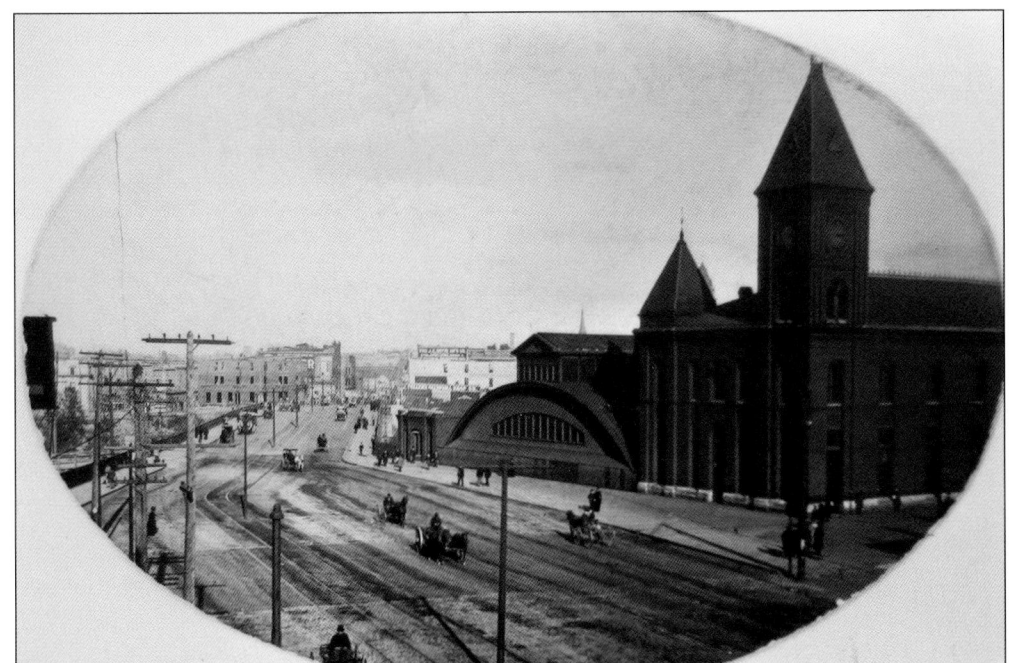

The Union Depot, located at the foot of Hennepin Avenue, opened in 1885. It served as a station for trains traveling over the Stone Arch Bridge into downtown Minneapolis. In 1892, journalists and politicians from all over the country converged on Union Depot on their way to the 1892 Republican National Convention, held just across the river in Minneapolis's Exposition Building. (Courtesy of the Minnesota Historical Society.)

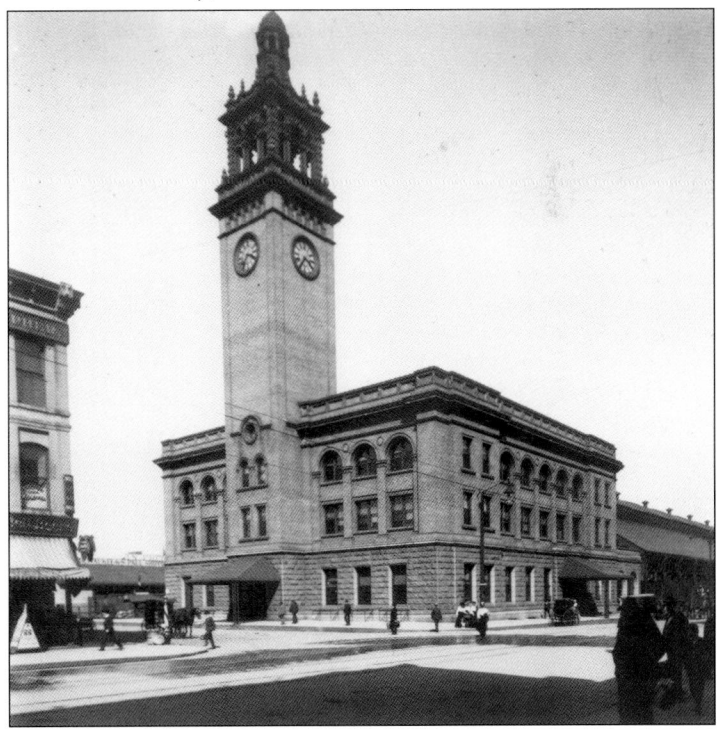

The Milwaukee depot was built for the Chicago, Milwaukee & St. Paul Railroad in 1899. The ornate pinnacle capping the station's clock tower, an early city landmark, was destroyed by high winds in 1941. The depot no longer serves as a train station. It has been repurposed as a hotel and event center. (Courtesy of Hennepin County Public Library Special Collections.)

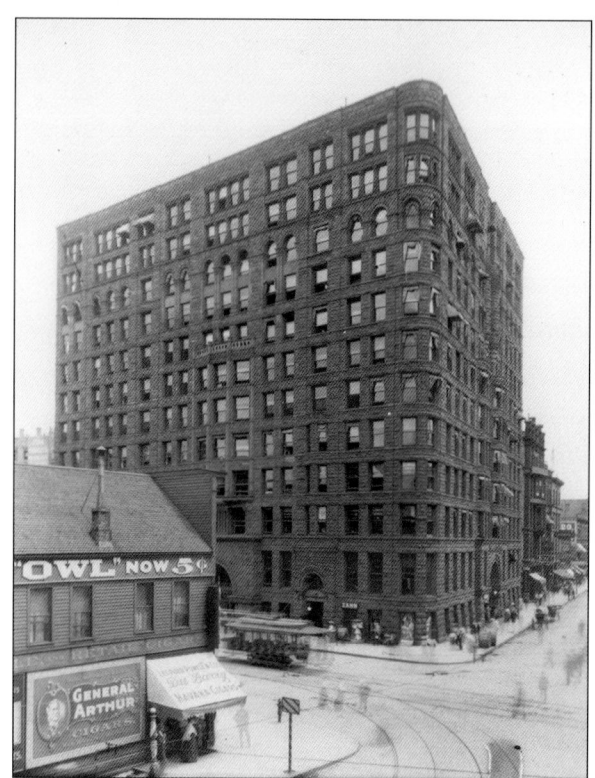

Considered Minneapolis's first skyscraper when it opened in 1886, the Lumber Exchange Building provided offices for the city's numerous lumber dealers. The building was designed by Long & Kees, the same architectural firm that built the Minneapolis City Hall. The Lumber Exchange continues to function as a downtown office building, looking very much as it did in 1886, at least on the outside. (Courtesy of Hennepin County Public Library Special Collections.)

Like the nearby Lumber Exchange Building, the Masonic Temple, now known as the Hennepin Center for the Arts, is one of a small group of downtown buildings from the 1880s that has survived into the 21st century. Long & Kees, the same architectural firm that designed the Lumber Exchange and Minneapolis City Hall, also built the Masonic Temple. The building is now operated as an artist center by the Art Space nonprofit group. (Courtesy of the Minnesota Historical Society.)

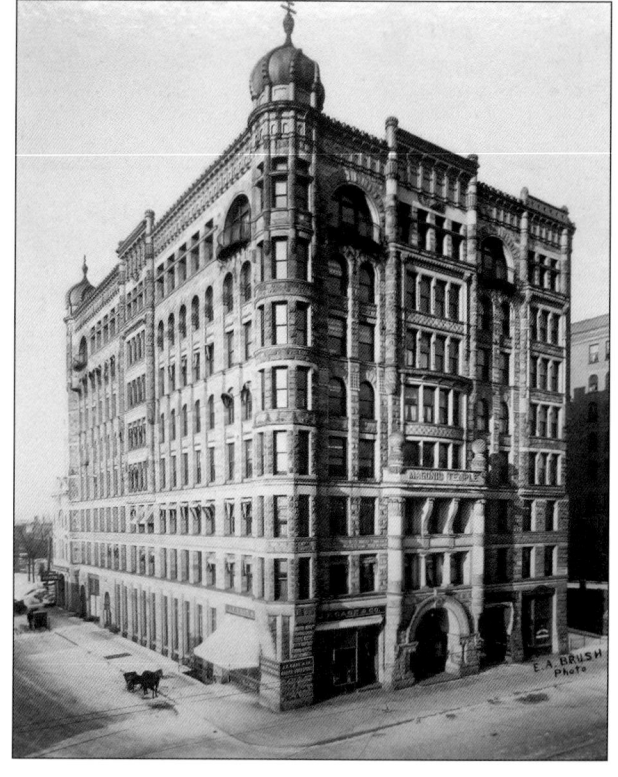

Originally known as the Northwestern Loan Guaranty Building, this 12-story structure, later renamed the Metropolitan Building, became a downtown architectural landmark when it opened in 1892. The Romanesque Revival building incorporated a rooftop garden and corner observation towers. (Courtesy of Hennepin County Public Library Special Collections.)

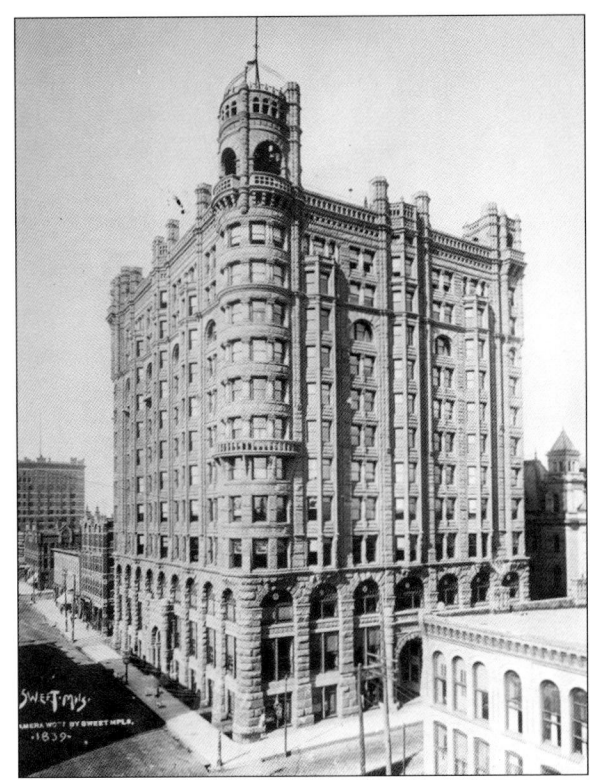

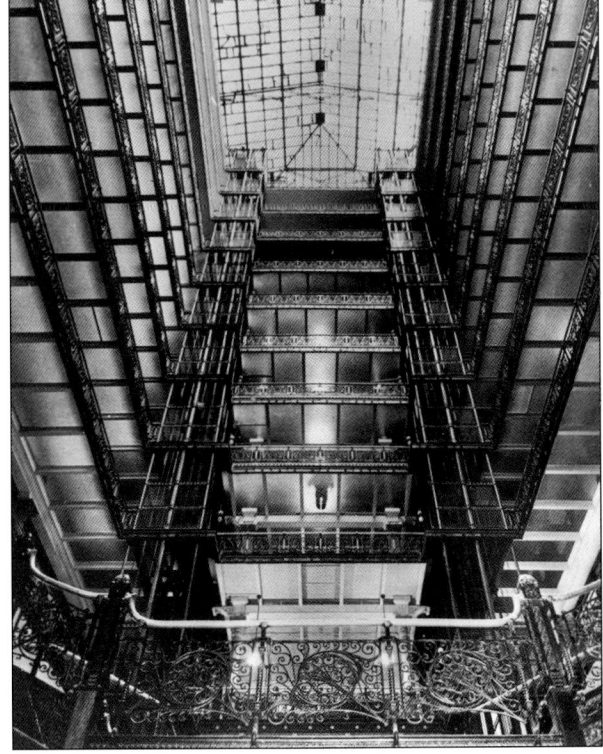

The Metropolitan was best known for its dramatic open court extending from the second floor to the ceiling. The city's preservationists lamented the building's demise when it was demolished during the urban renewal era of the early 1960s. (Courtesy of Hennepin County Public Library Special Collections.)

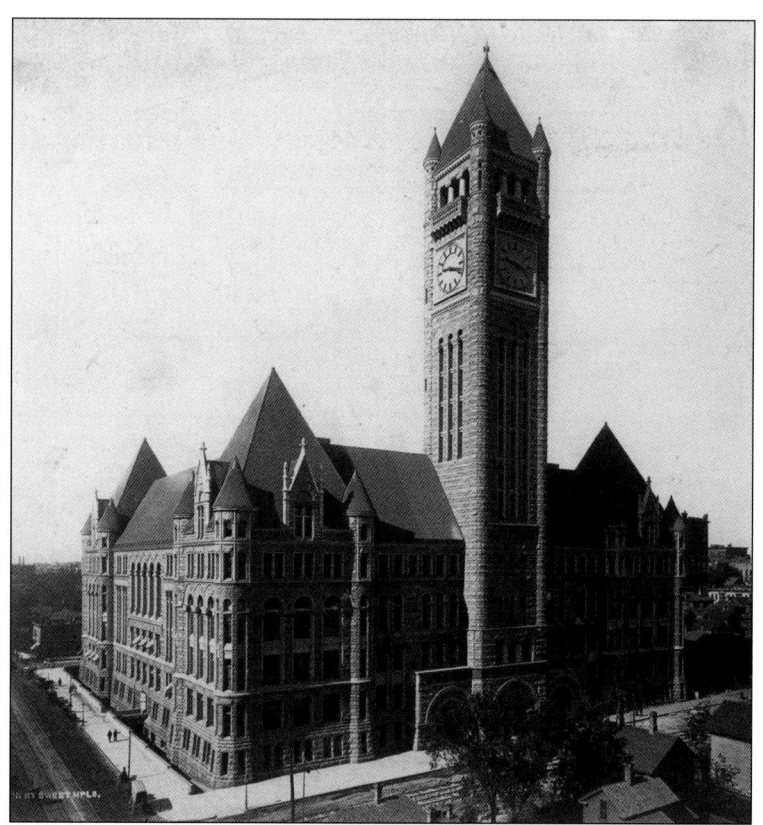

The Romanesque Revival city hall, officially known as the Municipal Building, was built over a 19-year period from 1887 to 1906. Architectural historian Larry Millet has described the building as "a thundering granite pile that when it arose block upon mighty block in the 1890s must have seemed like the city's dream of itself, powerful, resourceful, built for the ages." (Courtesy of Hennepin County Public Library Special Collections.)

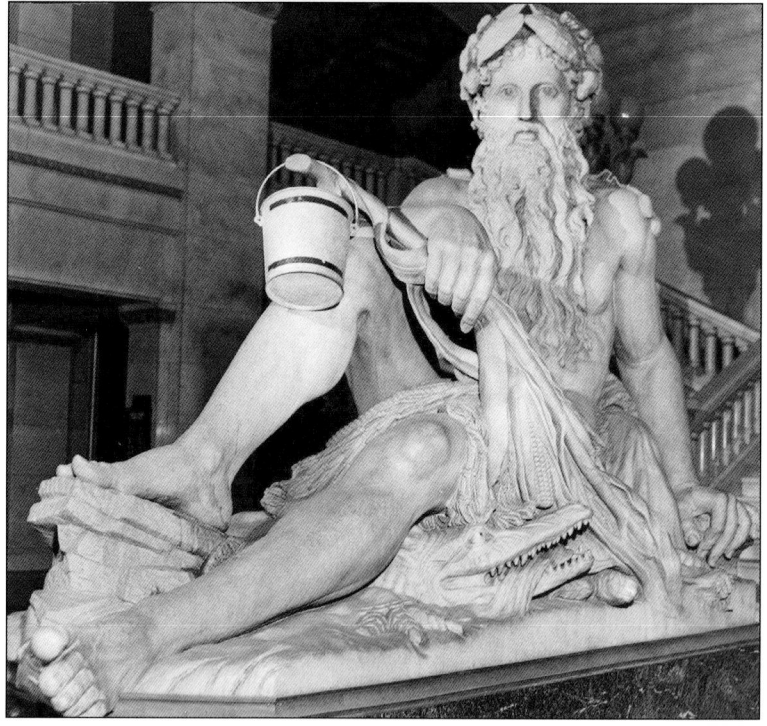

The *Father of Waters* at city hall symbolizes Minneapolis's close connection to the Mississippi River just a few blocks away. Noted American sculptor Larkin Mead created the sculpture from a single block of marble weighing 44 tons. Rubbing the Father's big toe is supposed to bring good luck. (Courtesy of Hennepin County Public Library Special Collections.)

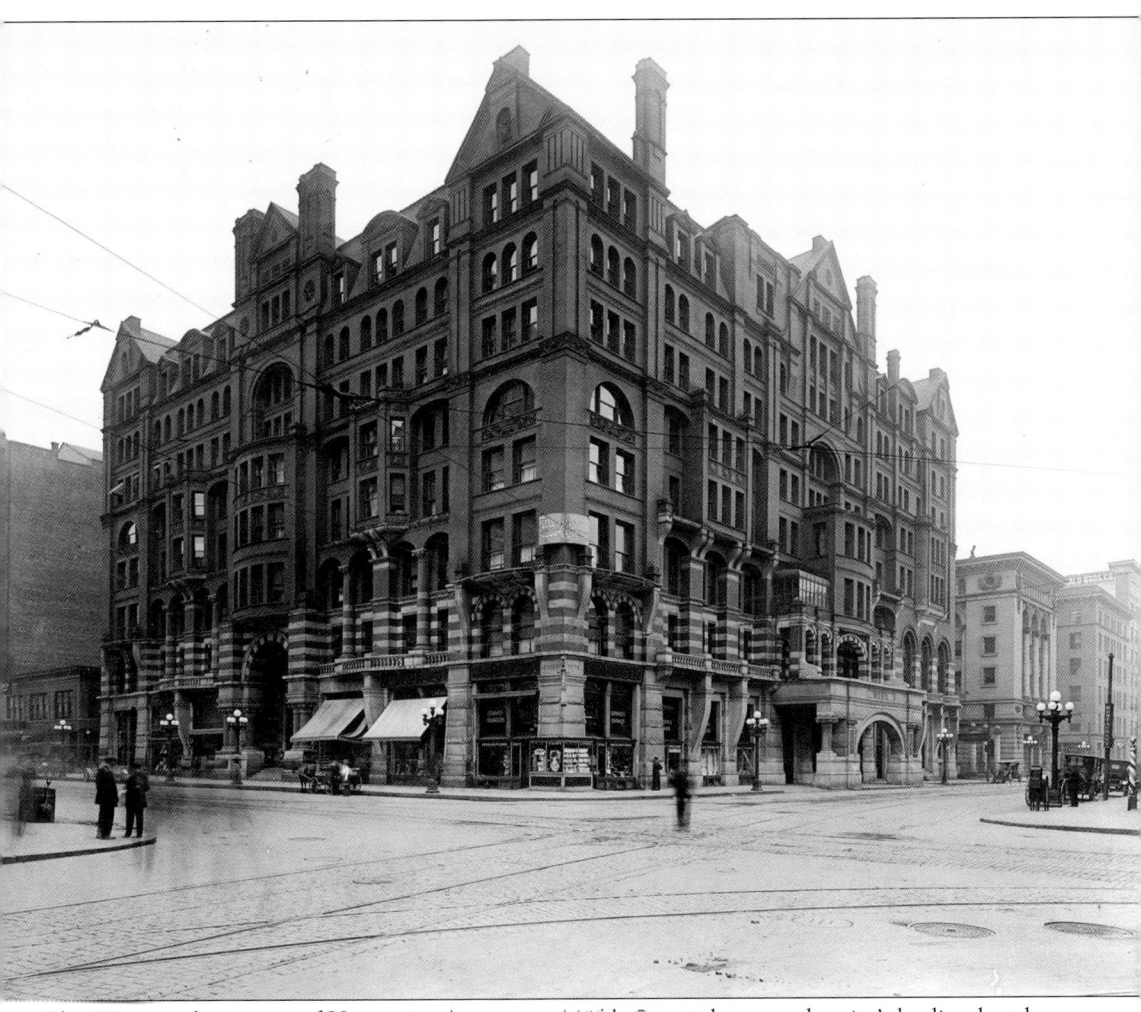

The West, at the corner of Hennepin Avenue and Fifth Street, became the city's leading hotel when it opened in 1884. Considered the most luxurious hotel west of Chicago at the time, the West had 407 rooms, 140 baths, and a large ornate lobby. Once a major downtown showplace, the hotel fell on hard times after World War I and was demolished in 1940. (Courtesy of Hennepin County Public Library Special Collections.)

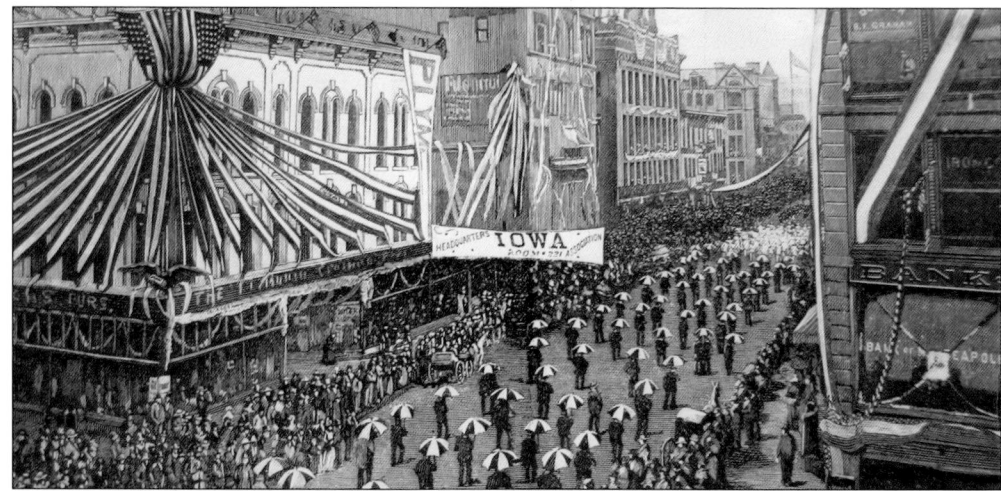

In 1892, Minneapolis was the site of the Republican National Convention, which nominated Benjamin Harrison for a second presidential term. The convention was held just across the river from downtown in the city's Exposition Building. Convention delegates are shown marching up Hennepin Avenue to the West Hotel. (Courtesy of the Minnesota Historical Society.)

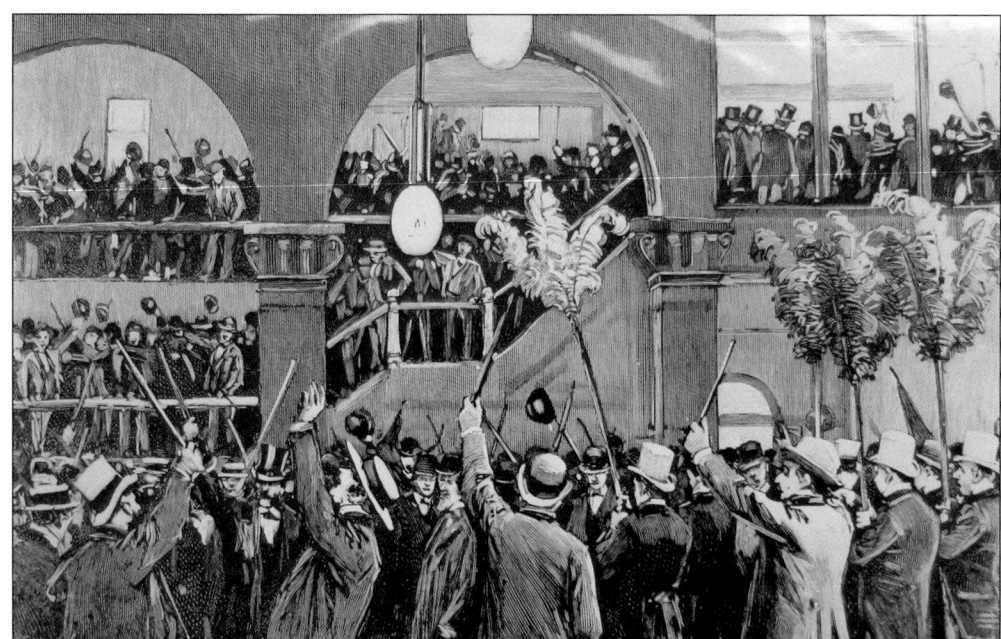

The West Hotel was at the center of action during the 1892 convention. "There is a constant ebb and flow of men, a constant hum of voices in the great rotunda," the *Minneapolis Tribune* reported. "The words being spoken in this great moving mass of humanity are making history and molding the men who will be future figures of American statesmanship." (Courtesy of the Minnesota Historical Society.)

Like many of his contemporaries, T.B. Walker arrived in Minnesota during the mid-1800s, full of ambition but with only a few dollars in his pocket. Walker soon began working his way up the economic ladder, rising from a clerk to become a powerful lumber baron. Among his other civic endeavors, Walker helped create the Minneapolis public library system and served as the library board's first chairman. (Courtesy of Hennepin County Public Library Special Collections.)

Walker was an avid art collector who used his large fortune to purchase exquisite paintings, tapestries, sculptures, and antique furniture. The wealthy businessman initially housed his collection in his sprawling downtown mansion on Hennepin Avenue. In 1927, Walker built his own museum in the exclusive Lowry Hill district. The Walker Art Center, now operated by a private nonprofit organization, still occupies the same Lowry Hill site today. (Courtesy of the Minnesota Historical Society.)

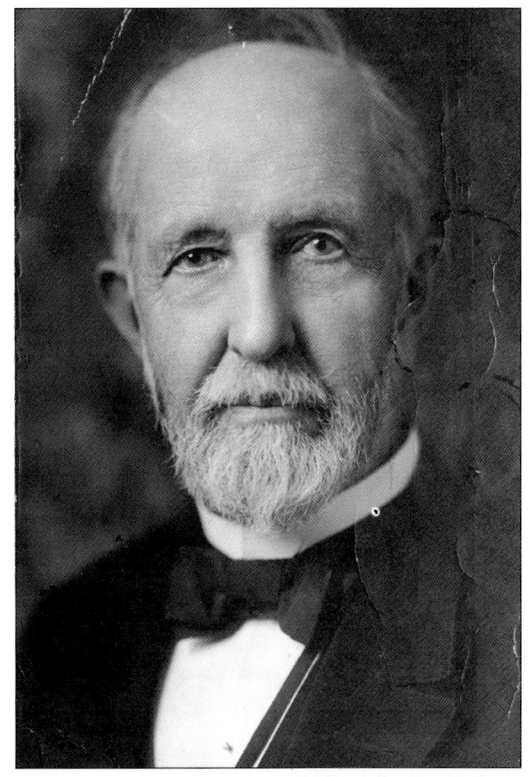

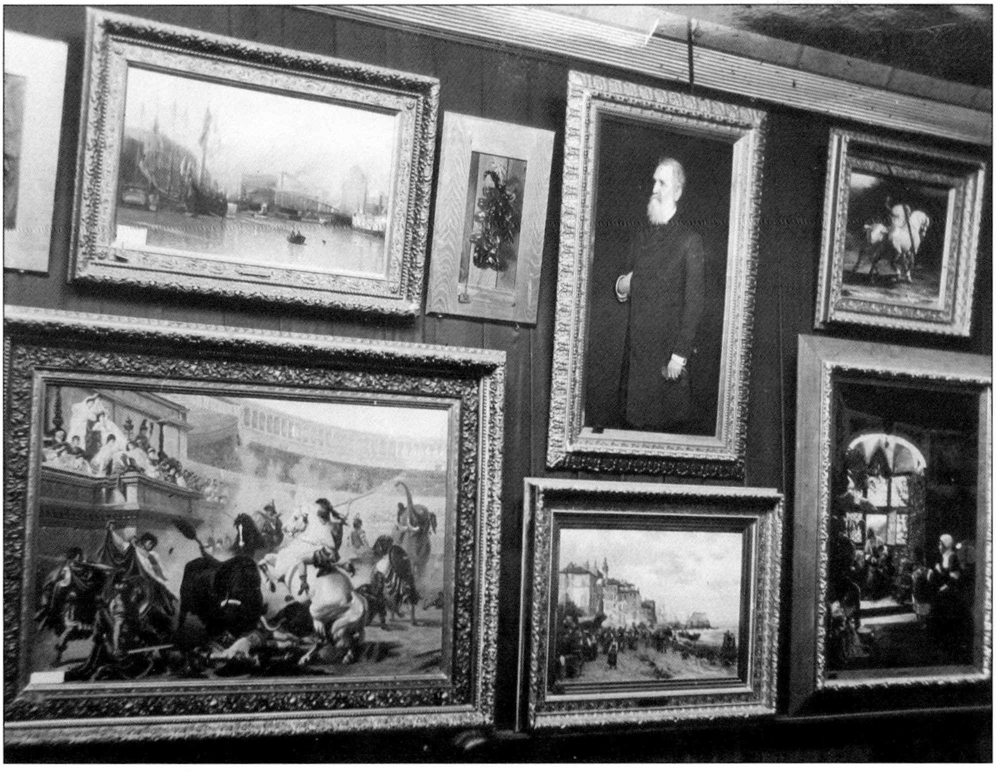

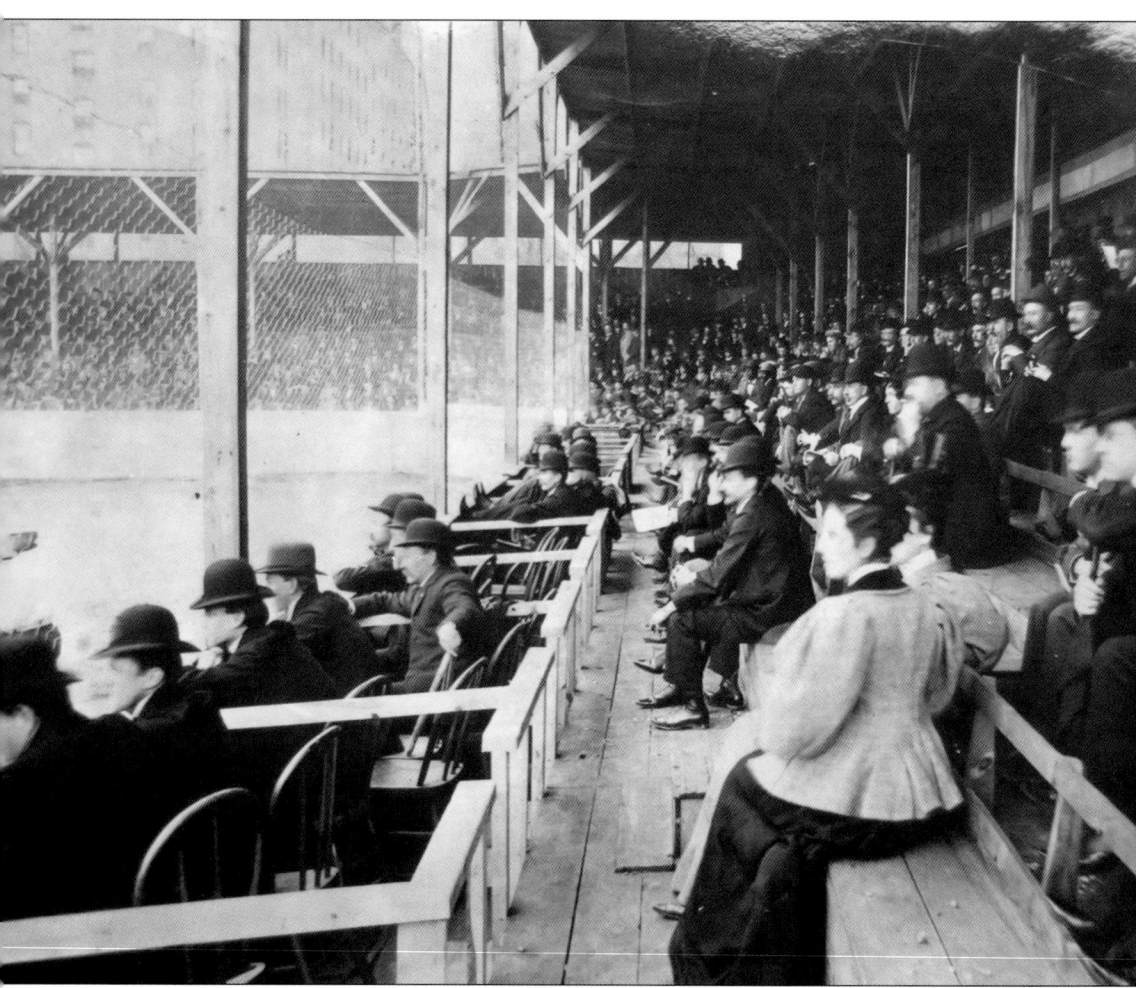

Athletic Park, at Fifth Street and First Avenue North, was the home of the Minnesota Millers baseball club from 1889 to 1896. Leisure attire was not yet in fashion at this game in 1892. The predominantly male fans are dressed in suits and ties. Women did not often attend the games, but two are seen here. (Courtesy of the Minnesota Historical Society.)

In the early 1880s, electric power came to downtown when the country's first hydroelectric power plant was built at St. Anthony Falls. The plant was built by local businessmen who formed the Minnesota Electric Light Company. In 1883, the Minneapolis company built a 275-foot tower at Bridge Square to promote electric power and demonstrate its safety. The tower was topped by eight electric arc lights that lit up the entire downtown at night. (Both, courtesy of Hennepin County Public Library Special Collections.)

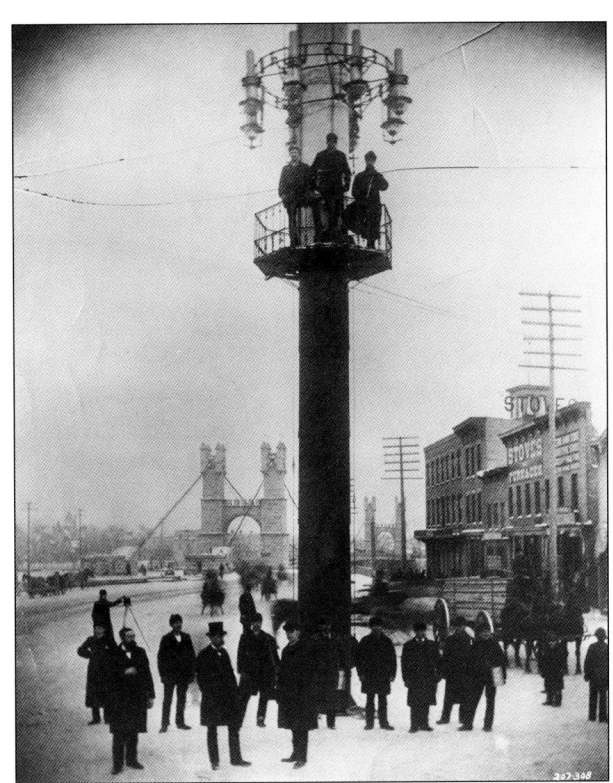

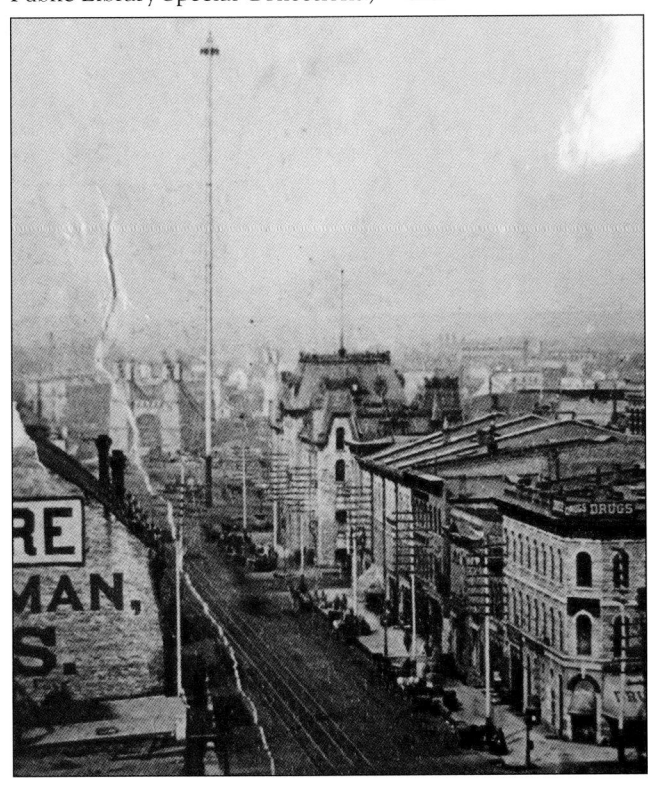

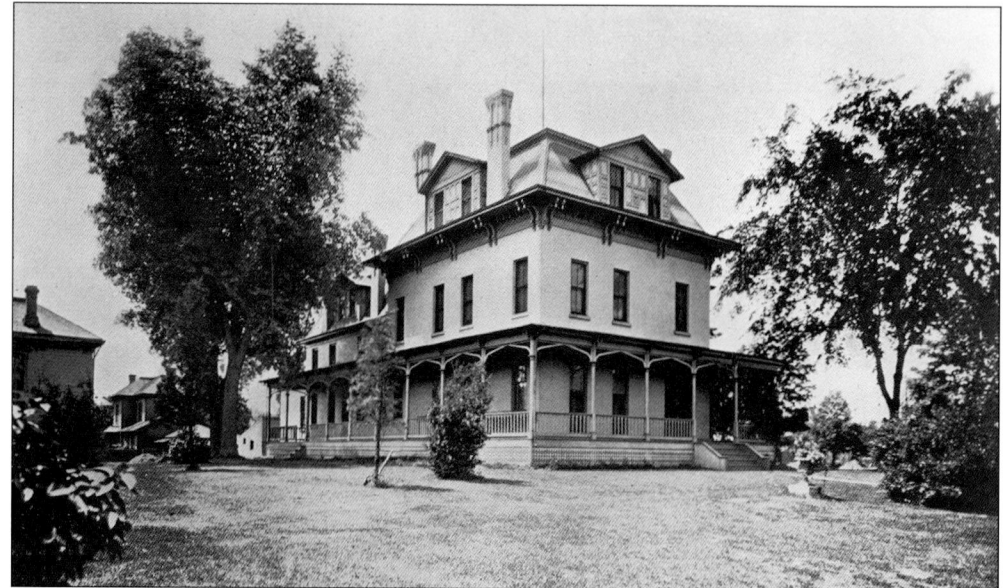

Soon after it opened in 1887, City Hospital quickly outgrew its cramped quarters in two modest frame buildings on Eleventh Avenue South. Recognizing the need for a more adequate medical facility, the city's Board of Charities and Corrections purchased the home of Russell Brackett, a wealthy local businessman, in 1893 and converted it to a new hospital. But even at its new location, City Hospital could not keep up with the rapidly rising demand for medical services. (Courtesy of Hennepin Medical History Center.)

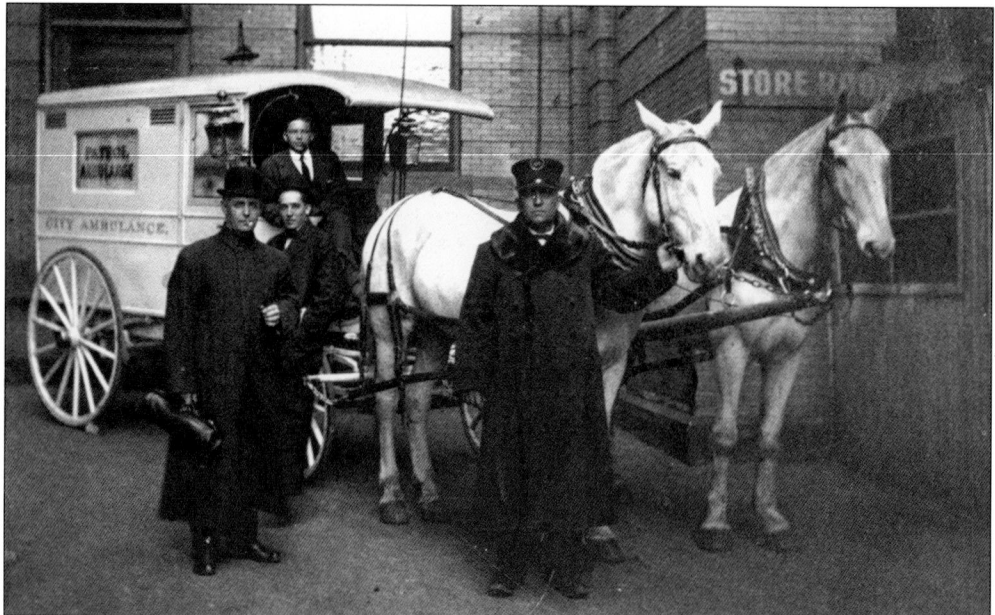

By 1898, city officials realized that the time had come to build a new facility from the ground up, one that was designed to function as a modern hospital. The Brackett Building was demolished and replaced with a new two-story hospital building. A staff doctor with the hospital's horse-drawn ambulance is shown here soon after the first of the new hospital buildings opened in 1900. (Courtesy of Hennepin Medical History Center.)

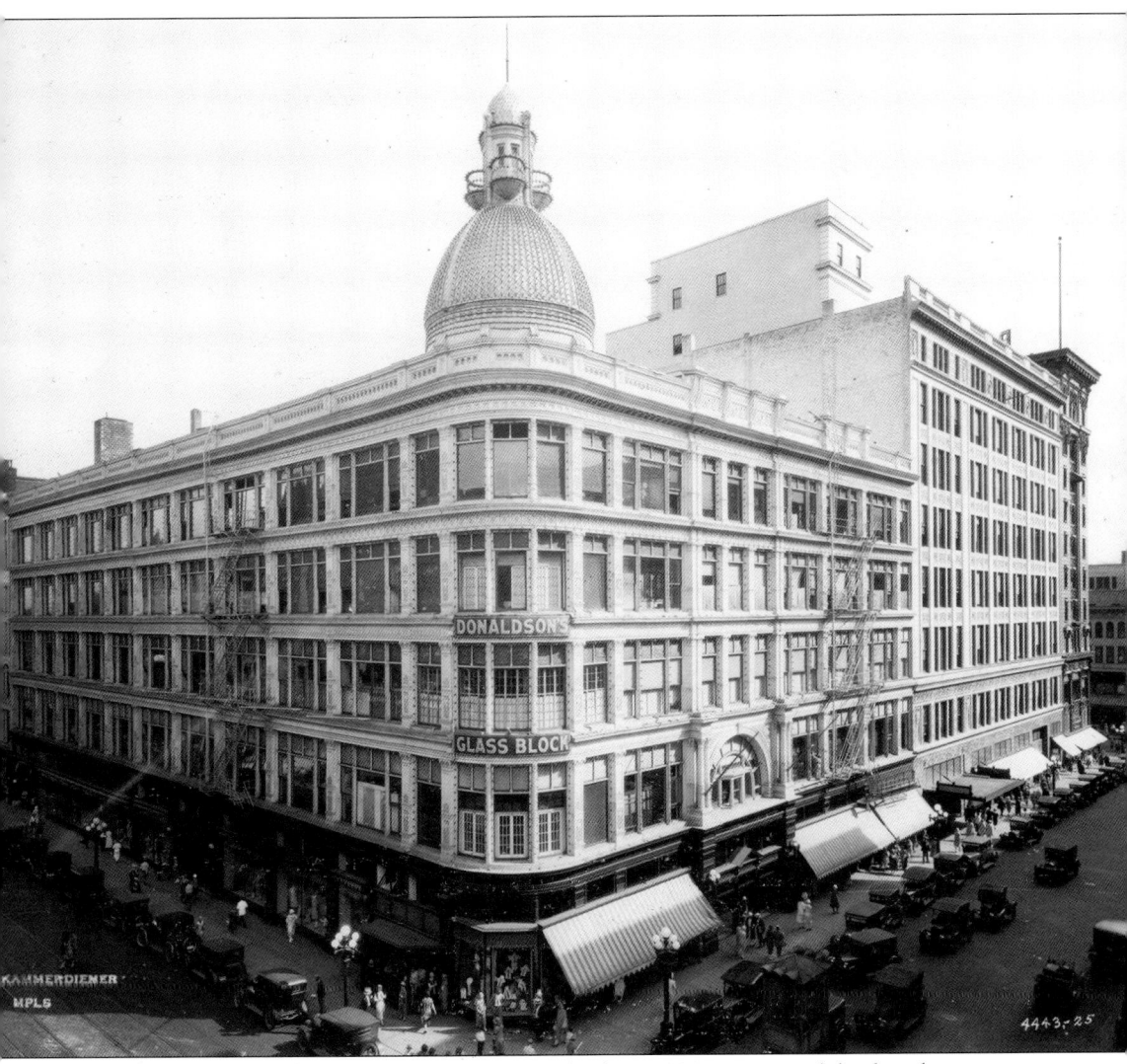

The L.S. Donaldson Company's department store, built in 1886, was one of the first downtown buildings to make extensive use of glass in its design. The building followed a style made popular by a group of Midwest architects known as the Chicago School. The department store's glass facade was responsible for its popular name, the Glass Block. (Courtesy of Hennepin County Public Library Special Collections.)

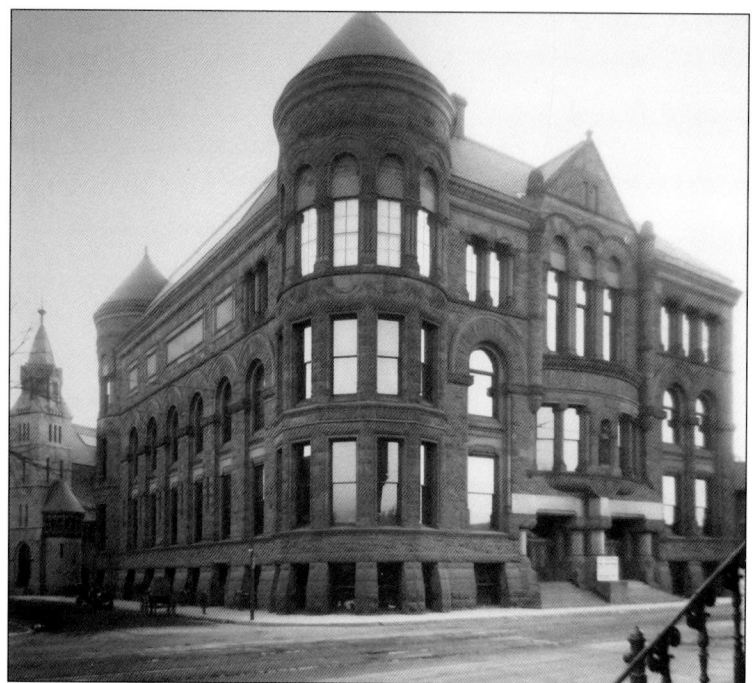

During the 1880s, the city's business leaders recognized the need for new public institutions to serve the growing population. The Minneapolis Public Library, created through an amendment to the city charter, was a key new public agency established during those years. The library board built its first library building in 1889. (Courtesy of the Minnesota Historical Society.)

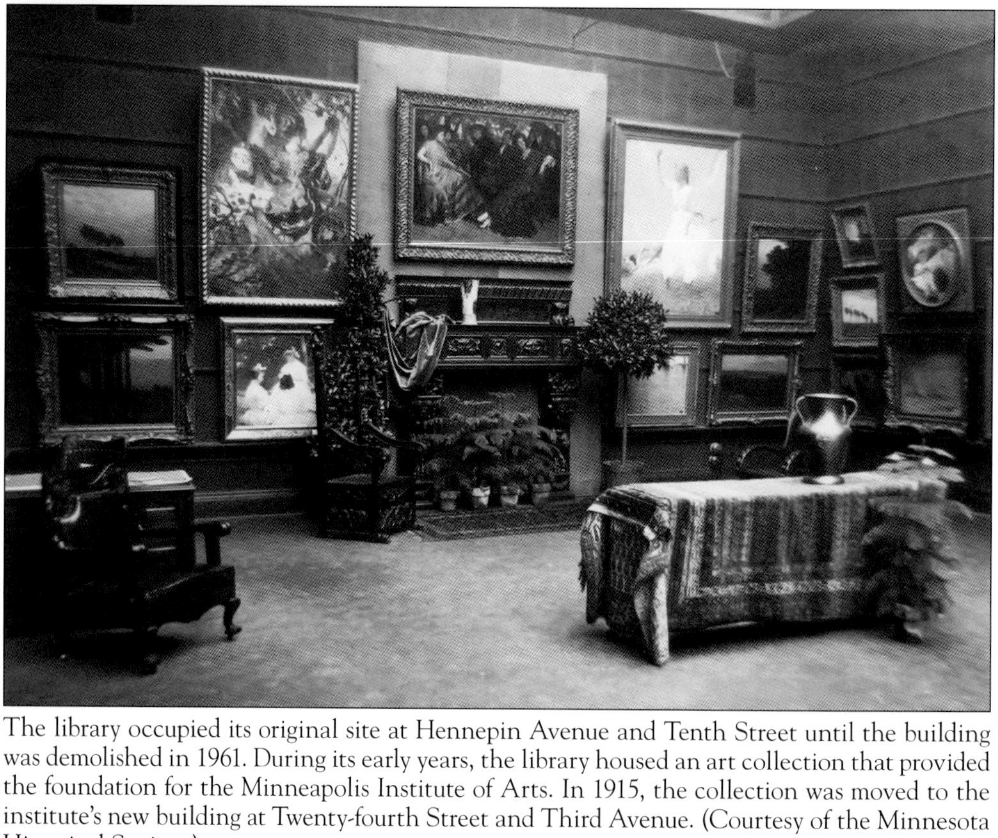

The library occupied its original site at Hennepin Avenue and Tenth Street until the building was demolished in 1961. During its early years, the library housed an art collection that provided the foundation for the Minneapolis Institute of Arts. In 1915, the collection was moved to the institute's new building at Twenty-fourth Street and Third Avenue. (Courtesy of the Minnesota Historical Society.)

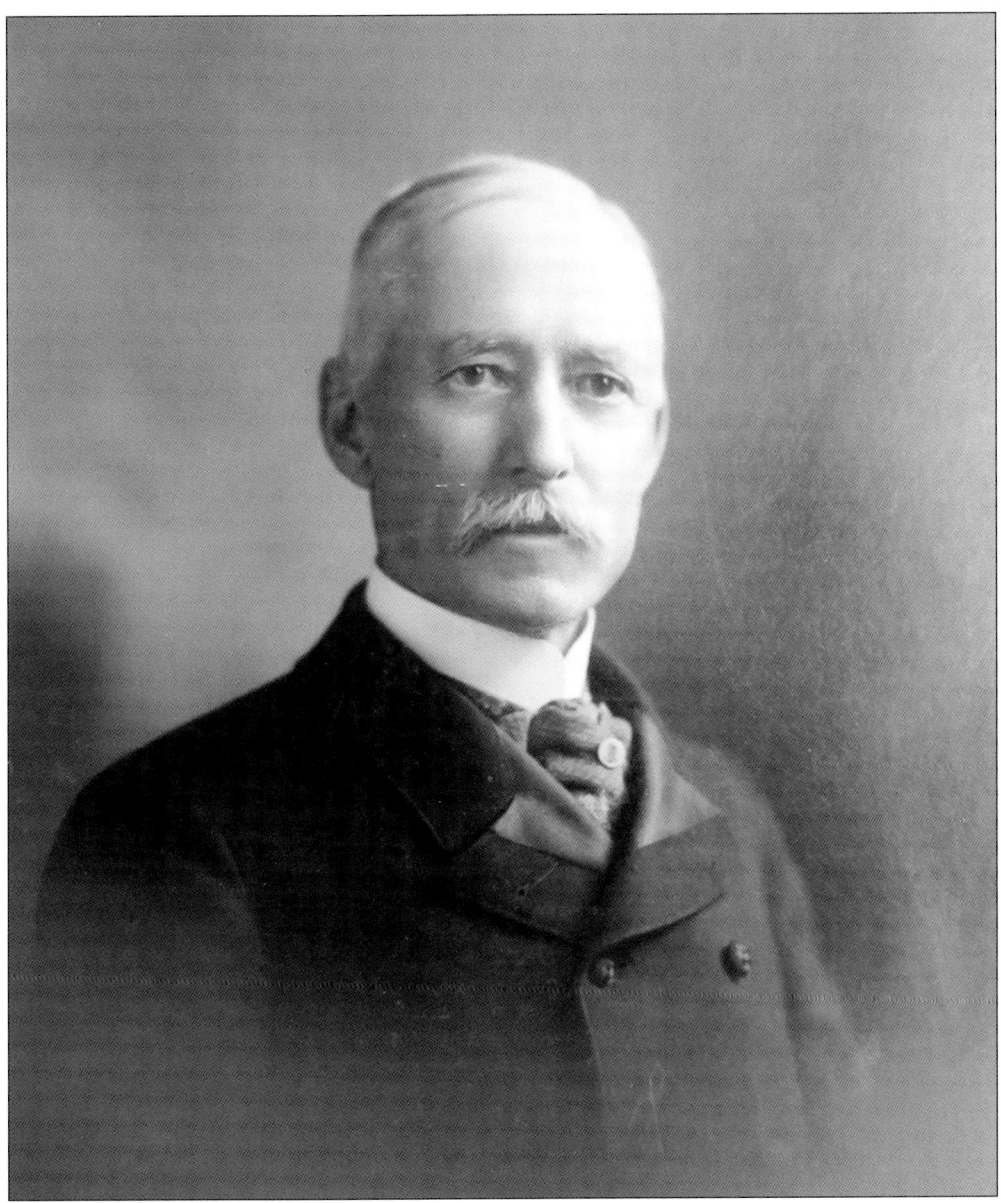
Like many of his fellow civic leaders, Charles Loring was a native of Maine who made his fortune in the flour-milling industry. Loring devoted his later years to civic concerns. He helped lead the effort to establish the Minneapolis park board. Later, he became the new public agency's first president. (Courtesy of the Minnesota Historical Society.)

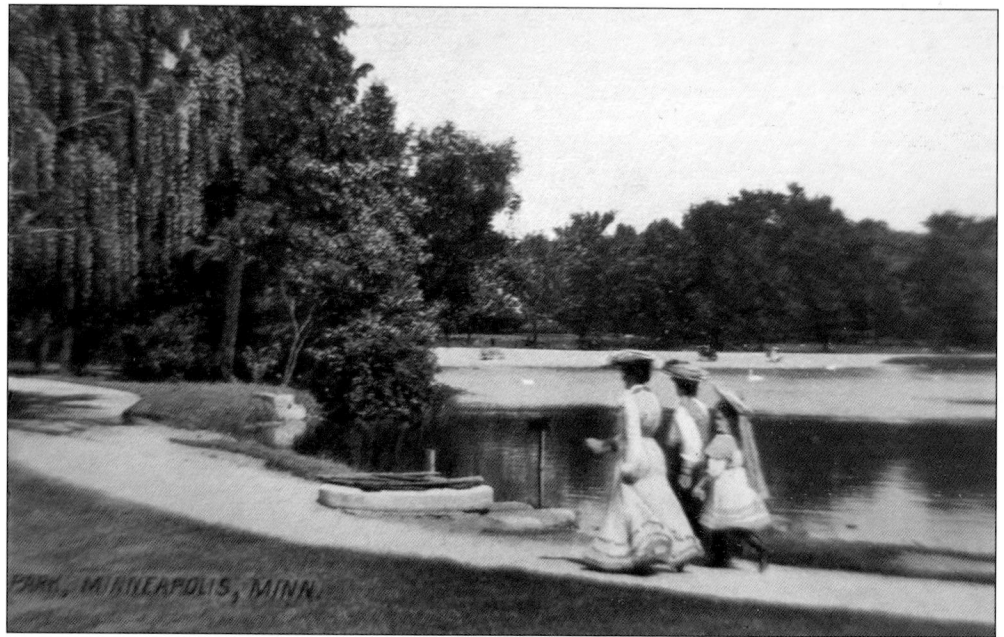

After the Minneapolis Board of Park Commissioners was established in 1883, land was acquired for a city park near the city's central business district. Originally, the green space was known as Central Park. In 1890, it was renamed Loring Park to honor Charles Loring. In 1906, the park board built the first permanent structure on parkland, a small two-story building in Loring Park used as a warming house in the winter and a community center during the warmer seasons. (Both, courtesy of the Minnesota Historical Society.)

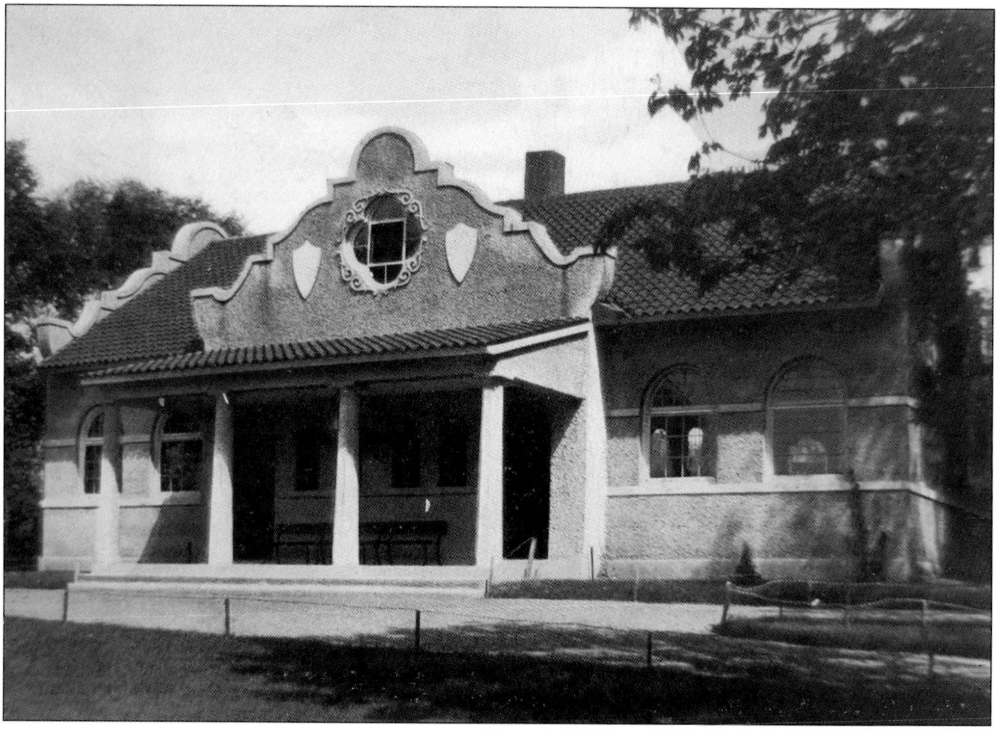

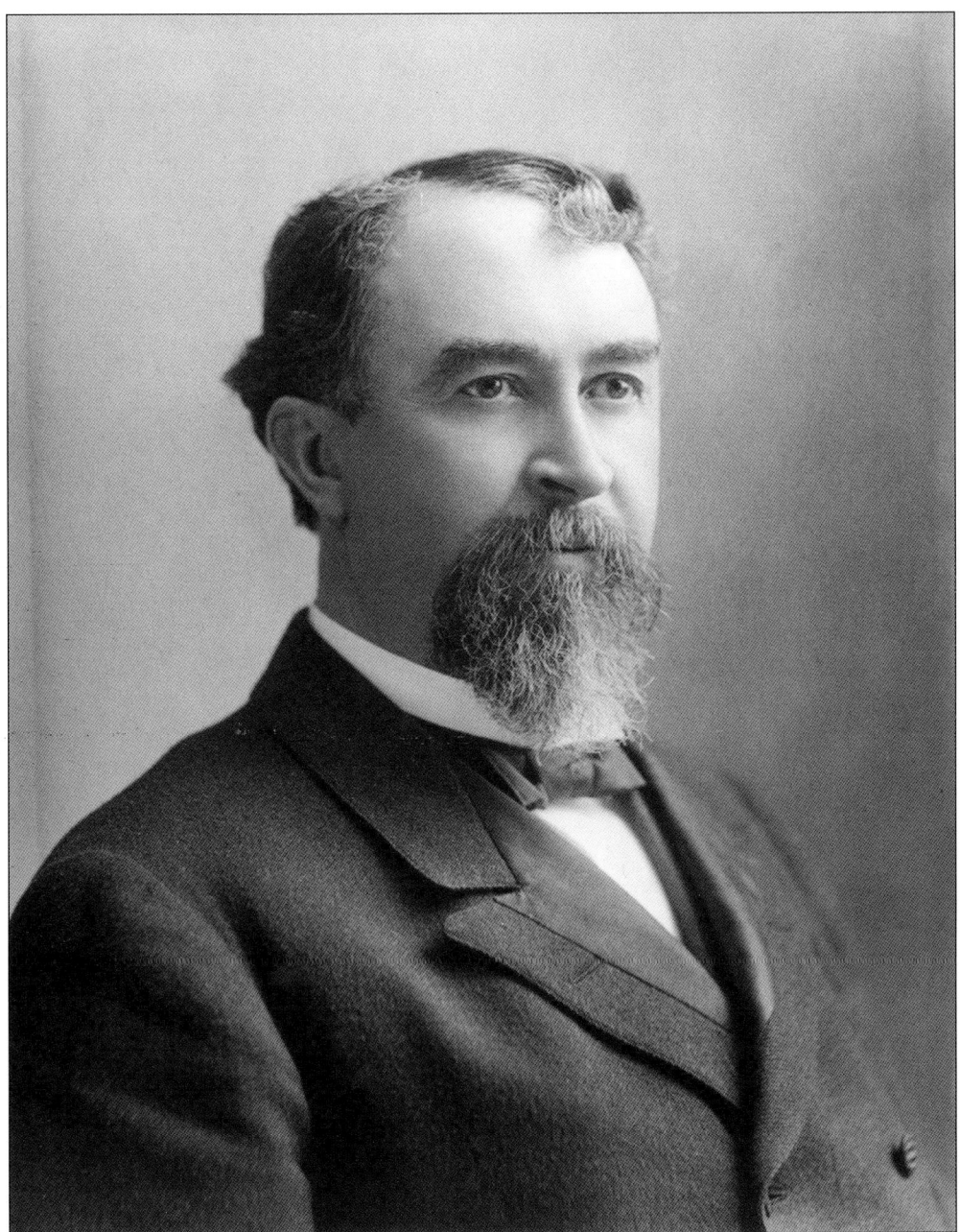

Thomas Lowry was a self-made businessman who built a small horsecar company into a major local concern called the Twin City Rapid Transit Company (TCRT). Lowry's company controlled public transportation in Minneapolis and St. Paul after the turn of the 20th century. Lowry continued to run the TCRT until his death in 1909. (Courtesy of Hennepin County Public Library Special Collections.)

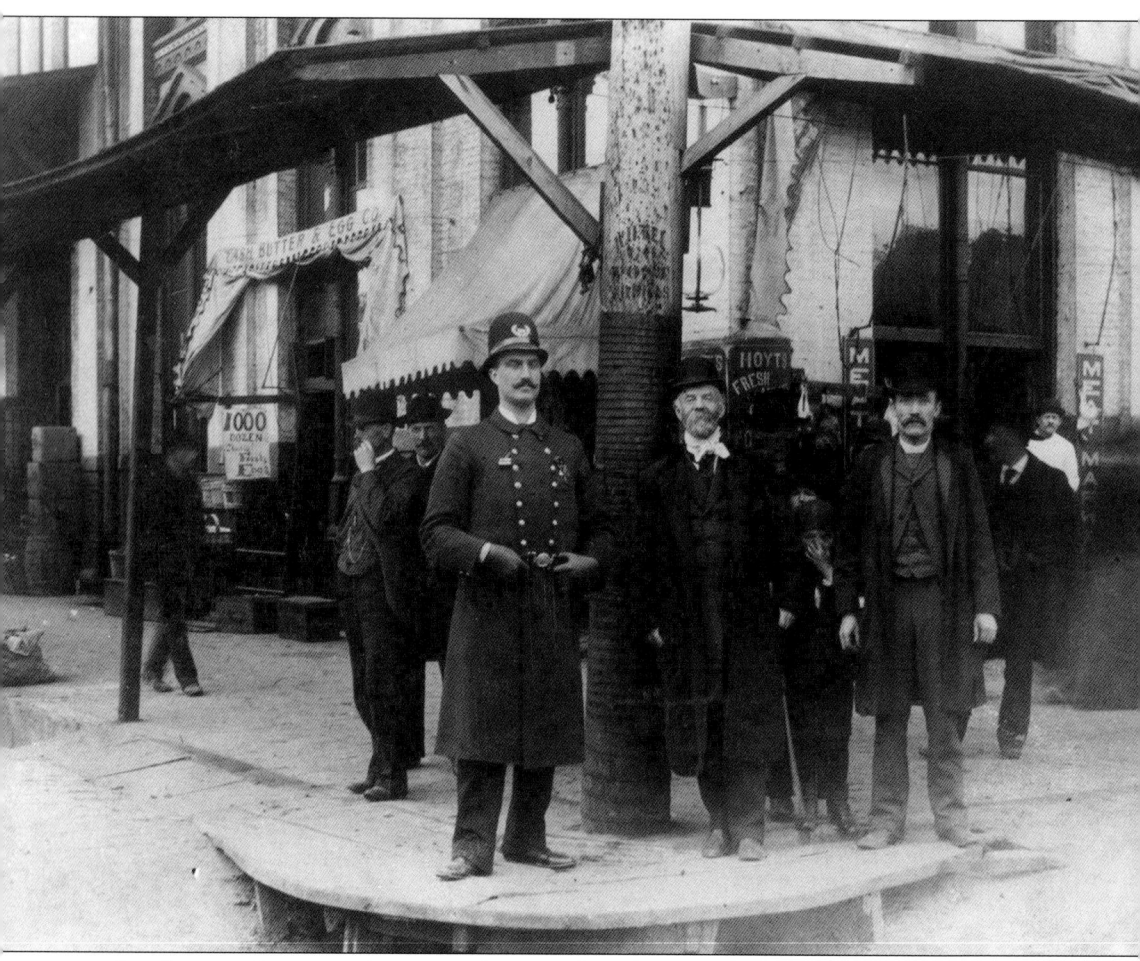

A stalwart policeman is shown standing guard at a busy intersection near Bridge Square. During the latter years of the 19th century, the police were kept busy patrolling the nearby vice district along the downtown riverfront. The police often found themselves buffeted between shifting city policies that alternated between abolishing prostitution and regulating it. (Courtesy of Hennepin County Public Library Special Collections.)

In the era before home delivery, the daily newspapers used boys, some as young as eight, to sell their papers on the streets of downtown Minneapolis. Shouting the current headlines, the newsboys would attract customers who usually paid a nickel for the daily paper. At the end of the day, the young boys would clear 25¢ or 30¢ for their day's work. This newsboy hawked his papers at a prime downtown corner on Hennepin Avenue. (Courtesy of Hennepin County Public Library Special Collections.)

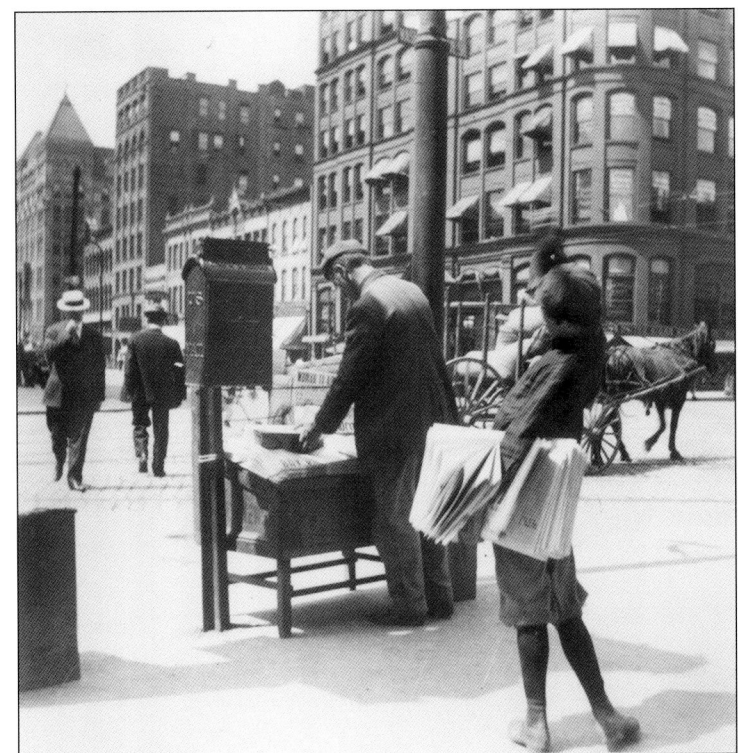

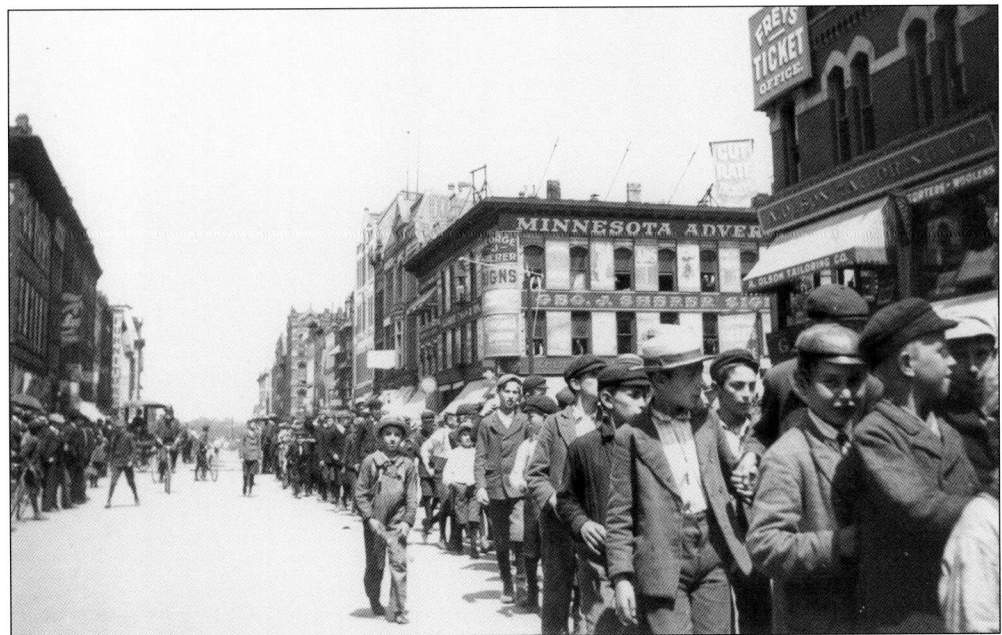

Many of the newsboys in this parade down Washington Avenue might have been homeless, fending for themselves on the streets of Minneapolis. In 1886, a group of civic-minded citizens established a newsboys' home. According to a newspaper report, the home was intended "to provide shelter and comfort for homeless boys. Left early in life to shift for themselves, educated only in the rough schooling of the streets." (Courtesy of Hennepin County Public Library Special Collections.)

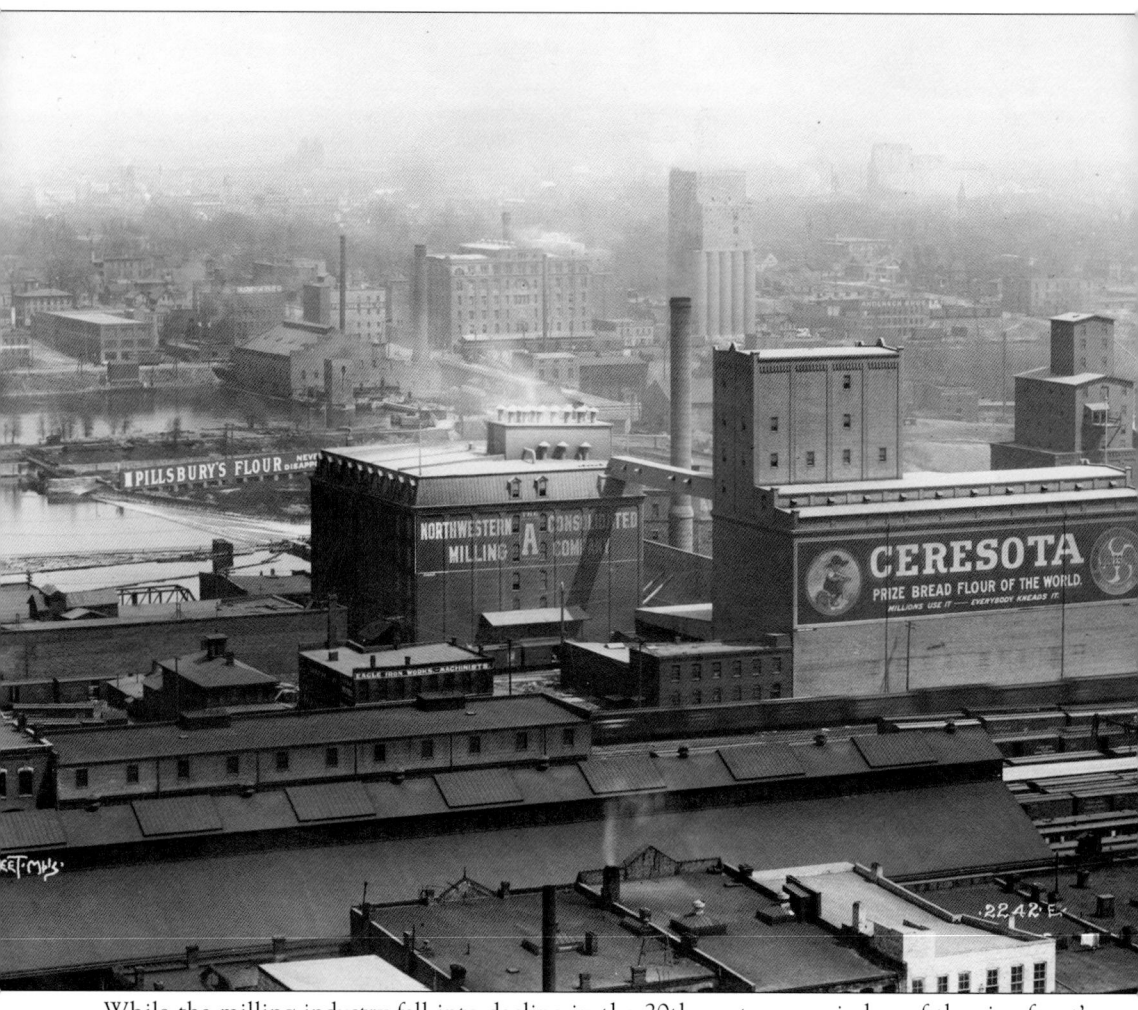

While the milling industry fell into decline in the 20th century, reminders of the riverfront's industrial past have been preserved into the 21st century. The Ceresota sign shown here has been restored and can still be seen today on the facade of a former grain elevator. (Courtesy of Hennepin County Public Library Special Collections.)

Three

THE NEW CENTURY

The 20th century brought important changes to downtown Minneapolis as new institutions began to influence urban life. Automobiles, initially a novelty and plaything for the rich, were soon seen driving up and down Minneapolis streets on a regular basis as Henry Ford's Model T brought motorcars within the reach of average Americans. Ford's company was soon producing 400 Model Ts a day at its 10-story plant on the western edge of downtown.

Those Minneapolitans who owned a motorcar could drive it downtown to take in a popular two-reeler at the movie theaters that lined Hennepin Avenue. Initially, the movies were shown in shabby storefronts and were not quite respectable. In an effort to upgrade the image of their new industry, theater owners soon began building elaborate movie palaces embellished with marble staircases and crystal chandeliers.

One block over from Hennepin, on Nicollet Avenue, a southern Minnesota real estate developer named George Draper Dayton established a major institution that carried his family's name. Throughout the 20th century, Dayton's Department Store anchored downtown and made Nicollet Avenue a major destination for shoppers from all over Minnesota.

Just beyond Nicollet, Marquette Avenue became the region's financial center as the city's major banks headquartered there extended their reach throughout the Upper Midwest. Downtown's financial role was strengthened when Minneapolis was named one of the regional headquarters for the newly created Federal Reserve System in 1914.

While upper Hennepin, Nicollet, and Marquette Avenues were thriving, Minneapolis's original downtown near the Mississippi riverfront was deteriorating. The streets around Bridge Square were now lined with shabby bars and hotels. In an effort to stem the tide of blight, city officials created Gateway Park on the site of Minneapolis's first city hall.

Minneapolis and its downtown continued to prosper during the early years of the 20th century. As a major financial and transportation center, downtown had become an economic magnet for the entire Upper Midwest.

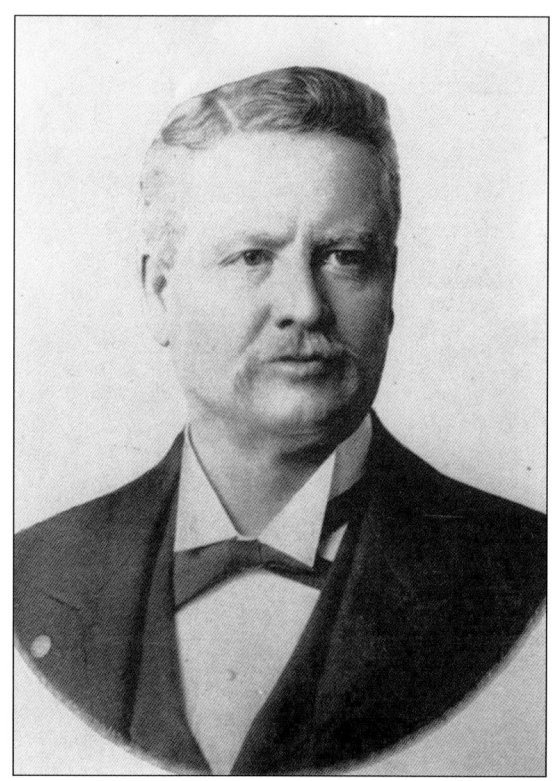

Albert Alonzo Ames, known as "Doc" Ames, served as mayor of Minneapolis off and on during the late 19th century. In 1900, he was elected to his final term. Together with his brother Fred, whom he appointed police chief, Doc Ames was caught up in a municipal corruption scandal that shocked the city's upstanding citizens. Ames was finally driven from office by a crusading grand jury foreman named Hovey Clarke. (Courtesy of the Minnesota Historical Society.)

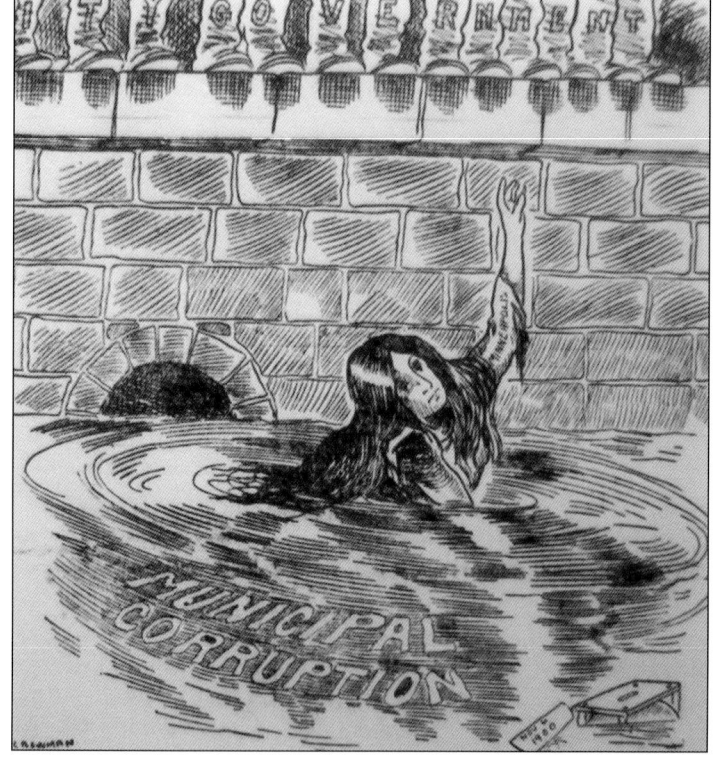

This 1902 cartoon shows Minneapolis sinking into a cesspool of corruption as a result of the Ames scandal. In the title to his work, the cartoonist asked, "Did she jump in or was she pushed?" The cartoon shows a ballot box floating in the cesspool, a reference to the 1900 election that returned Doc Ames to office. (Courtesy of Hennepin County Library.)

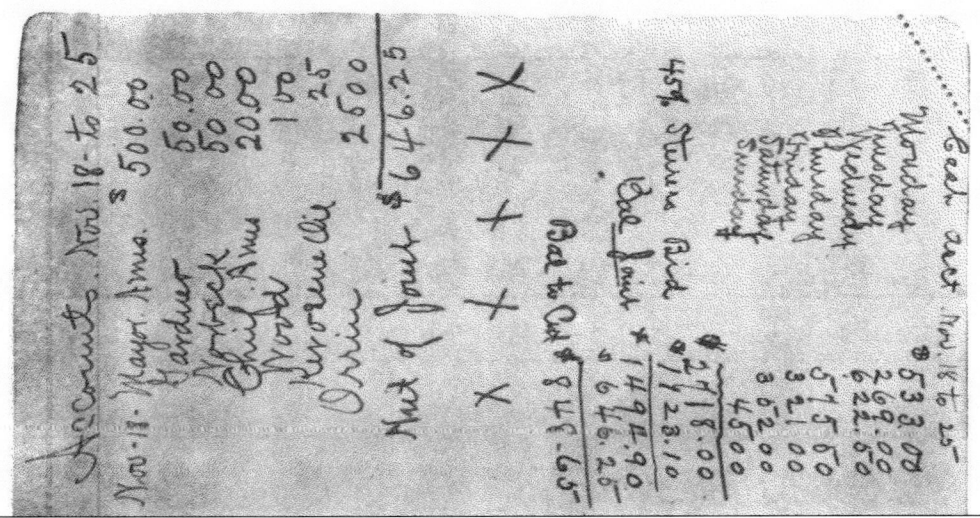

Noted American journalist Lincoln Steffens brought unwanted notoriety to Minnesota's largest city with his 1903 article "The Shame of Minneapolis," published in *McClure's Magazine*. The exposé was later included in a book titled *The Shame of the Cities*, which highlighted the problem of municipal corruption in America at the turn of the last century. (Courtesy of Hennepin County Public Library.)

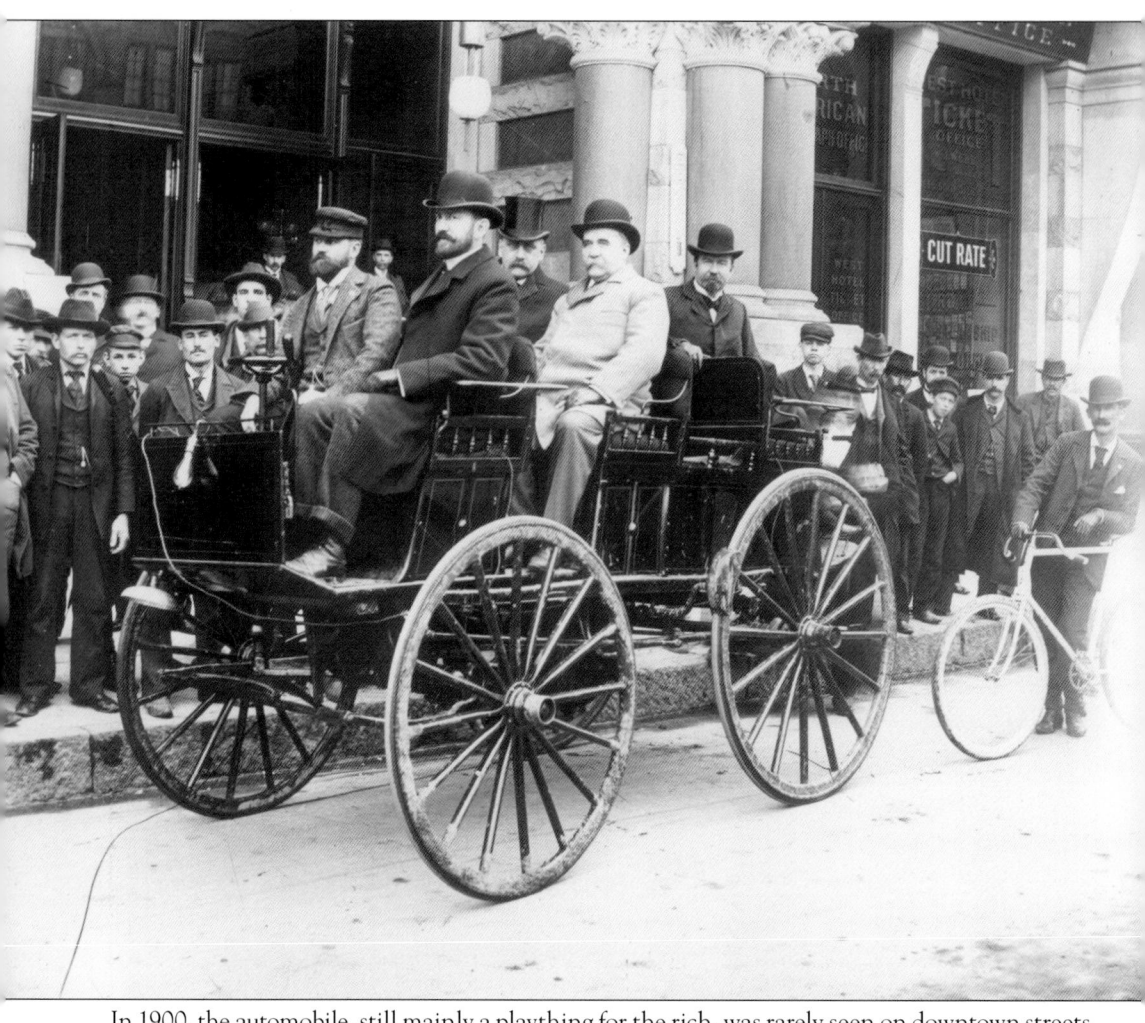

In 1900, the automobile, still mainly a plaything for the rich, was rarely seen on downtown streets. That year, the manager of the Minnesota State Fair issued an open invitation to all automobile owners to participate in a parade through the fairgrounds. "Some of the leading society men who own automobiles have interested themselves in the event and will try to secure a large attendance," the *Minneapolis Tribune* reported. (Courtesy of Hennepin County Public Library Special Collections.)

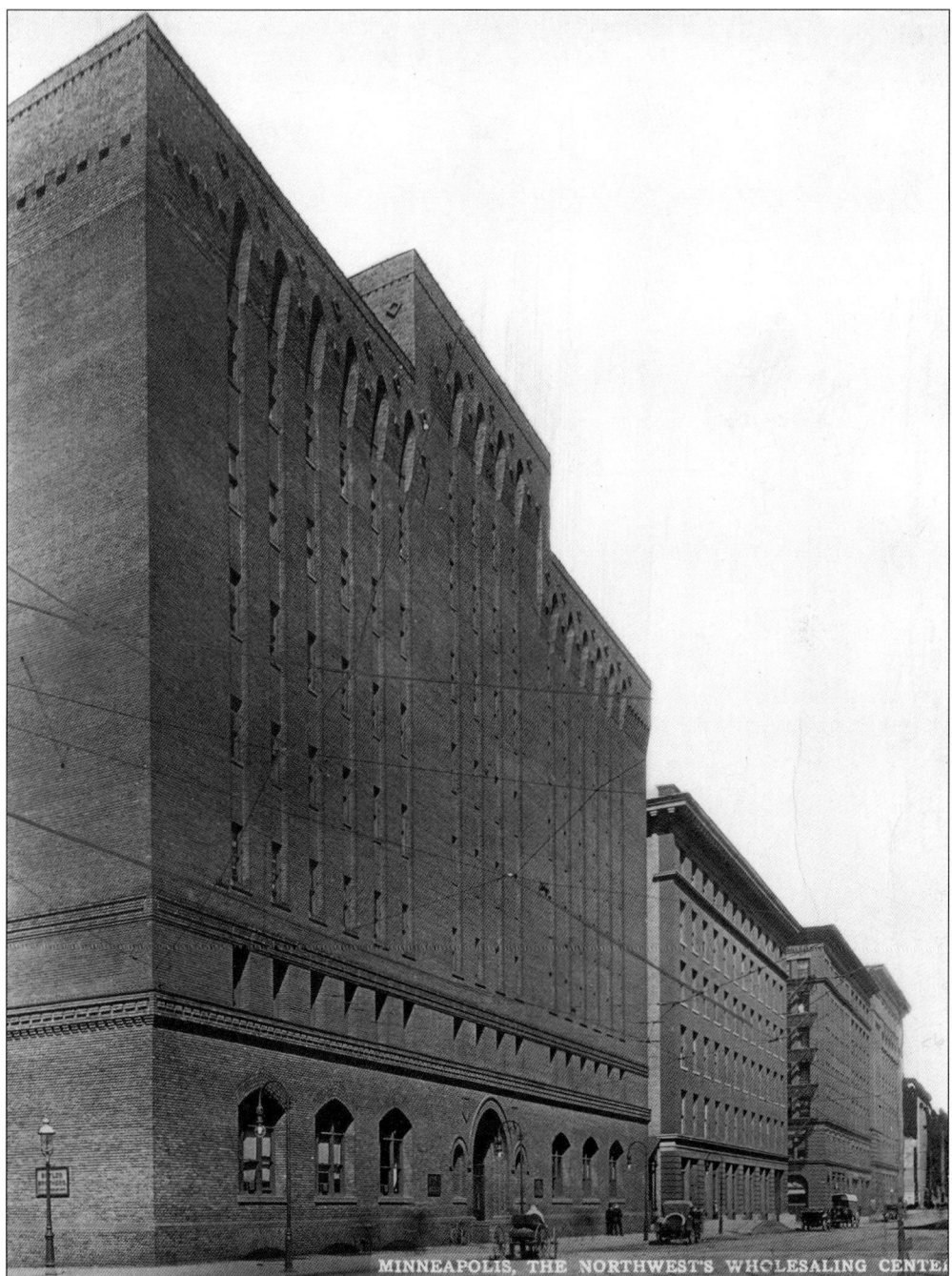

Butler Square was built in 1906 as a warehouse for an eastern wholesale distributing company. The warehouse was located in what was then the center of the city's market district. When it was renovated starting in 1976, Butler Square was one of the first downtown buildings to use historic preservation as a marketing tool to help attract tenants. The renovation maintained the building's original facade but carved out an interior atrium to create a lighter, more open feel for the historic structure. (Courtesy of Hennepin County Public Library Special Collections.)

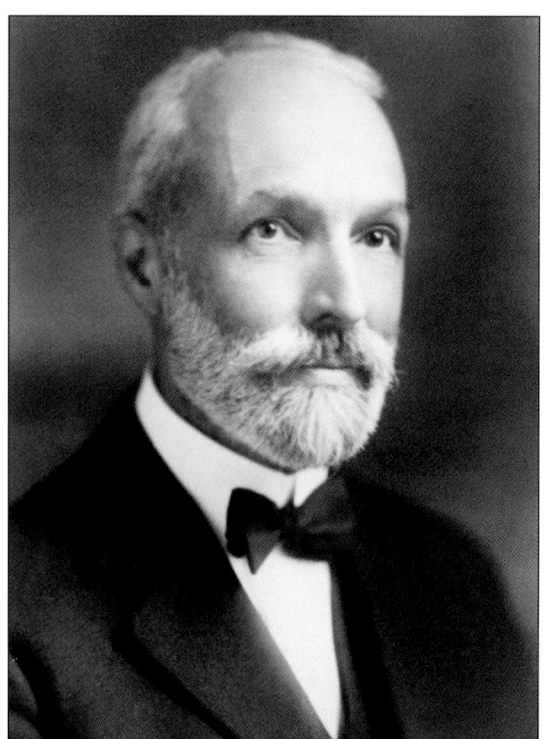

George Draper Dayton was a real estate developer who began purchasing property on Nicollet Avenue as an investment in the 1890s. When fire destroyed the Westminster Presbyterian Church at Nicollet Avenue and Seventh Street, Dayton bought the vacant site from the church and built a six-story commercial building at that corner. In order to attract an anchor tenant to his new development, Dayton purchased an interest in a downtown retail store, Goodfellow Dry Goods. (Courtesy of the Okabena Company.)

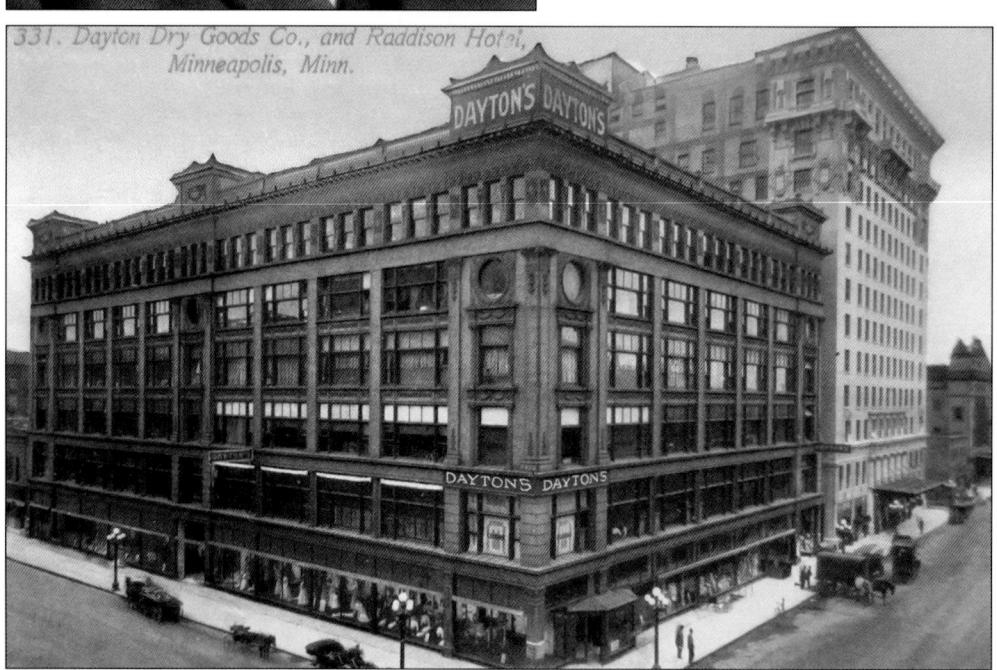

In 1903, Dayton bought out the remaining partners in Goodfellow and took over management of the store. Renamed Dayton's Dry Goods, the store evolved into a major local institution. Later known as Dayton's Department Store, the Nicollet Avenue building would continue to display the family name until 2001, when the store was again renamed, first as Marshall Field's and later as Macy's. (Courtesy of the Minnesota Historical Society.)

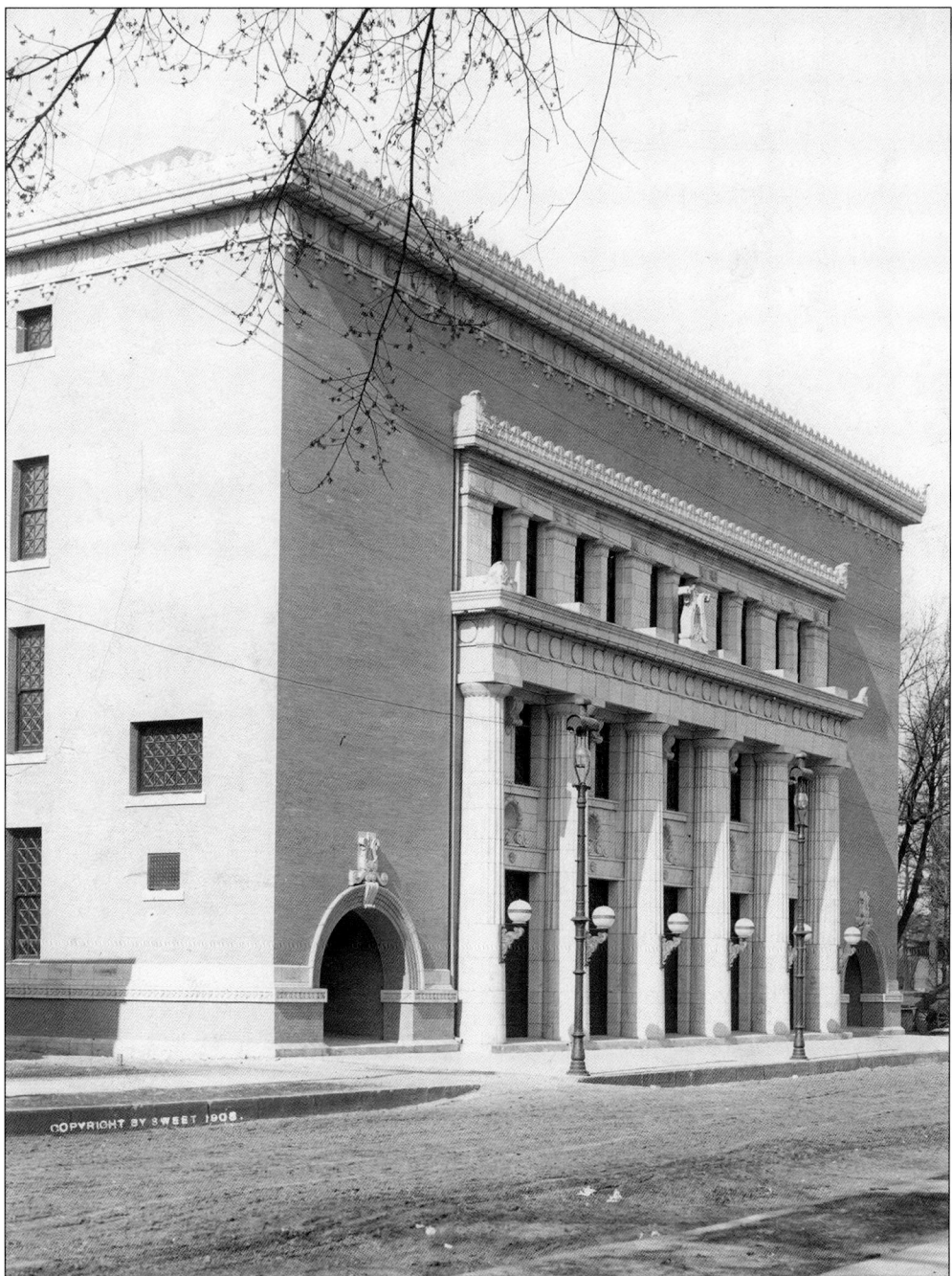

The Minneapolis Auditorium, built in 1905, was the city's first public building used for a broad range of civic events, from musical and theatrical performances to political rallies. Later, it became a venue for live theater when a new, larger auditorium was built at Second Street and Thirteenth Avenue South. (Courtesy of Hennepin County Special Collections)

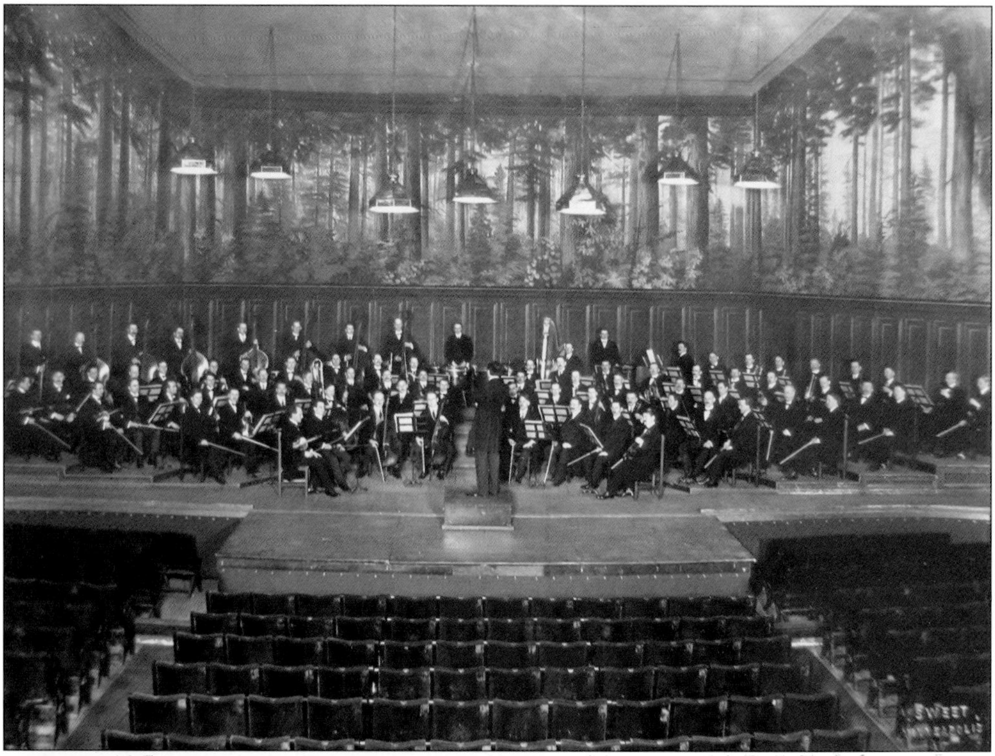

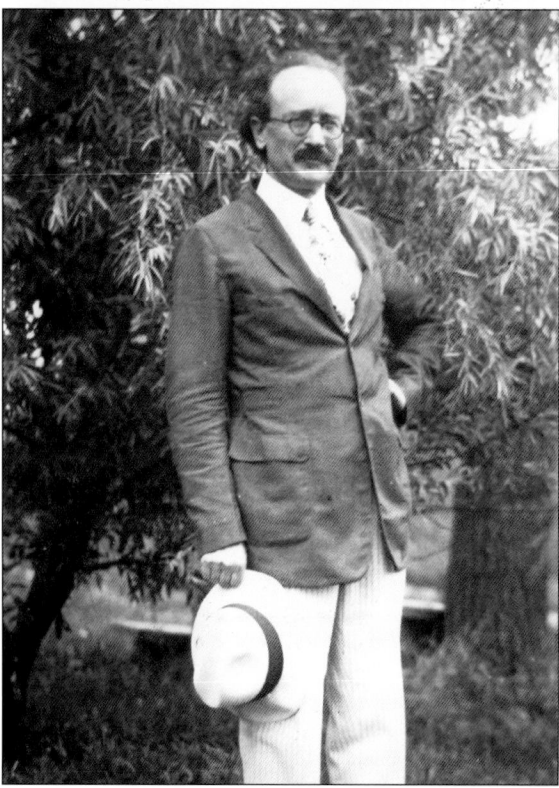

The Minneapolis Symphony Orchestra gave its inaugural concert in 1903. Two years later, the orchestra obtained a permanent home when it moved to the newly built Minneapolis Auditorium. The orchestra would remain there for the next 20 years. The symphonic group gained national acclaim under its first conductor, Emil Oberhoffer. (Courtesy of the Minnesota Historical Society.)

The German-born Emil Oberhoffer led the Minneapolis Symphony for its first 19 years. Oberhoffer was born into a musical family in 1867 and immigrated to the United States while still in his teens. He moved to St. Paul and worked as a teacher and concert performer before founding the Minneapolis Symphony. (Courtesy of the Minnesota Historical Society.)

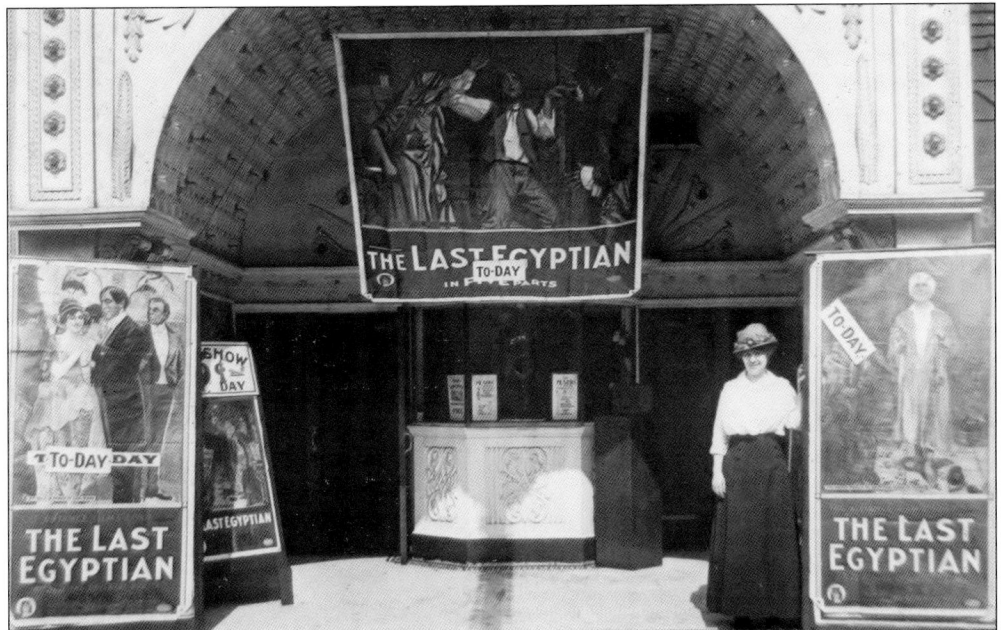

By the 20th century's teen years, the movie theaters were providing a new reason for people to come downtown. As many as 20,000 Minneapolitans were attending the movies each week. For a nickel or a dime, moviegoers could spend an hour or so watching the popular one- and two-reelers. The early films created a new class of entertainers—movie stars. (Courtesy of the Minnesota Historical Society.)

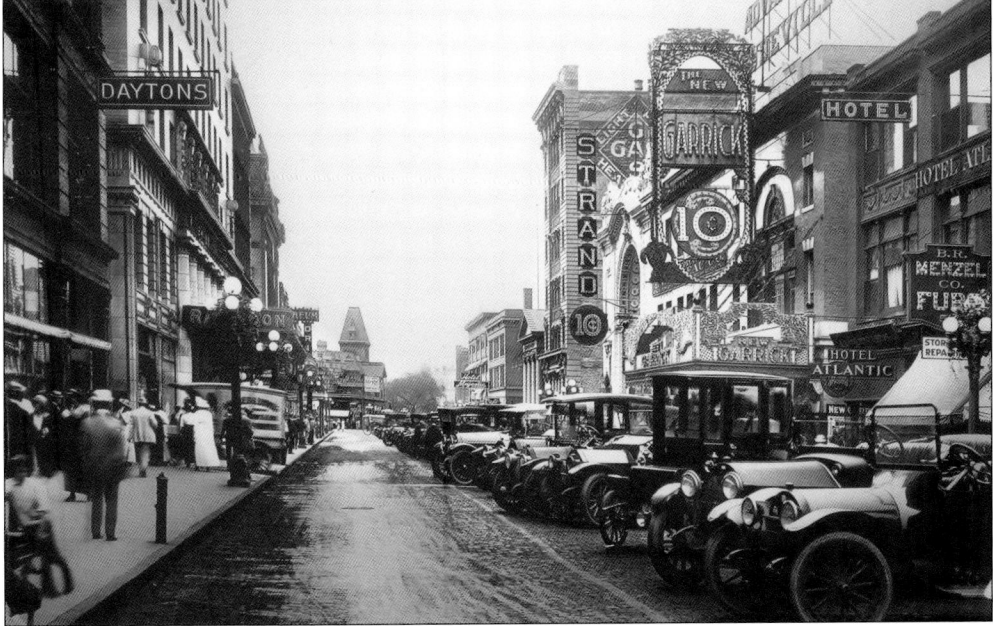

In 1916, Seventh Street between Nicollet and Hennepin Avenues was an extension of Minneapolis's Great White Way. The Grand and the Garrick theaters advertised their 10¢ admission charge. Dayton's Department Store, on the left, is the only remaining building from the World War I era on this section of Seventh Street. (Courtesy of the Minnesota Historical Society.)

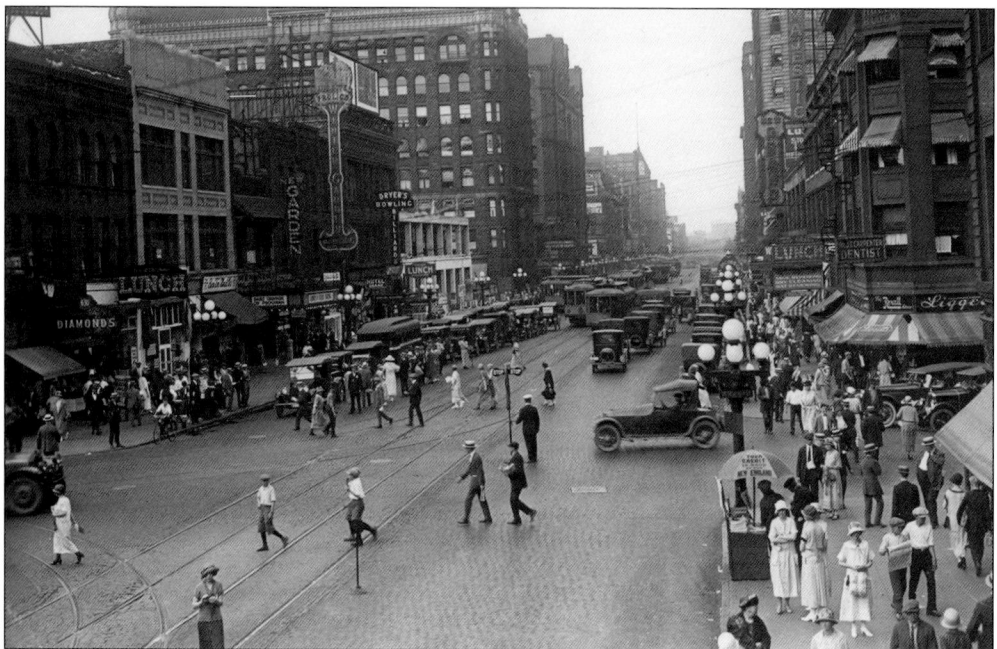

By 1920, cars were clogging downtown streets, as seen in this busy Hennepin Avenue scene. A key landmark from that era, the Masonic Temple, is on the left. The line of storefronts approaching the Masonic Hall would later become the notorious Block E, a collection of sleazy bars, billiard parlors, and flophouses. (Courtesy of the Minnesota Historical Society.)

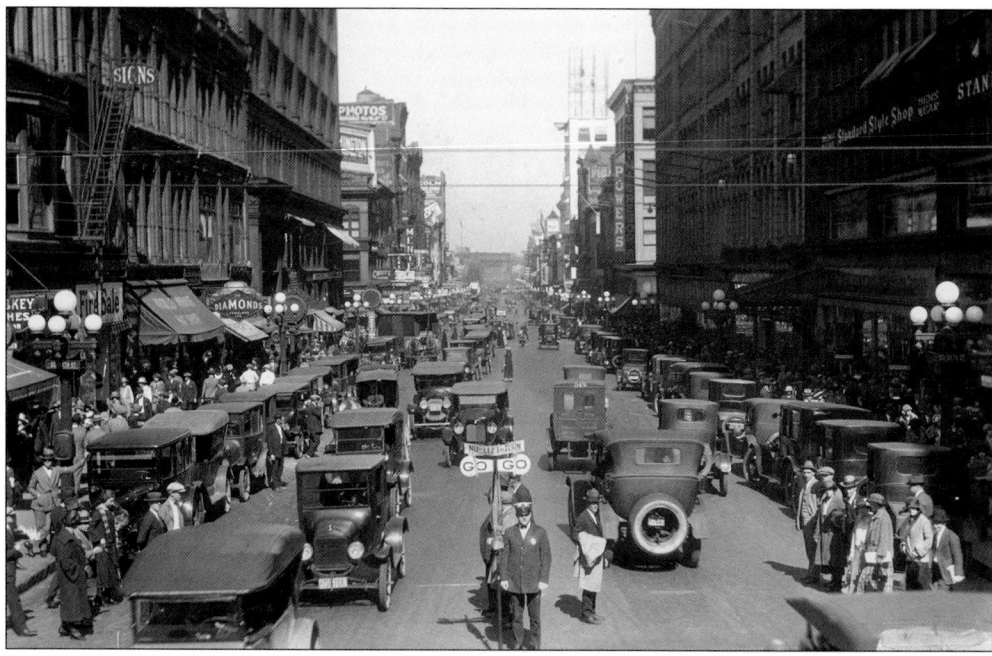

A Minneapolis policeman directs traffic on Nicollet Avenue in this 1920 photograph. Pedestrians are waiting for him to signal that they can cross the busy street. Powers Department Store is on the right. Powers continued to anchor the corner of Nicollet Avenue and Fifth Street until the store closed in 1985. (Courtesy of the Minnesota Historical Society.)

As Henry Ford's Model T continued to break sales records, his company began building new regional production facilities, including this one in Minneapolis at the western end of downtown. Even before construction was completed, the Ford Motor Company began making plans to expand its 14-story plant. Soon, Ford was producing 400 Model Ts a day in Minneapolis. (Courtesy of Hennepin History Museum.)

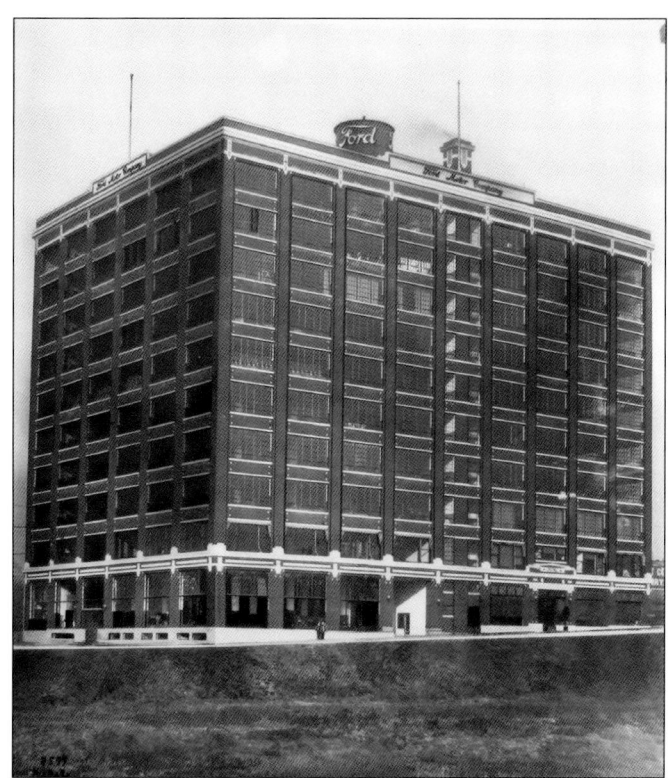

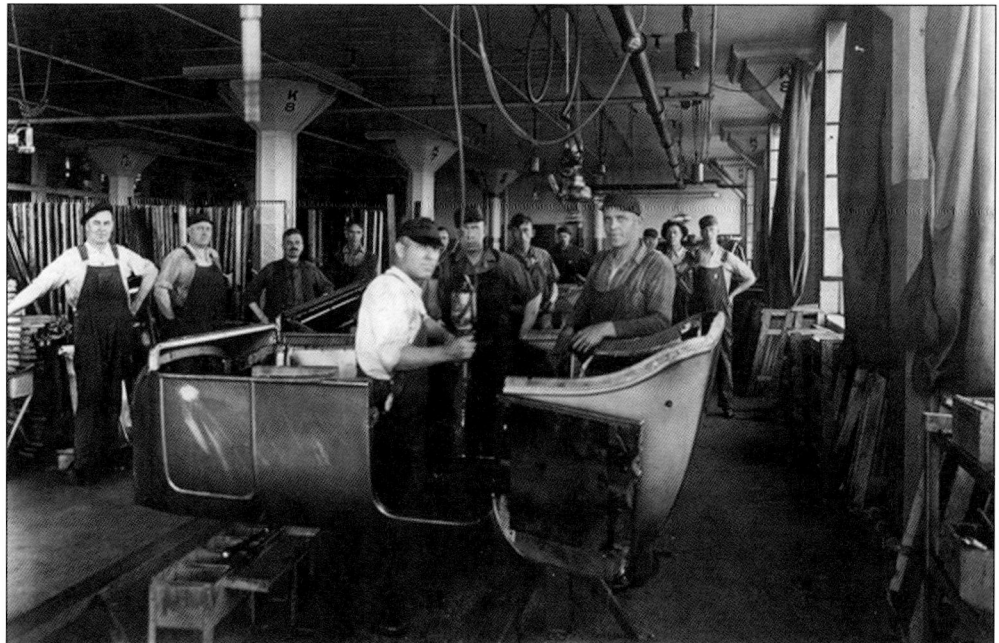

Workers at the Minneapolis plant had to keep pace with the assembly line, a production technique Ford introduced at his early auto factory in Michigan. These line workers benefitted from Ford's $5 daily wage, more than twice what most industrial concerns were paying at that time. (Courtesy of Hennepin History Museum.)

Minneapolis' Selection for Big Regional Bank Hailed as Great Boon to the Whole Northwest

BANKING POWER OF SIX STATES TO CENTER HERE

Minneapolis Chosen as One of Twelve Cities for Reserve Institution.

In 1914, Minneapolis became the headquarters of the Federal Reserve System's Ninth District. The district covered an area stretching from Northern Michigan to Montana. As a district headquarters, Minneapolis was able to solidify its position as the region's financial center. (Courtesy of Hennepin County Public Library.)

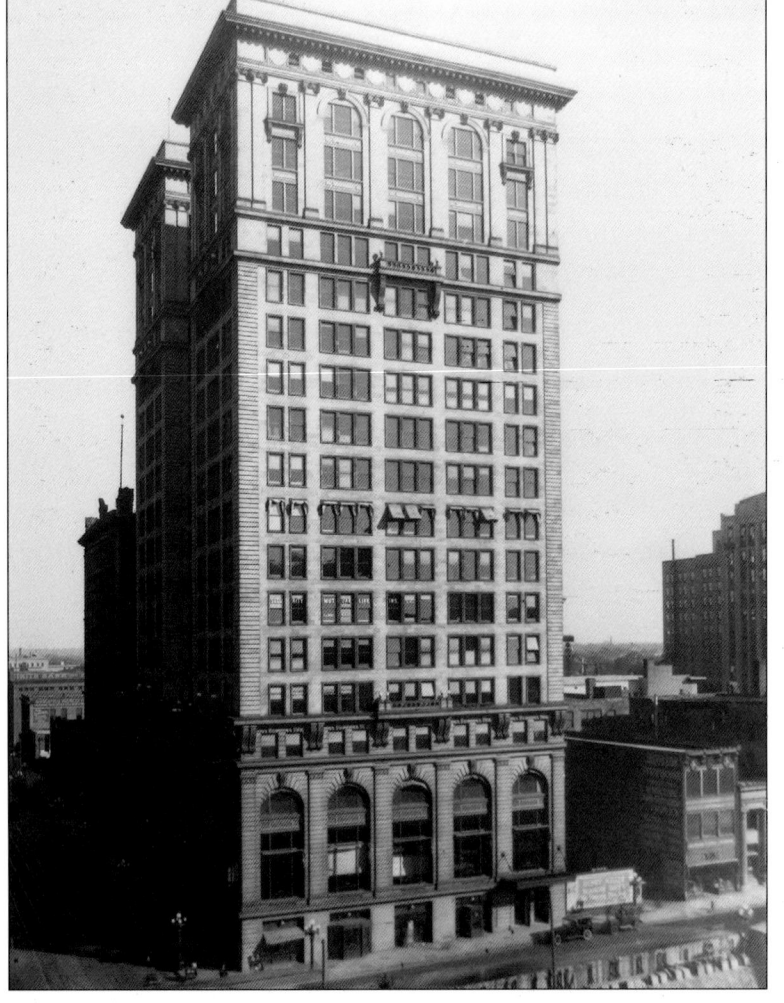

In 1914, one of Minneapolis's largest financial institutions, First National Bank, completed work on a new downtown headquarters building it shared with the Soo Line Railroad. Then the city's tallest office tower, the First National Bank–Soo Line Railroad building retained that title until it was upstaged by newer, taller towers in the late 1920s. (Courtesy of the Minnesota Historical Society.)

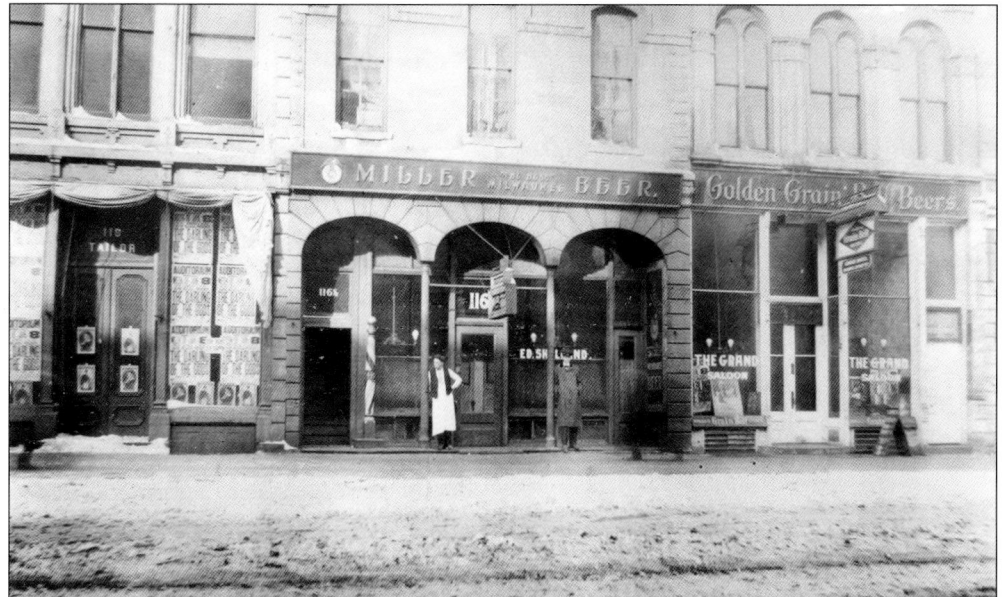

As downtown retailers moved away from the riverfront after the turn of the 20th century, the blocks along lower Hennepin and Nicollet Avenues slid into decay. Shabby bars and hotels surrounded Bridge Square. First Street at the riverfront had become the city's vice district. (Courtesy of the Minnesota Historical Society.)

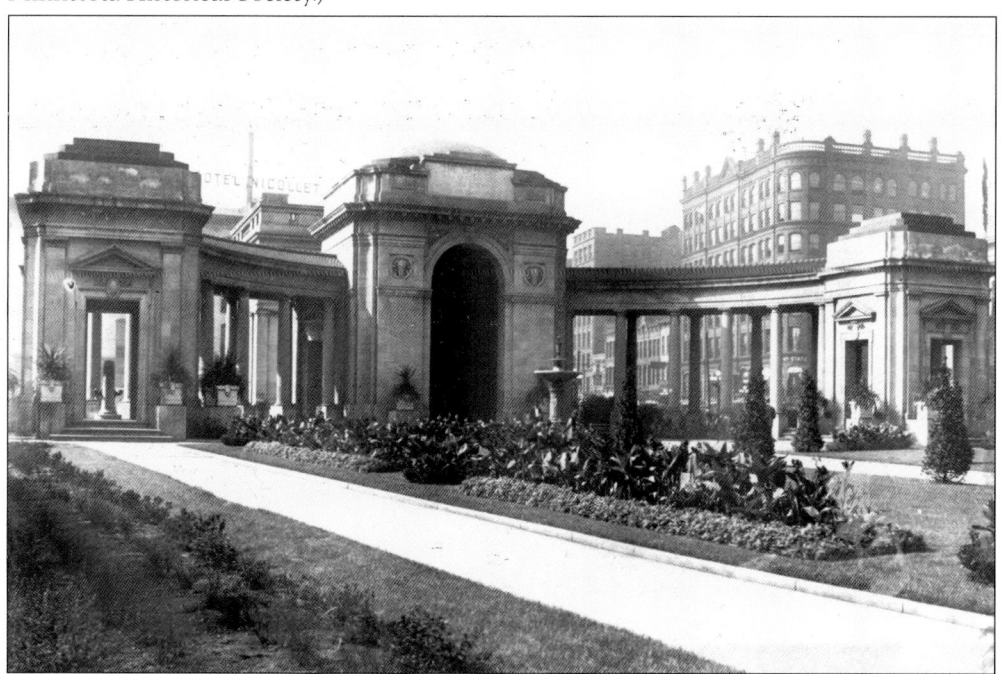

The Gateway Park and Pavilion, built in 1915, represented an effort to bring a new urban planning movement known as City Beautiful to Minneapolis. The block-long project consisted of a classical pavilion fronting a small tree-lined park. City leaders hoped that Gateway Park would combat the urban blight that had enveloped the area, but those hopes were never realized. (Courtesy of Hennepin County Library Special Collections.)

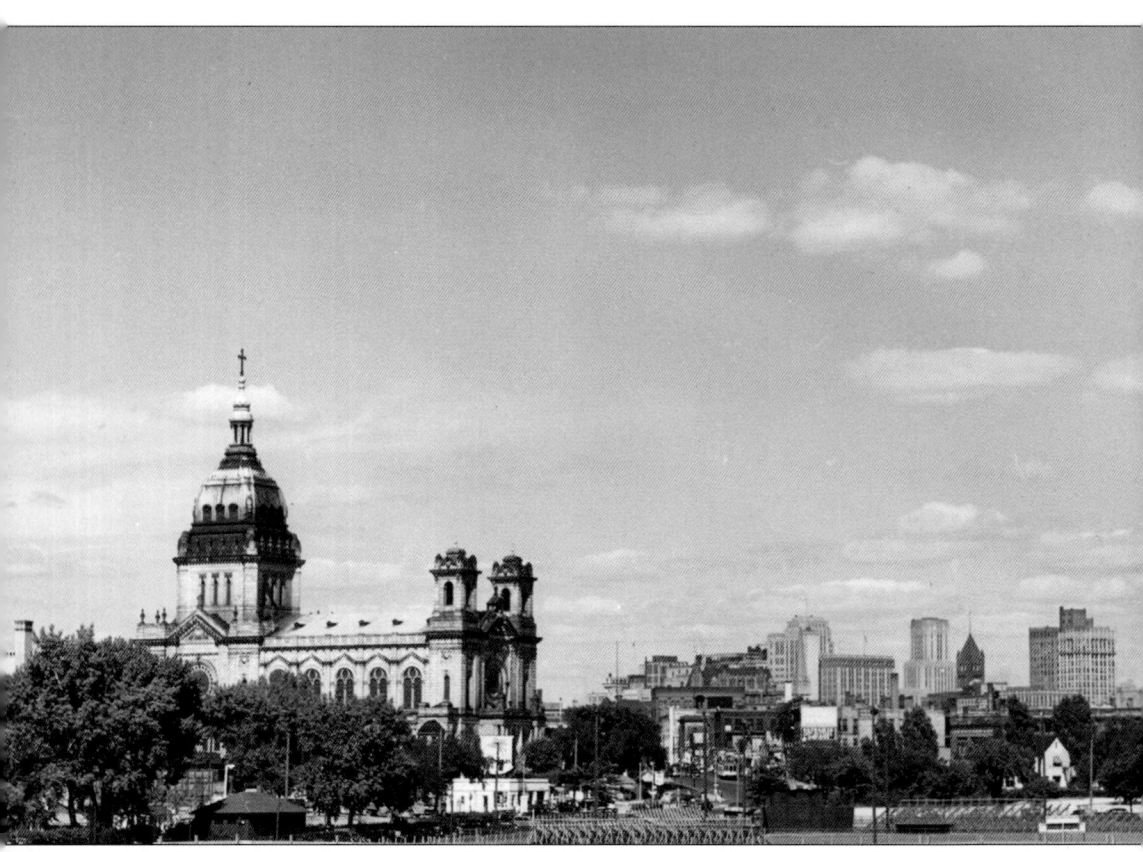

The Basilica of St. Mary was built in 1914 by Emmanuel Masqueray, the architect who also designed the St. Paul Cathedral. Combining Neoclassical and Baroque styles, the church serves as procathedral for the St. Paul diocese. The basilica was damaged by the construction of nearby Interstate 94 in the 1980s and underwent extensive renovations starting in the 1990s. (Courtesy of Hennepin History Museum.)

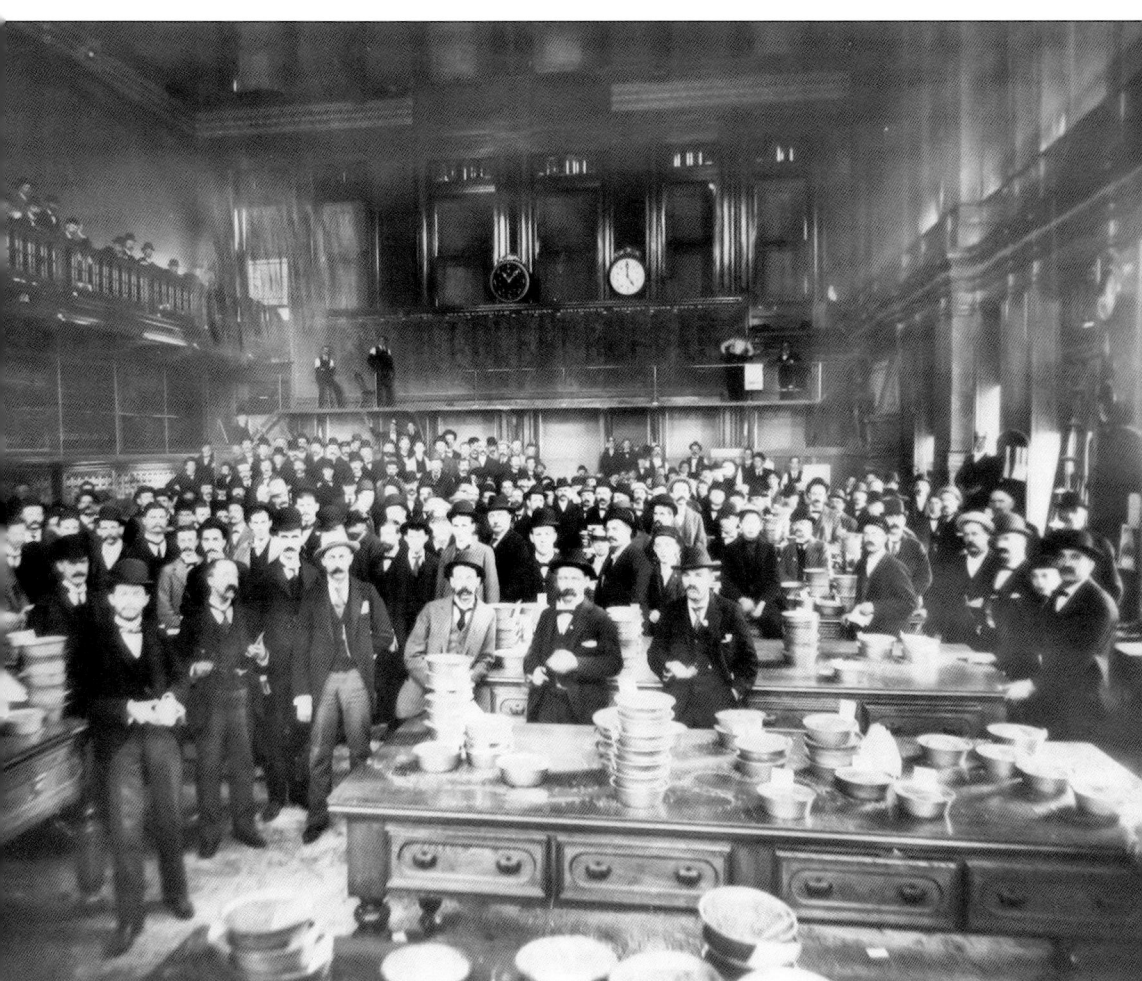

The origins of the Minneapolis Grain Exchange extend back to 1881, when it was known as the Minneapolis Chamber of Commerce. The exchange was established to eliminate wide swings in grain prices by enabling buyers and sellers to agree on a price for the grain to be delivered at a future time. Through most of the exchange's history, grain futures were bought and sold on its open trading floor. The bowls seen on the tables in front contain various grades of wheat and other grains. (Courtesy of the Minnesota Historical Society.)

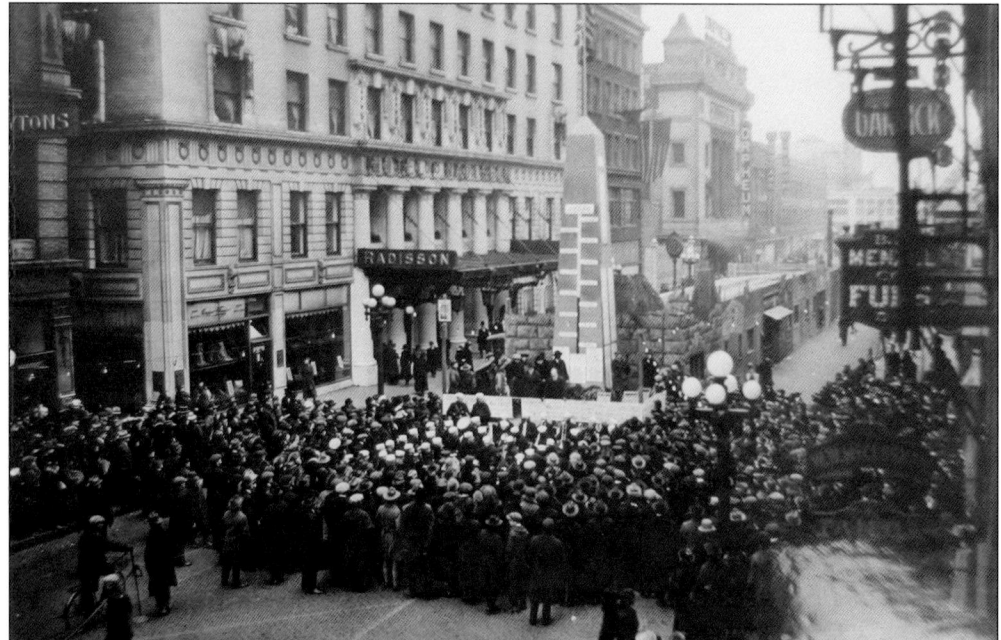

When the United States declared war on Germany in 1917, the federal government faced the need of financing the rapid expansion in federal activities. Minnesotans could demonstrate their support of the war effort by purchasing Liberty Bonds, used to finance the war. This Liberty Bond rally was held in the middle of Nicollet Avenue. (Courtesy of the Minnesota History Society.)

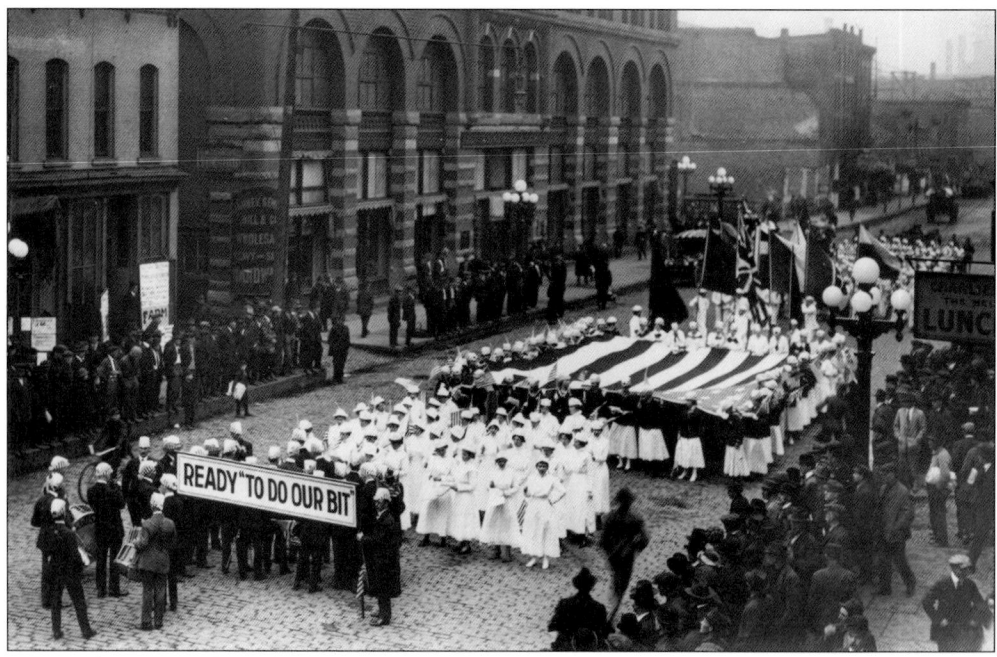

During the year and a half that the United States was a combatant in World War I, downtown Minneapolis was the site of a series of patriotic parades intended to support the Minnesota men who were fighting in the trenches of France. By Armistice Day, the war had claimed the lives of more than 2,000 Minnesotans. (Courtesy of Hennepin County Public Library Special Collections.)

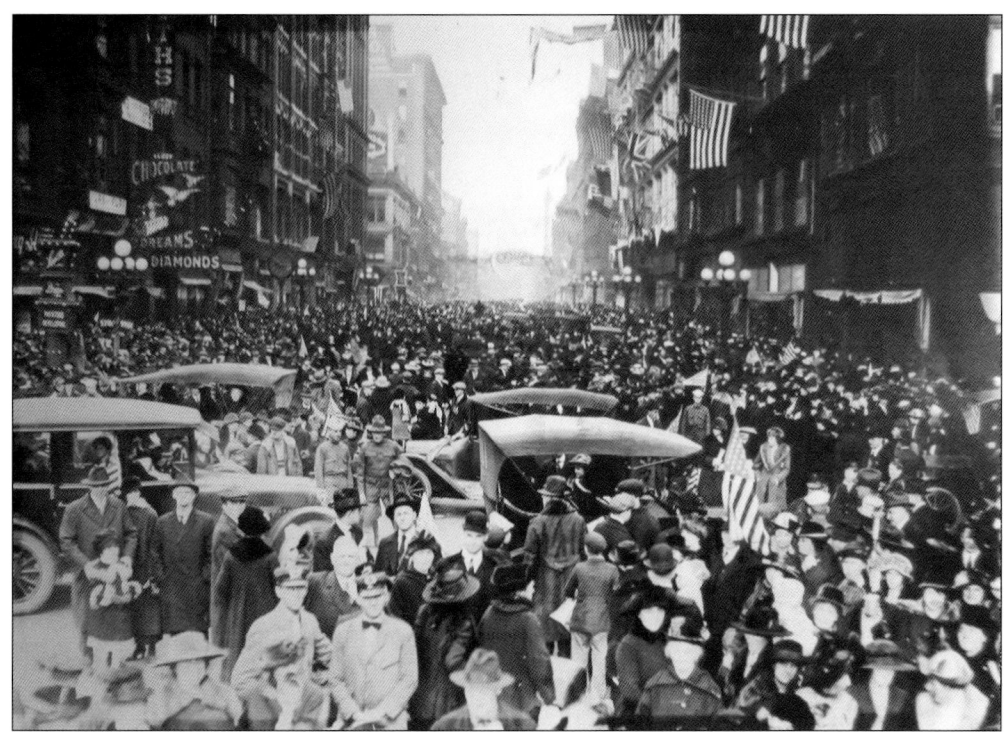

News of the Armistice, which ended World War I, reached Minneapolis just before 2:00 in the morning on November 11, 1918. "By 4 AM, the downtown streets were clogged with merrymakers," the Minneapolis Journal reported. "Everyone was brimming over with good humor and feeling of fellowship for every other man, be the struggling newsboy working his way through the crowd or the sedate banker off the hill." (Both, courtesy of Hennepin County Public Library Special Collections.)

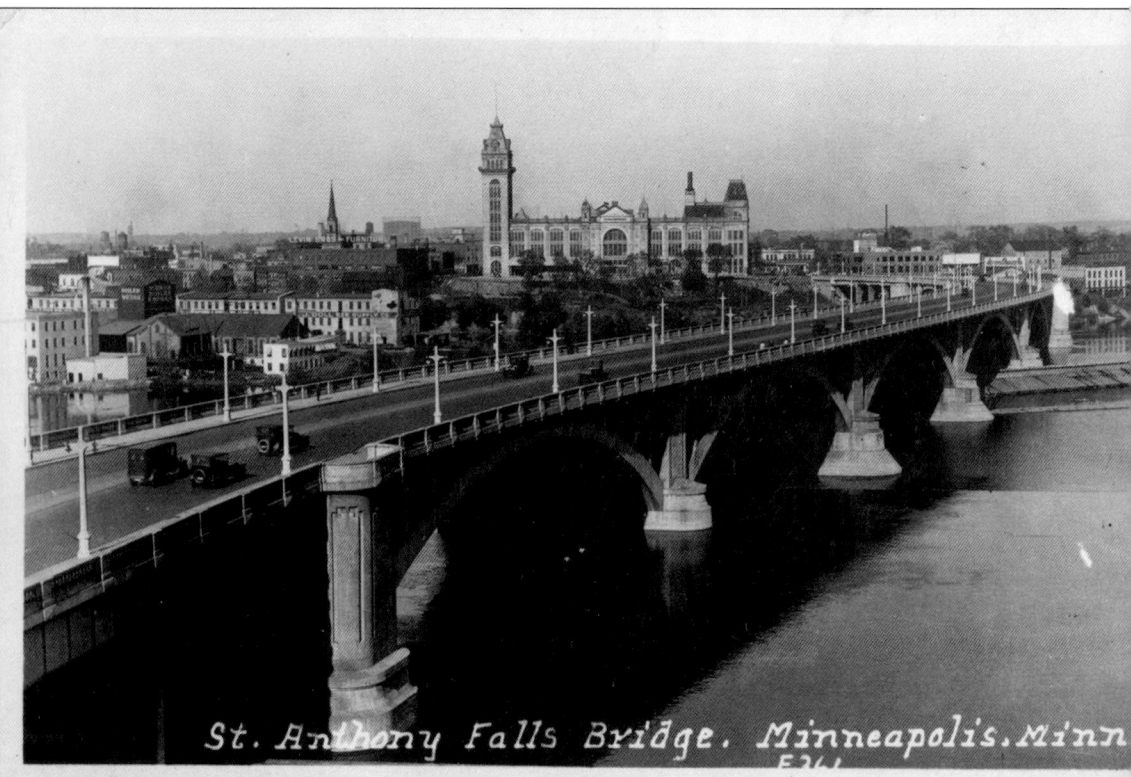

The Minneapolis riverfront gained a second arched span over the Mississippi when the Third Avenue Bridge opened in 1918. Highway planners curved the bridge as it passed over the river to prevent the bedrock supporting the bridge piers from fracturing. In this photograph, the large structure with the tower is the Exposition Building, the site of the 1892 Republican National Convention. (Courtesy of Hennepin County Public Library Special Collections.)

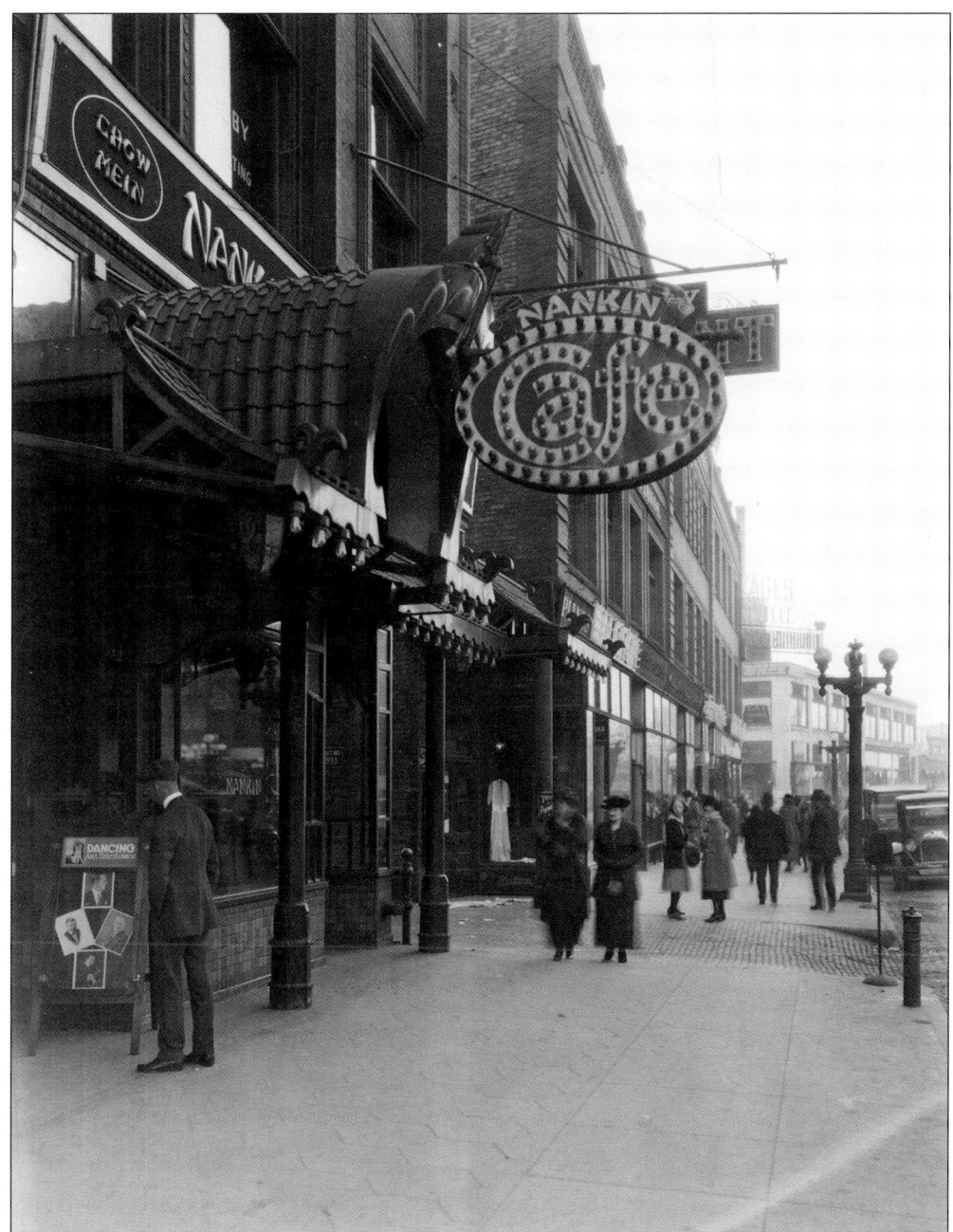

Starting in 1919, when it first opened, the Nankin Café introduced generations of Minnesotans to such Chinese American delicacies as egg rolls, fried rice, and chow mein. With its elaborate Oriental decor, the Nankin brought an exotic touch to downtown in an era when ethnic restaurants were still a rarity in the Midwest. After an 80-year run, the Nankin closed in 1999. (Courtesy of Hennepin History Museum)

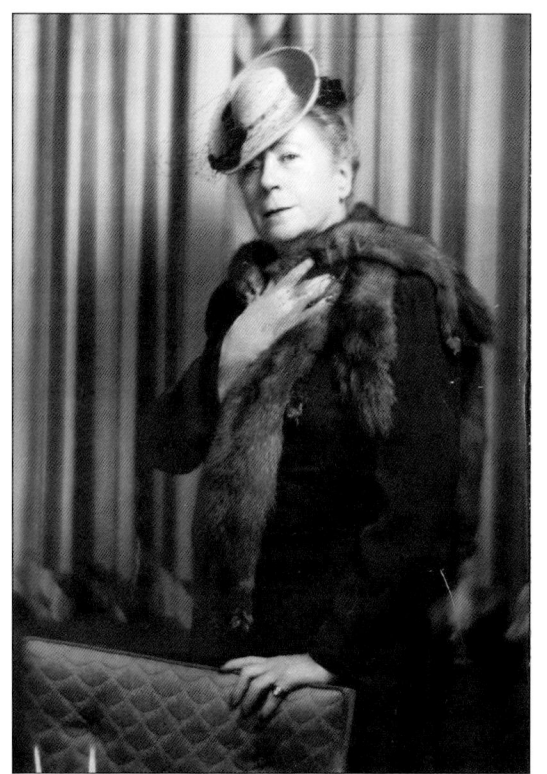

Elizabeth Quinlan worked her way up from a $10-a-week clerk in the Goodfellow Dry Goods store to a premier position at the top of Minneapolis's fashion world. In 1894, Quinlan left Goodfellow and opened the city's first women's specialty store in partnership with Fred Young, another former Goodfellow employee. The Young Quinlan store soon became the place to shop for fashionable women throughout Minnesota. (Courtesy of Hennepin County Public Library Special Collections.)

The Young Quinlan Building, which opened in 1924, brought high-fashion style to Nicollet Avenue. The five-story building, located at the corner of Nicollet Avenue and Ninth Street, exemplified the Renaissance Revival style popular in the 1920s. It is one of the few downtown buildings from the 1920s that has survived virtually intact into modern times. (Courtesy of Hennepin County Special Collections.)

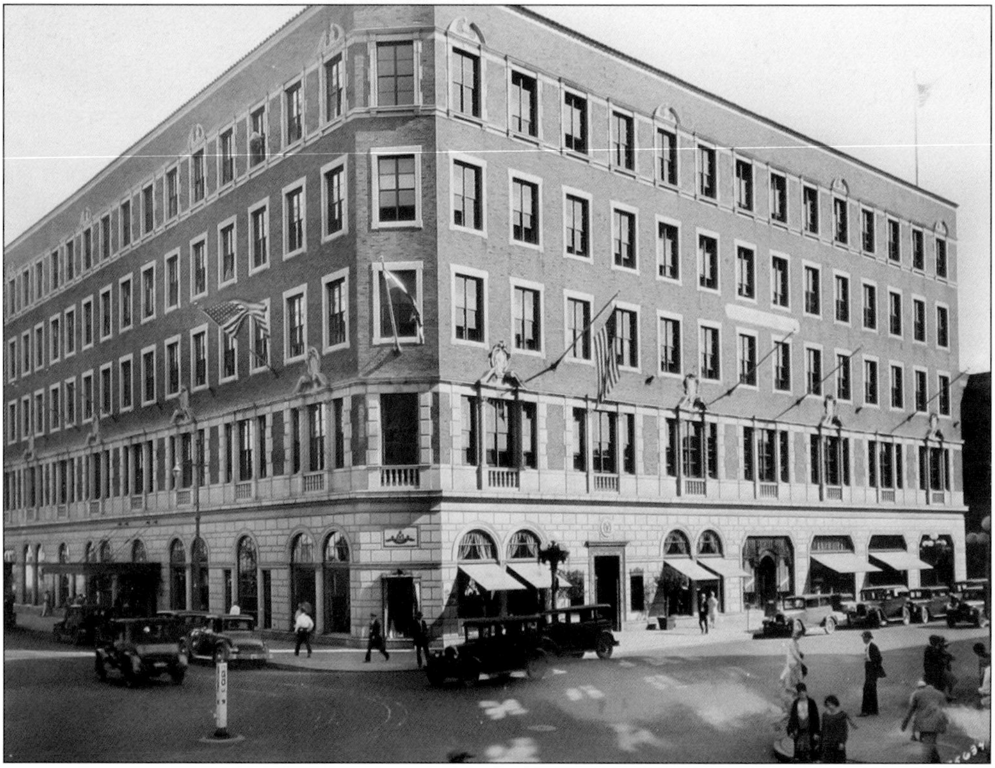

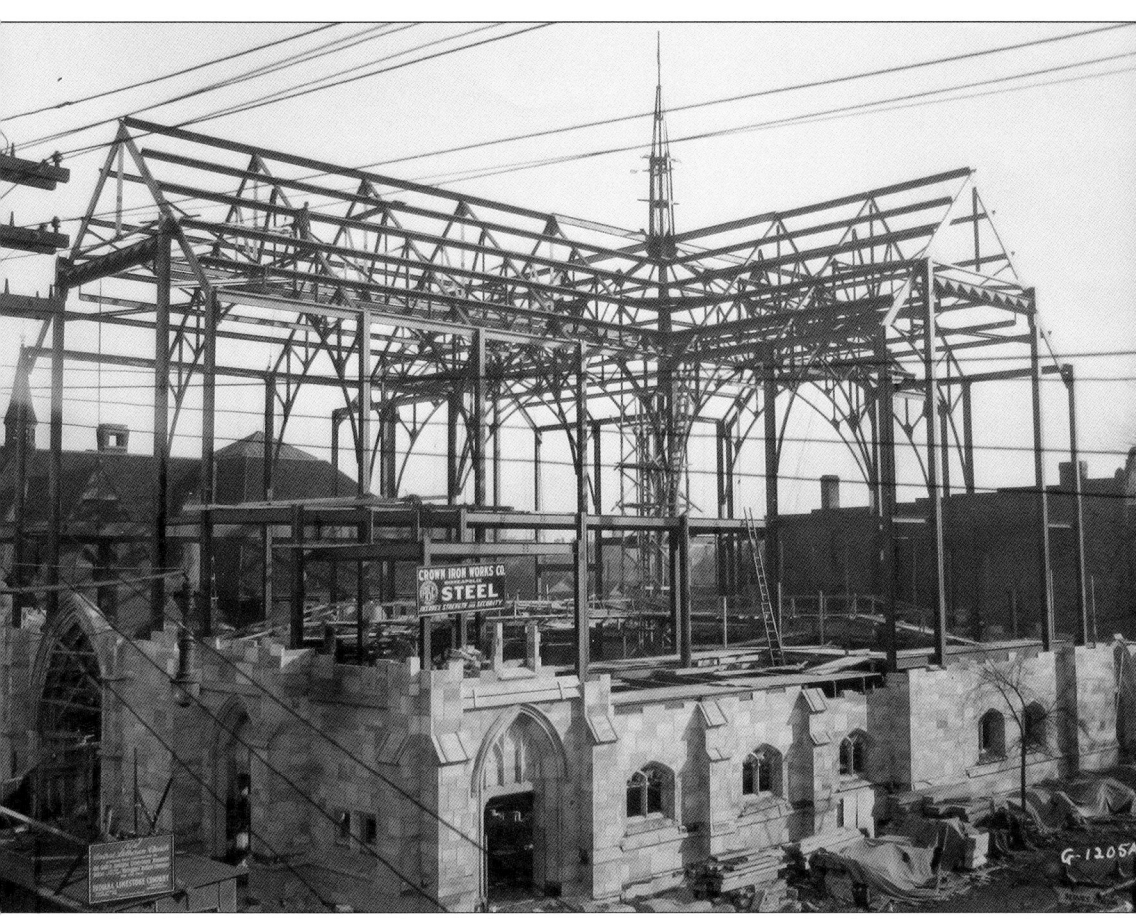
Central Lutheran Church, shown here under construction in 1926, was founded by a group of Norwegian American laymen who wanted a Lutheran presence in downtown Minneapolis. At a time when many Norwegian American Lutheran congregations worshipped in Norwegian, Central Lutheran's founders determined that the future of Lutheranism in America lay in the use of English. (Courtesy of the Minnesota Historical Society.)

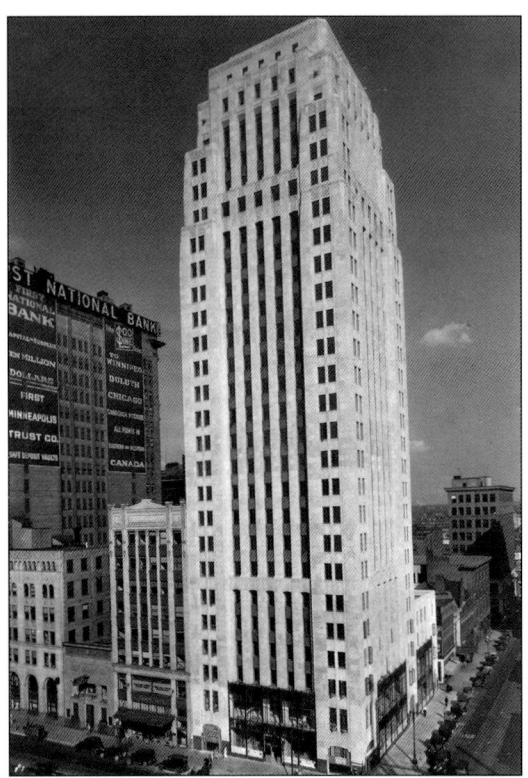

The Rand Tower, downtown's bow to the Art Deco era, provides an architectural reminder of the Roaring Twenties. The building was designed by Holabard & Root, the Chicago firm that also designed St. Paul's Art Deco city hall. The Rand Tower's small lobby is embellished with a star-studded terrazzo floor, an elegant spiral staircase, and ornamental elevator doors. (Courtesy of Hennepin County Public Library Special Collections.)

One of downtown's most prominent artworks, the bronze sculpture known as *Wings* is displayed in the lobby of Rand Tower. The sculpture reflects the interests of the building's developer, Rufus Rand, an aviation enthusiast. Rand flew with the Lafayette Flying Corps during World War I. *Wings* creator Oskar J.W. Hansen is shown at work on the sculpture. (Courtesy of Hennepin County Public Library Special Collections.)

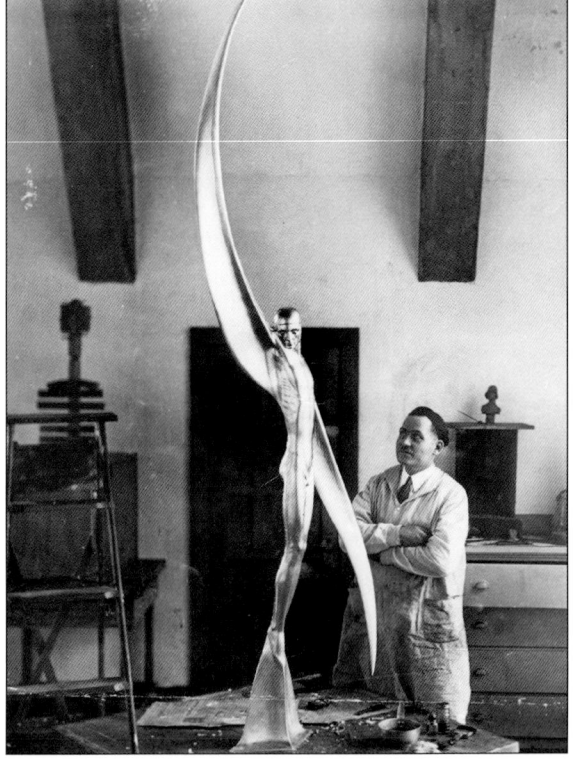

Four

TUMULTUOUS DECADES

In 1929, a flamboyant developer named Wilbur Foshay built an office tower modeled after the Washington Monument that would dominate the city's skyline for more than 40 years. Foshay inaugurated his downtown landmark with an extravagant three-day celebration over Labor Day weekend. Two months later, the stock market crashed, and Foshay was sent to jail for tax evasion.

While the city was hard hit by the Depression, its downtown core survived the economic turmoil of the 1930s. Minneapolis's major banks remained open during those years except for a brief period in March 1933, euphemistically known as a bank "holiday."

As the Depression took hold, city hall was able to keep its public services functioning despite a sharp drop in municipal revenues. Minneapolis residents who faced hard times were able to get a respite from the Depression at the downtown city park and library, which remained open throughout the 1930s.

In 1934, the streets of downtown Minneapolis were rocked with violence as labor union members clashed with police during a bitter truckers' strike that claimed the life of two strikers and a sheriff's deputy. Pressure from the Roosevelt Administration helped end the strike four months after it began.

The advent of World War II brought major changes in the lives of most Minnesotans. Families stood by as their sons and daughters marched off to war. Rationing made a trip to the grocery store something of an ordeal. Downtown soon became a staging point for victory parades, military recruitment campaigns, and Liberty Bond rallies.

The industrial buildup accompanying the war brought an end to the Depression and boosted household incomes, but goods were in short supply in downtown stores. With money in their pockets during the wartime years, people flocked to Hennepin Avenue's Great White Way and its string of movie theaters showing Hollywood's latest productions.

Minneapolitans celebrated in the streets of downtown when VJ Day, August 14, 1945, brought an end to the war. Like Americans everywhere, they looked forward to a new era of peace and prosperity.

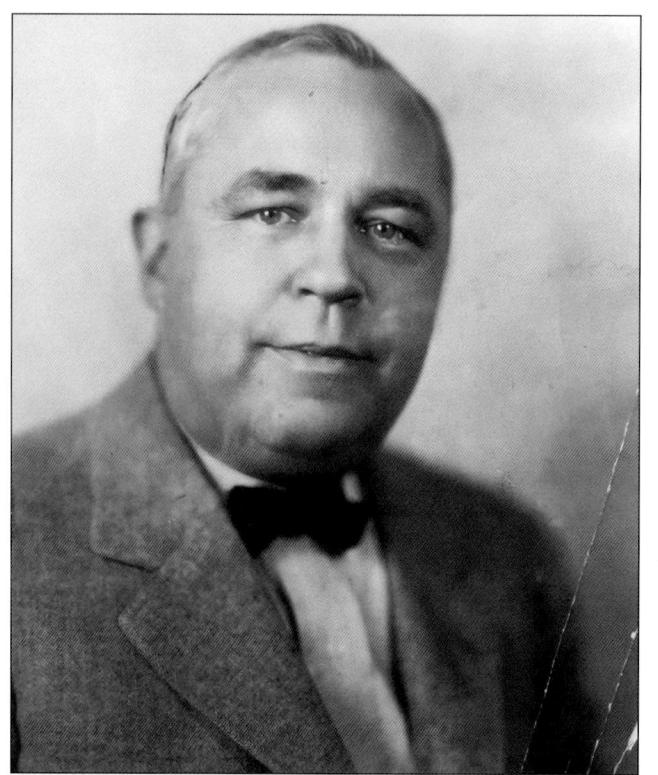

Wilbur Foshay was a Minnesota businessman who made his fortune buying utility companies throughout the Midwest. Shortly after completing the downtown office tower that bore his name, Foshay was convicted of stock fraud. Because of good behavior, he served only three years of his 15-year sentence. In 1947, Foshay received a full pardon from Pres. Harry Truman. (Courtesy of the Minnesota Historical Society.)

Over Labor Day weekend in 1929, Foshay organized a lavish three-day celebration to inaugurate his new building. The celebration featured a fireworks display and a two-hour concert with a march written and directed by John Phillip Sousa for the occasion. During the celebration, Foshay unveiled a bronze statue known as *Scherzo* that he had commissioned for the building. In the 1940s, *Scherzo* was moved to the entrance of a downtown restaurant, where it became a well-known local landmark. (Courtesy of the Minnesota Historical Society.)

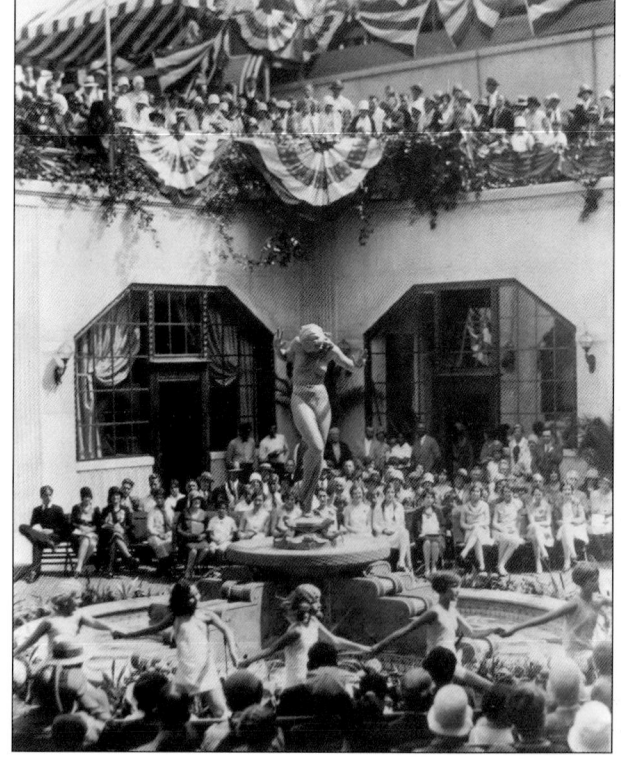

Foshay built his 447-foot-tall office building to resemble the Washington Monument. Much to the chagrin of the city's conservative business leaders, the flamboyant businessman carved his name in 10-foot-high letters at the top of the building. The Foshay Tower continued to dominate the downtown skyline well into the 1970s, when it was overshadowed by a new group of taller buildings. (Both, courtesy of Hennepin County Public Library Special Collections.)

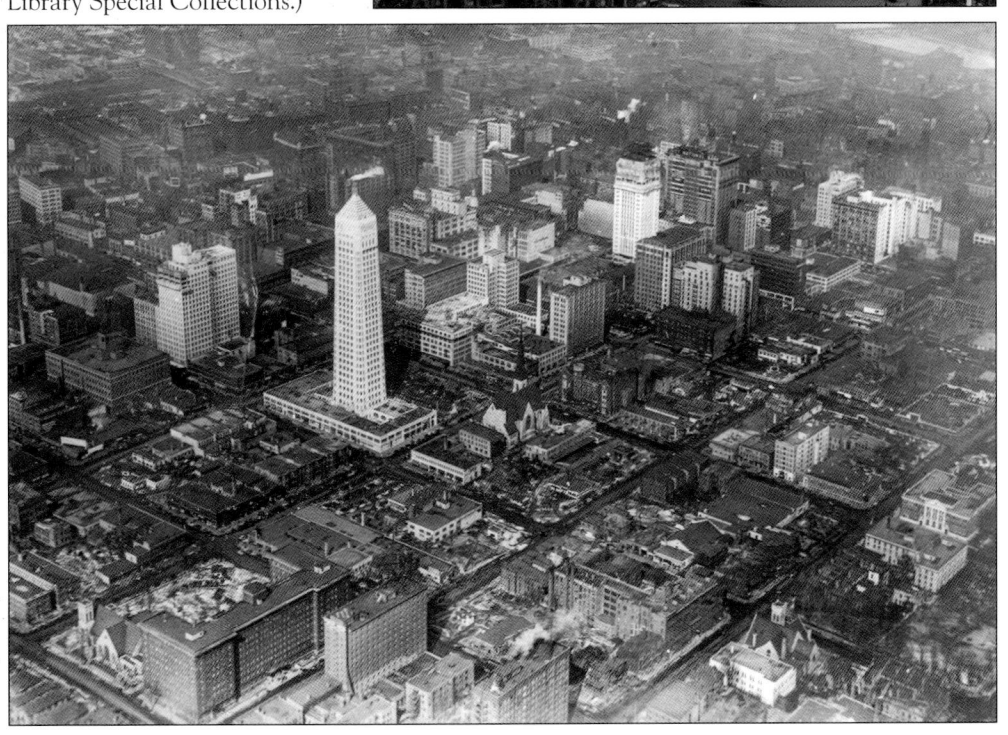

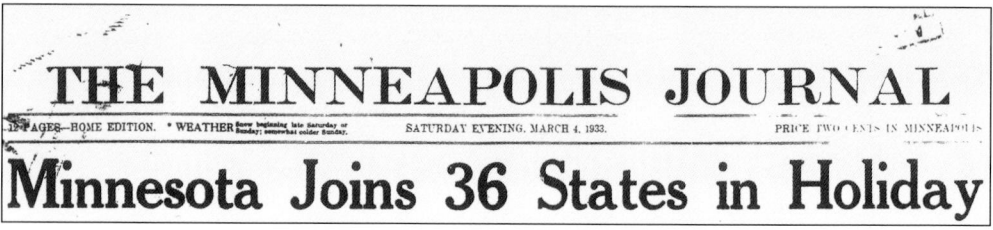

On March 4, 1933, Minneapolis became the 37th state to close its banks in an effort to prevent a financial panic. The next day, the newly inaugurated president, Franklin Roosevelt, nationalized the bank "holiday" by extending it to the entire country. Donaldson's and other downtown stores told their customers that they would accept government-issued scrip if the banks stayed closed. (Both, courtesy of Hennepin County Public Library.)

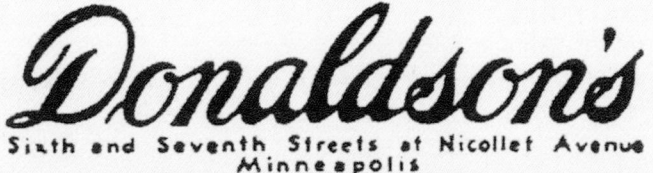

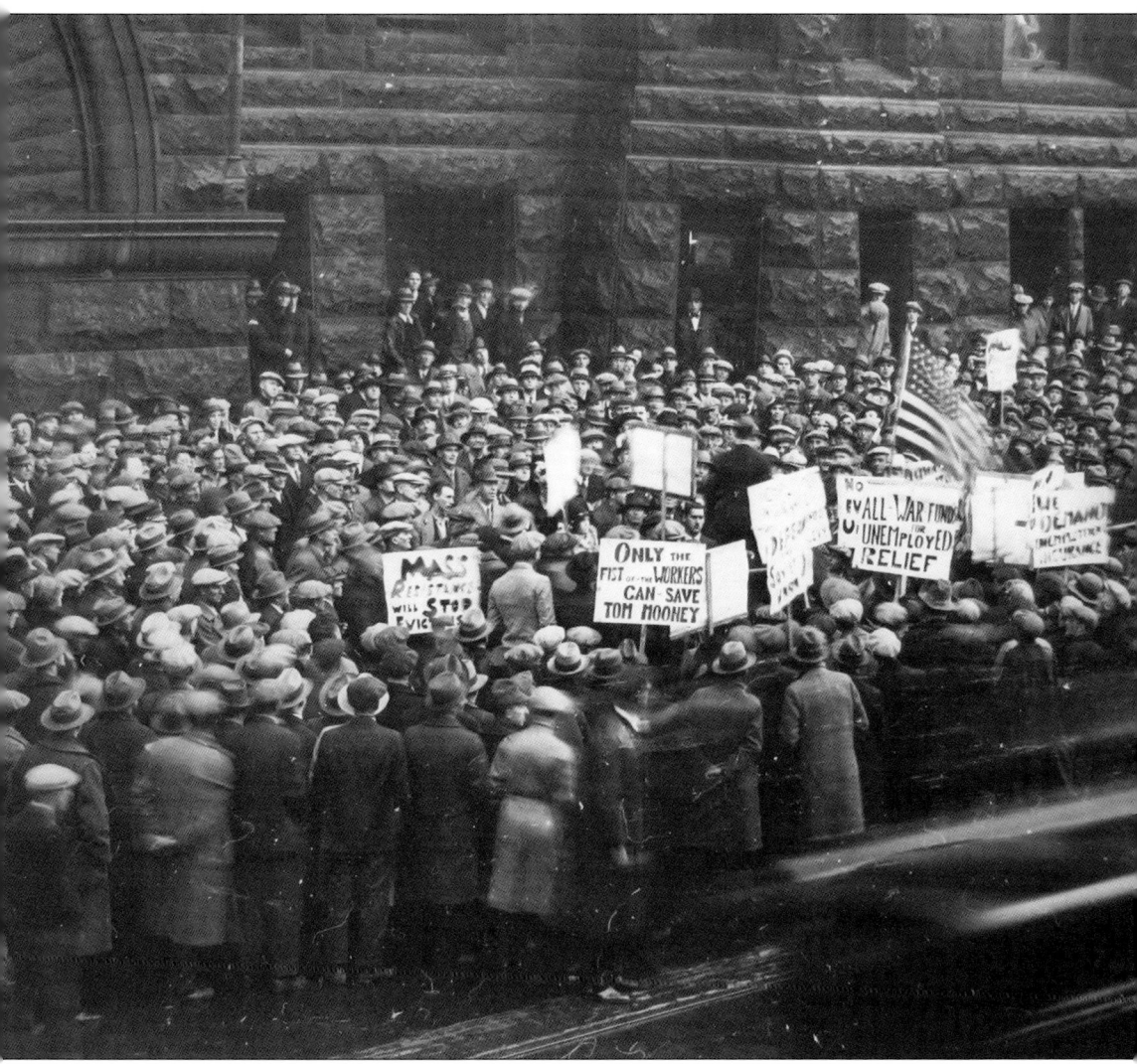

In 1932, city hall was the scene of angry confrontations as throngs of unemployed men protested cuts in city relief. As the Depression intensified, relief became an increasingly contentious political issue when some members of the city council began objecting to providing local funds for people they viewed as "shirkers and malcontents." (Courtesy of the Minnesota Historical Society.)

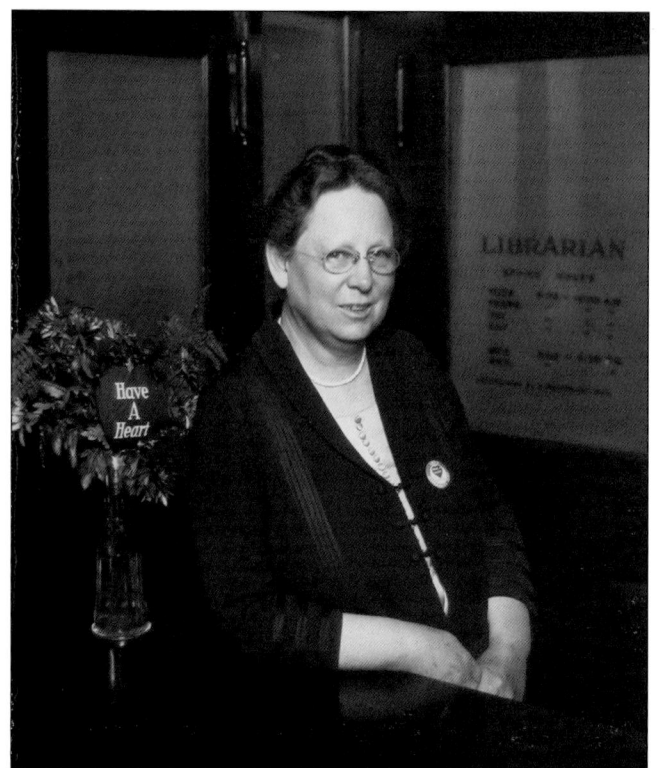

Gratia Countryman served as head of the Minneapolis library system from 1904 to 1936. Citing a revenue shortfall, the Minneapolis City Council tried to close the city's libraries during the summer of 1933. Countryman rallied support and persuaded the council to keep the libraries open. (Courtesy of the Minnesota Historical Society.)

During the Depression, Minneapolis residents used the library and its newspaper files to hunt for jobs. The downtown library provided respite for many Minneapolitans who faced hard times in the 1930s. The library's free services were particularly welcome during those years. (Courtesy of the Minnesota Historical Society.)

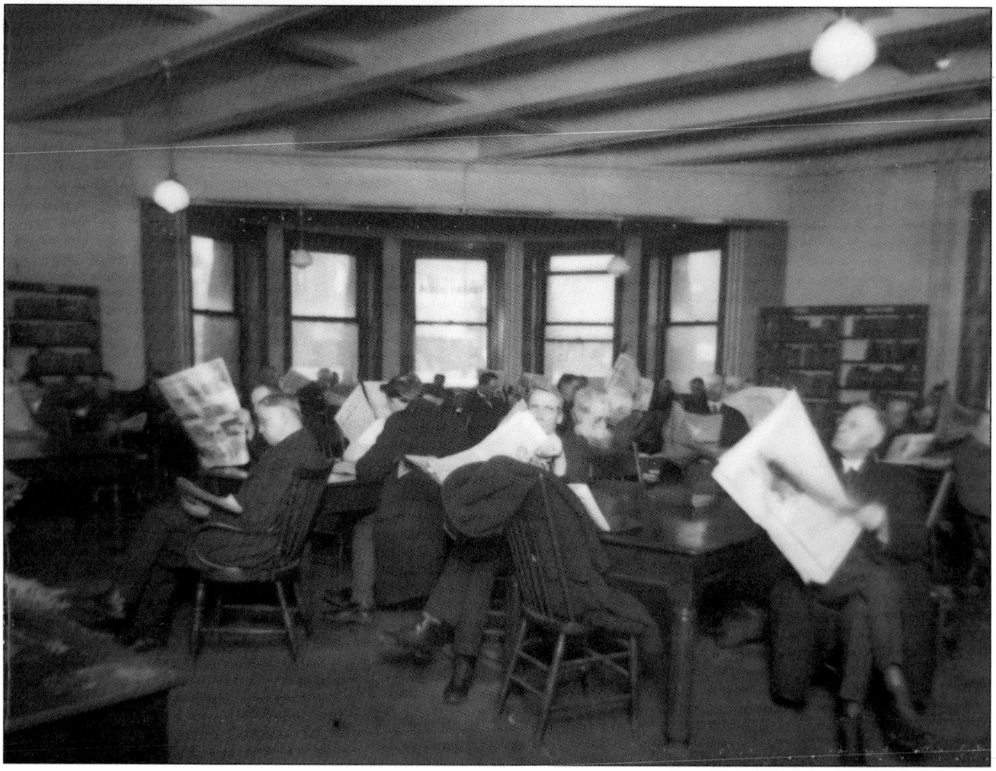

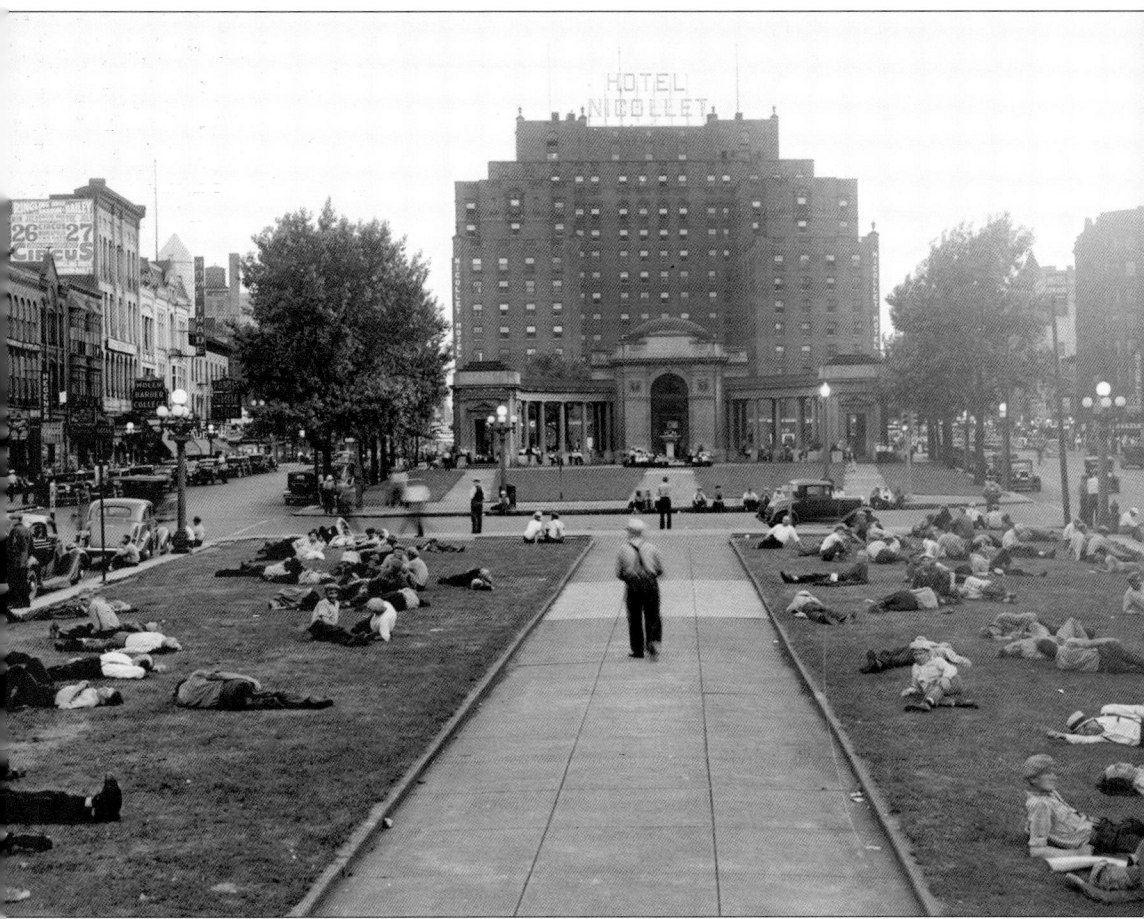

The Nicollet Hotel was built on the site of the original 1858 Nicollet House. While the hotel, which opened in 1924, attracted an upscale clientele, it was surrounded by the increasingly decrepit Gateway district. During the Depression, the park across from the hotel was a gathering place for the unemployed. After standing vacant for several years, the Nicollet Hotel was demolished in 1991. (Courtesy of Hennepin County Library Special Collections.)

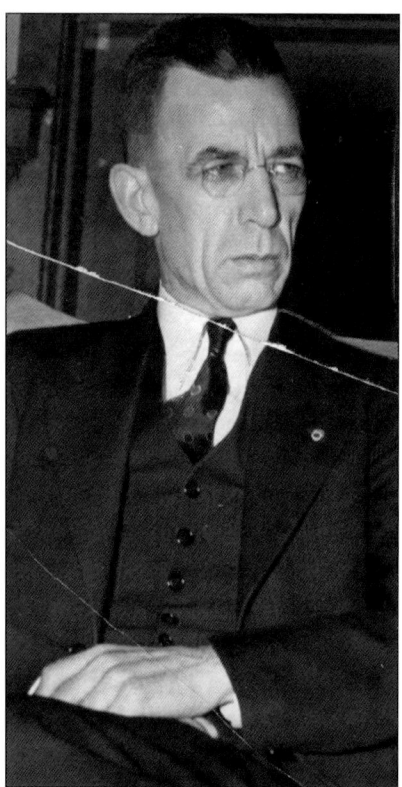

A charismatic leader and shrewd tactician, Vine Dunne spearheaded a bitter strike by Teamsters Local 574 that convulsed downtown Minneapolis in 1934. Dunne and his supporters battled the powerful Citizens Alliance, a business organization established in the early 1900s to thwart union organizing. While Dunne was battling the alliance, he also had to fend off attacks from the national Teamsters leaders who disapproved of his tactics. (Courtesy of Hennepin County Public Library Special Collections.)

Over a four-month period in the summer of 1934, the strikers clashed with the police and their deputies in the city warehouse district. During one violent clash in July, the police opened fire, killing two strikers and wounding 67 others. The strike ended when the Roosevelt Administration pressured Minneapolis business leaders to reach a settlement with the local Teamsters. (Courtesy of the Minnesota Historical Society.)

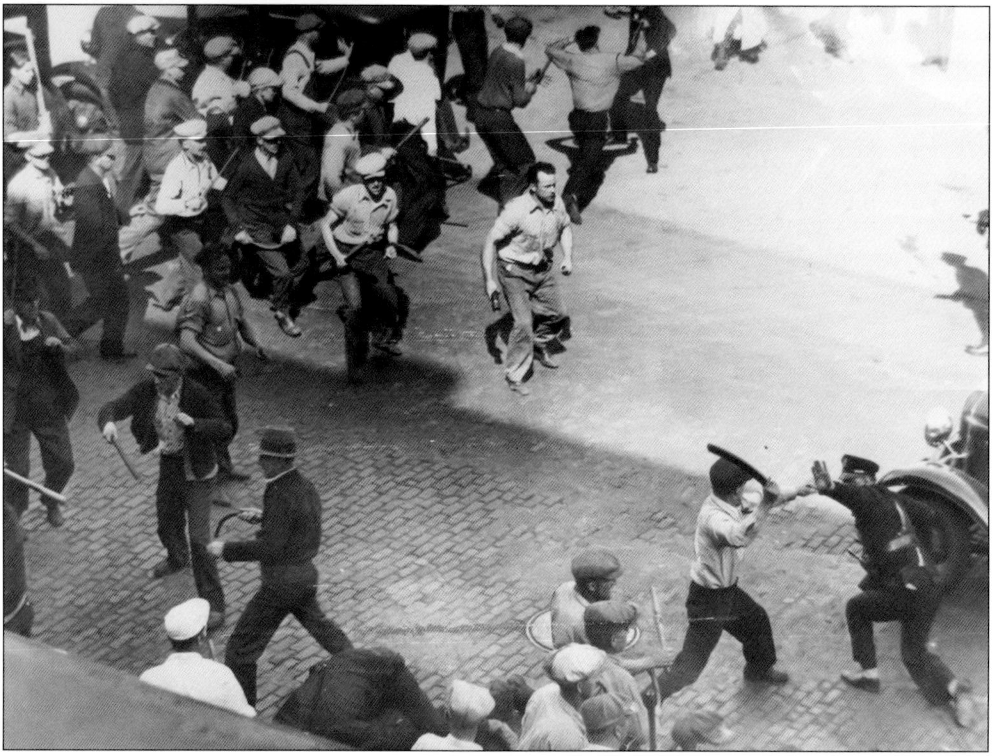

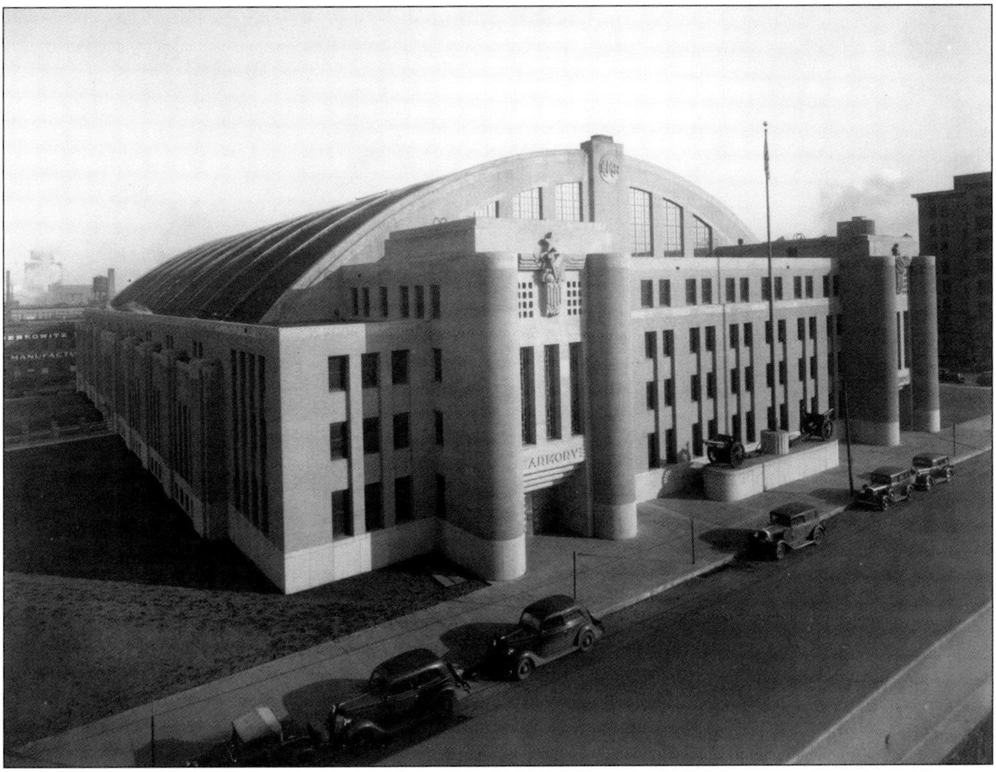

The Minneapolis Armory, downtown's link to the New Deal era, was built in 1936 with funds from the Public Works Administration. The building's design, known as PWA Moderne, features a pair of huge stone eagles presiding over the front entrances. During its earlier years, the amory housed a unit of the Minnesota National Guard. After sitting vacant for a time, it was converted to a parking garage in 1998. (Both, courtesy of Hennepin County Public Library Special Collections.)

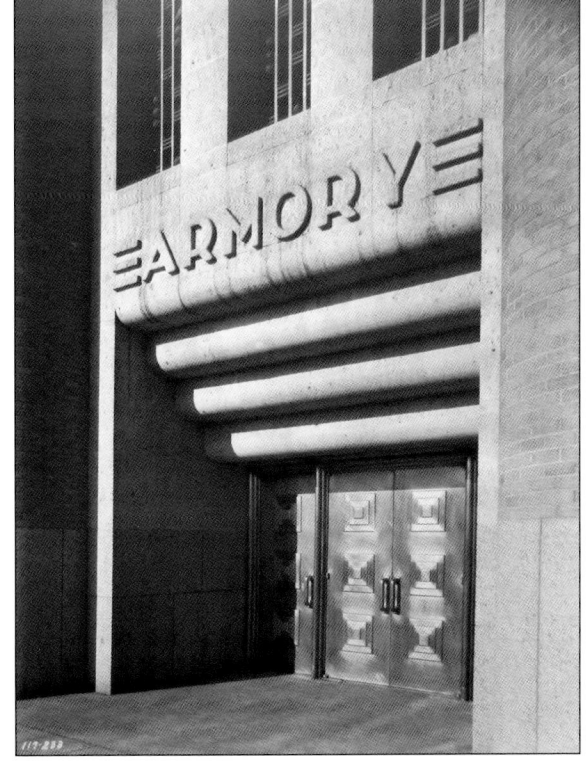

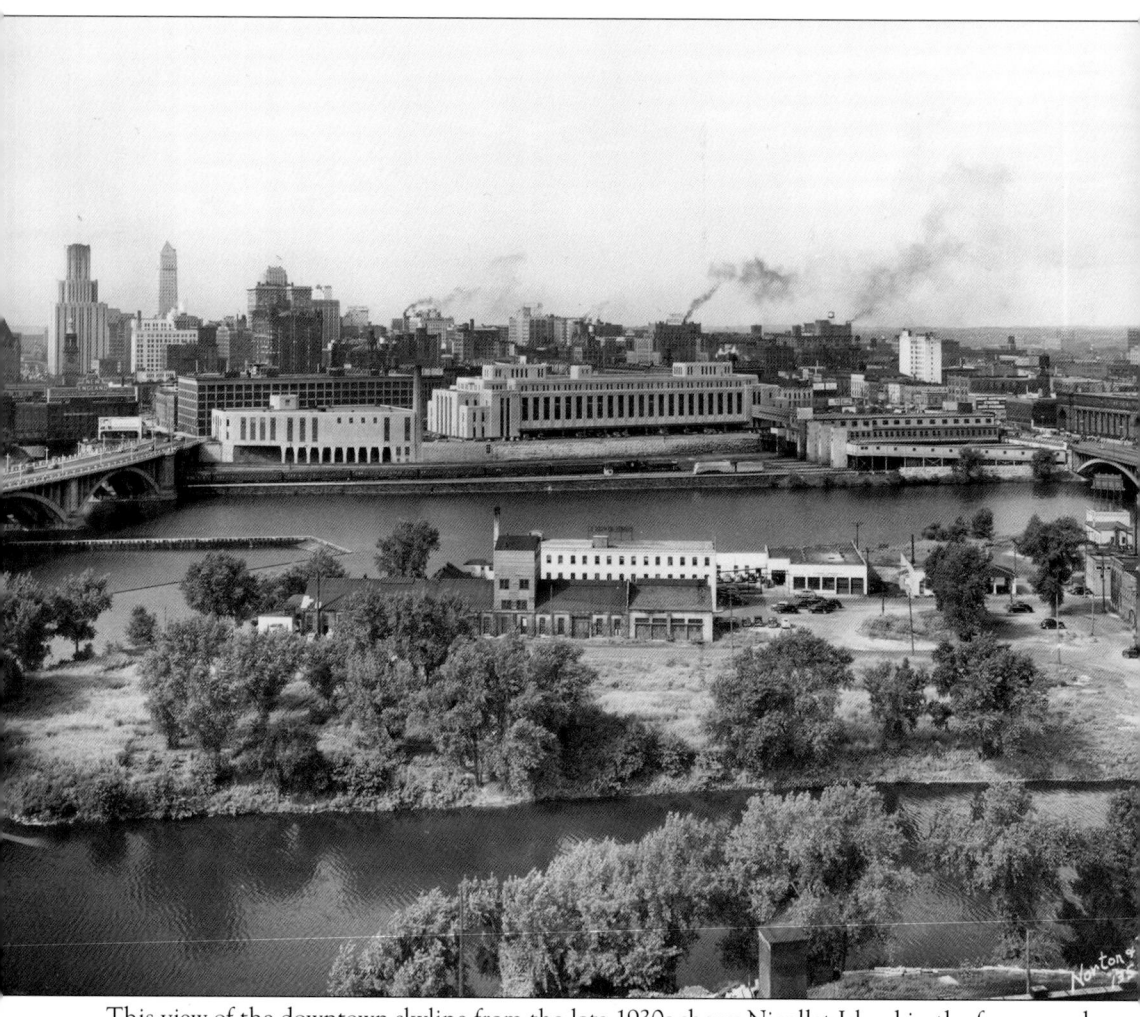

This view of the downtown skyline from the late 1930s shows Nicollet Island in the foreground. Across the river, the Minneapolis Post Office is the long, low building with the vertical window bays. Built in 1934, the post office occupied the site that had been the city's red light district at the turn of the 20th century. (Courtesy of Hennepin History Museum.)

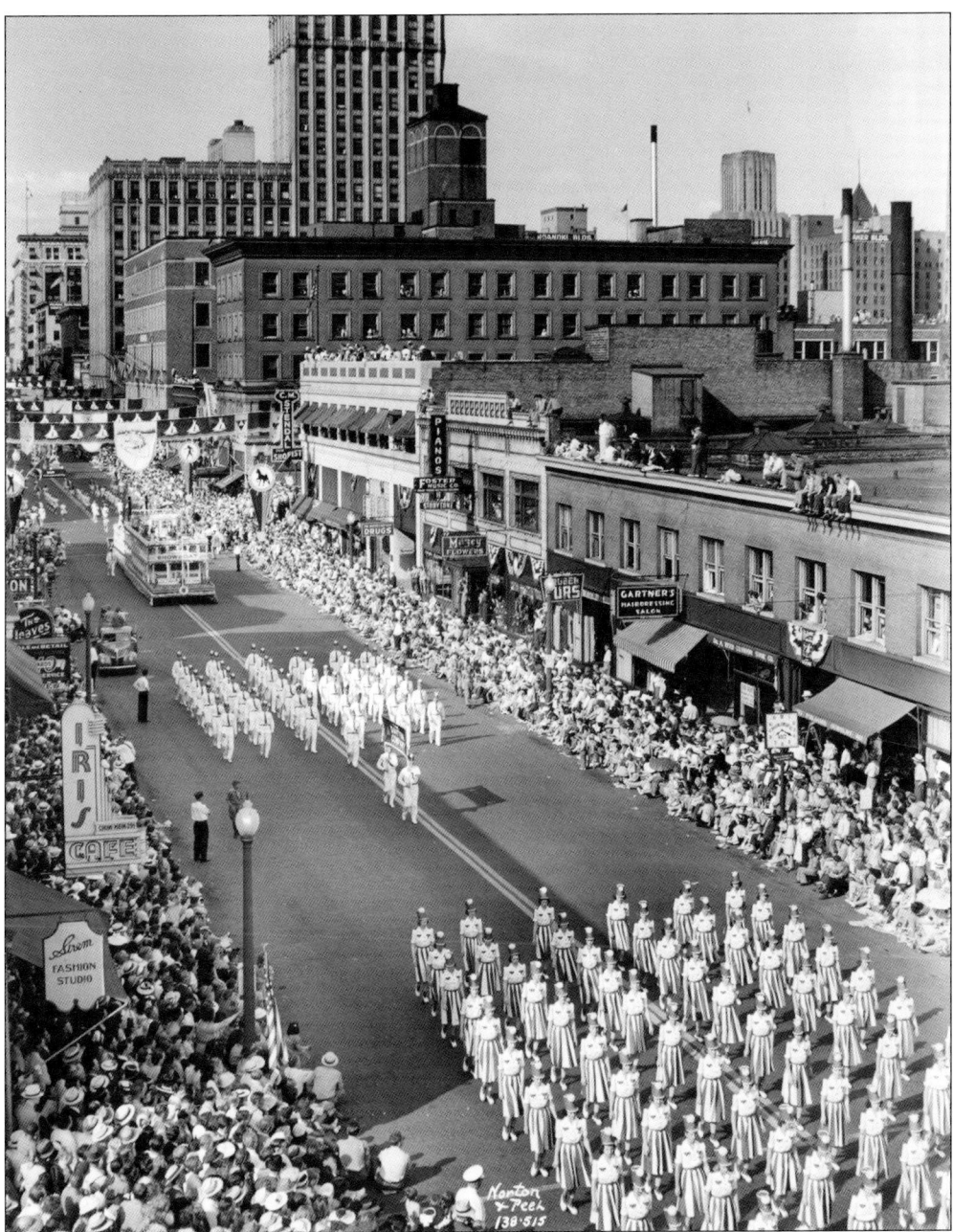

Minneapolis's annual midsummer festival, the Aquatennial, was held for the first time in 1940. The civic event celebrates the city's lakes and rivers. The parade through downtown Minneapolis is one of the highlights of the summertime celebration held during the third week in July. (Courtesy of Hennepin County Public Library Special Collections.)

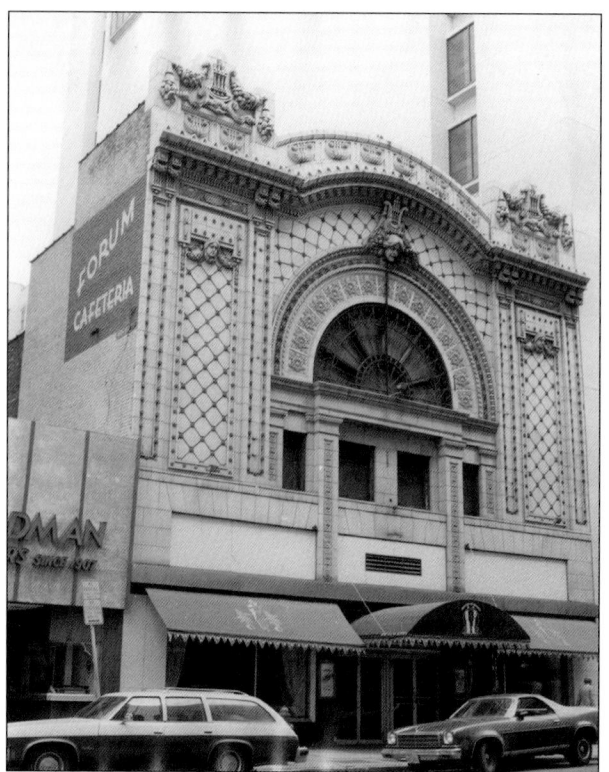

The Forum Cafeteria was a culinary landmark, noted more for its Art Deco decor than its assembly line food. The downtown eatery was built inside the shell of the former Strand Theater. While the building housing the Forum was eventually demolished, the period furnishings were removed and installed in later restaurants that occupied the site. (Both, courtesy of Hennepin County Public Library Special Collections.)

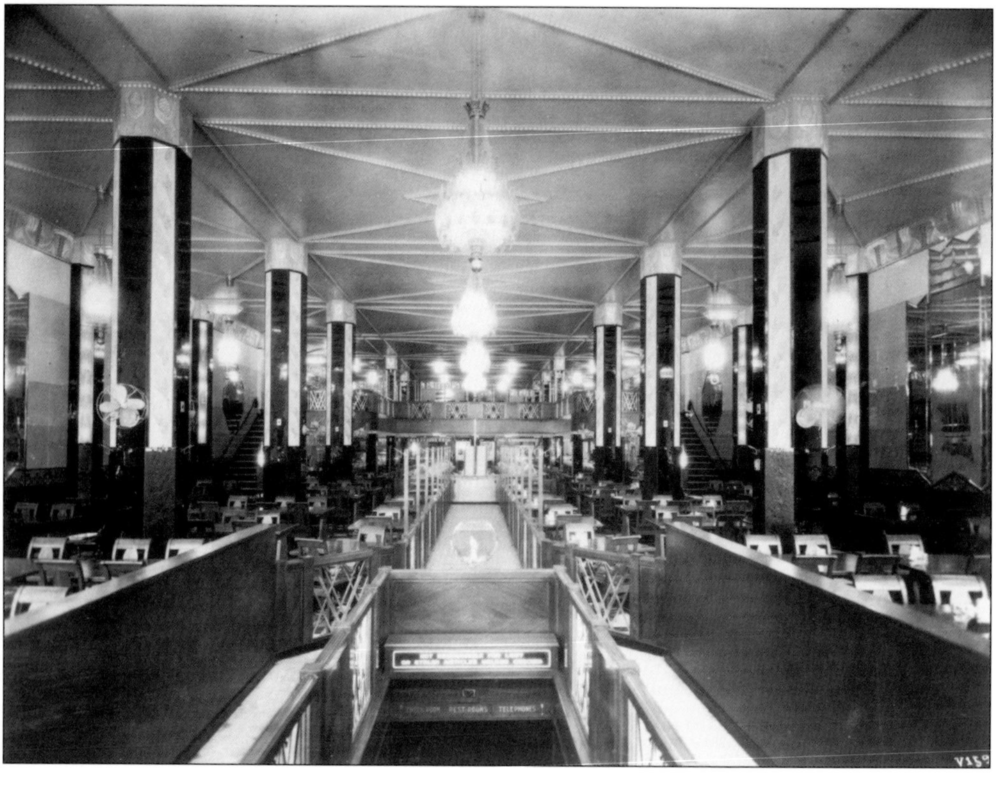

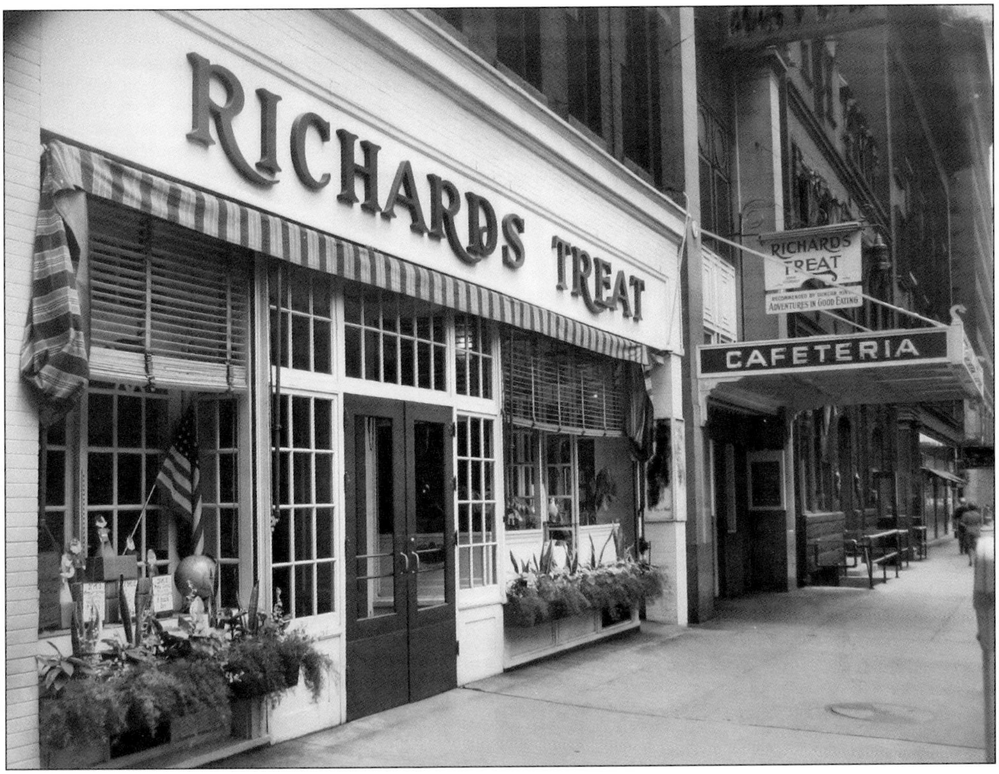

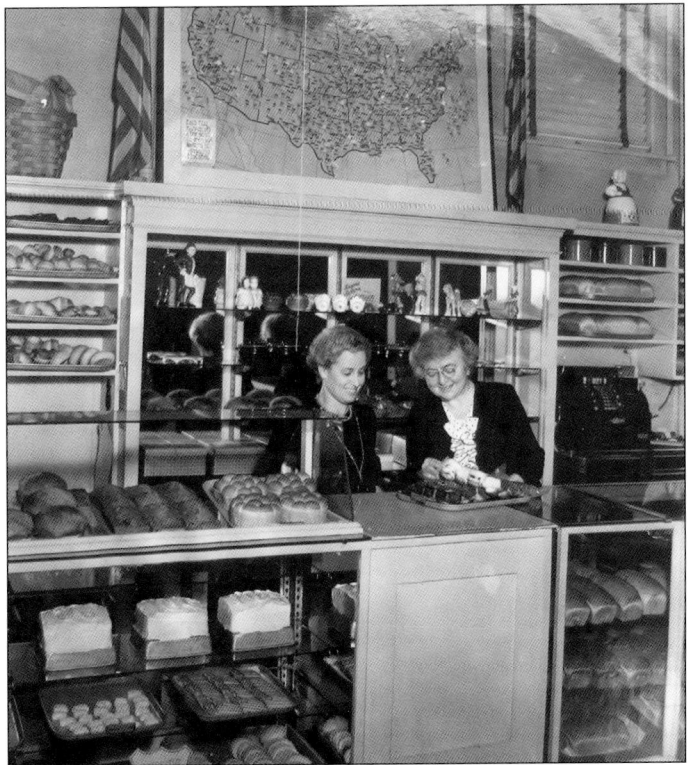

Richards Treat Cafeteria on Sixth Street was operated by two former home economics teachers, Lenore Richards and Nola Treat. The cafeteria served the comfort food of its era—meat loaf, chicken potpie, and roast turkey, with strawberry shortcake and ice cream sundaes for desert. The cafeteria closed in 1957 after a 33-year run. (Both, courtesy of the Minnesota Historical Society.)

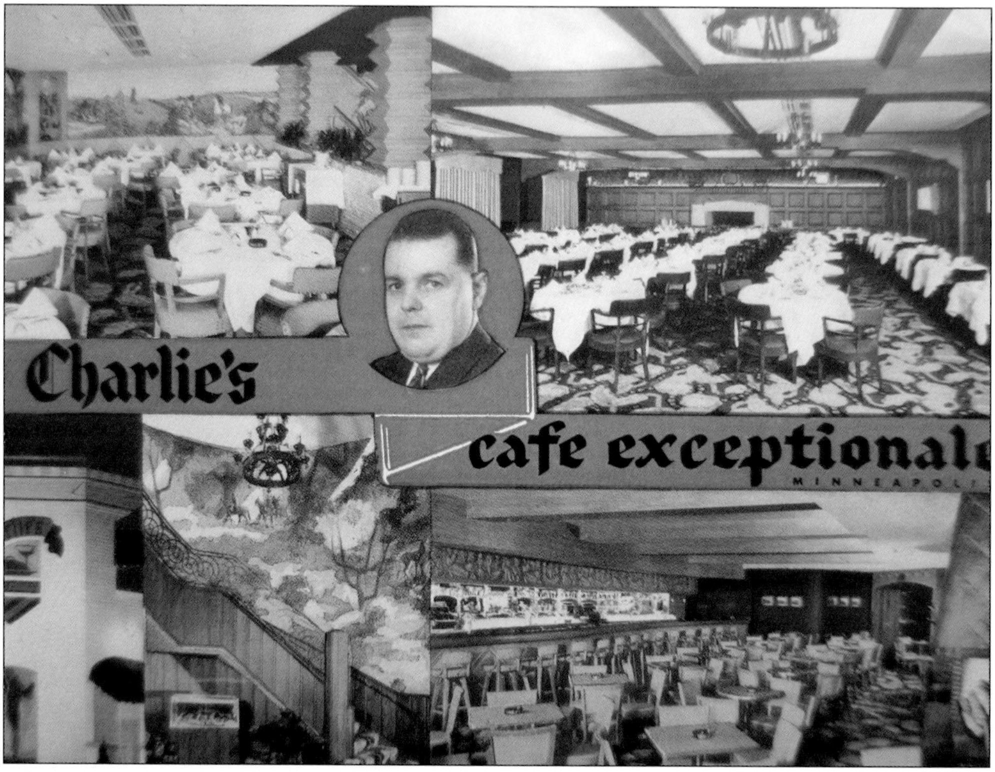

Charlie's Café Exceptionale was downtown's special occasion restaurant for nearly 50 years, until it closed in 1982. The café was run by Minneapolis's larger-than-life restaurateur Charlie Sanders and, later, by his wife, Louise. The statue of the naked nymph, *Scherzo*, originally created for the Foshay Tower, was prominently displayed at the entrance to Charlie's. (Courtesy of the Minnesota Historical Society.)

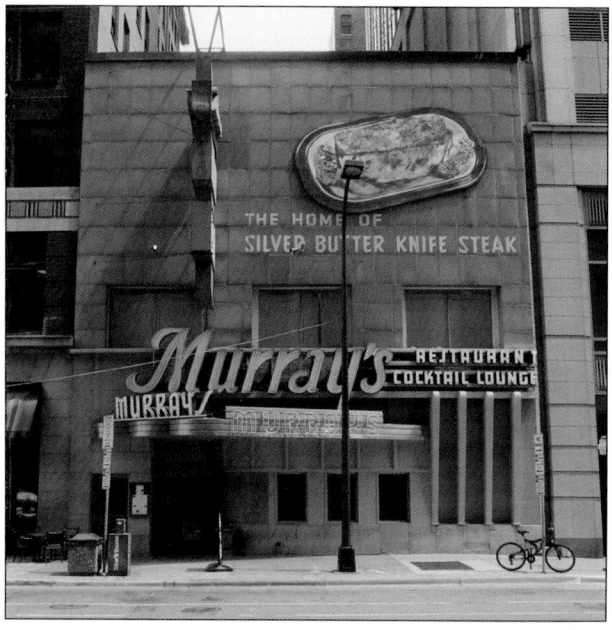

Murray's is downtown's last surviving restaurant and cocktail lounge from the 1950s. The restaurant's "silver butter knife steak," its signature dish, still draws a steady stream of customers, just as it did when the restaurant opened more than 70 years ago. (Author's collection.)

Farmers and Mechanics Bank was the last downtown building constructed before the start of World War II. The building's facade features bold relief sculptures of a farmer and a mechanic flanking the front entrance. The wheat shaft symbolizes Minnesota's agricultural heritage. No longer a bank, the Art Deco Moderne building was converted to a Westin hotel in 2007. (Right, author's collection; below, Hennepin County Public Library Special Collections.)

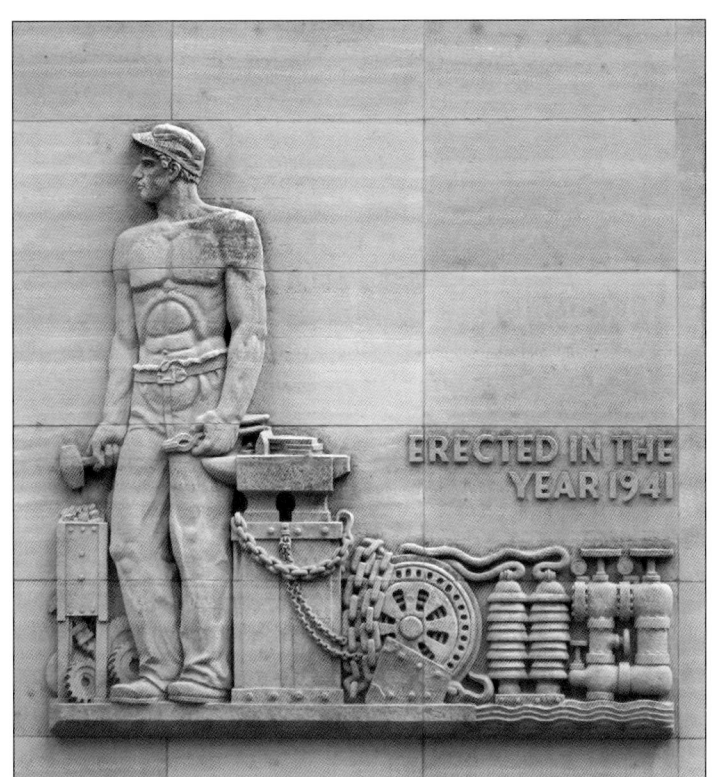

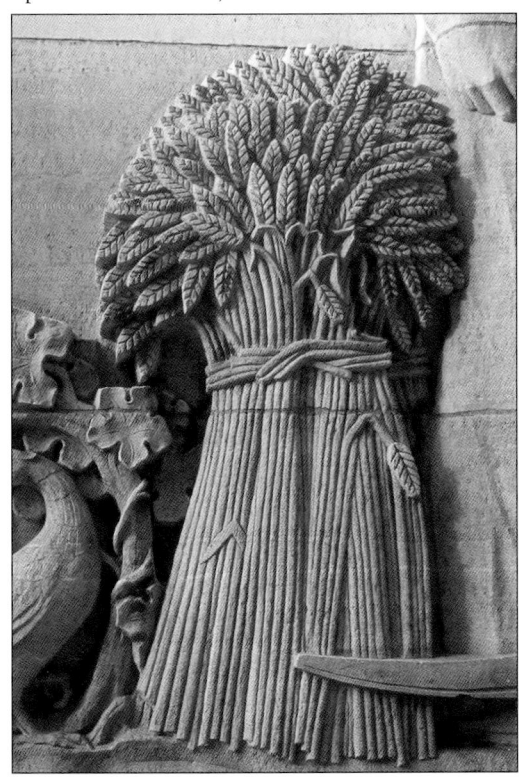

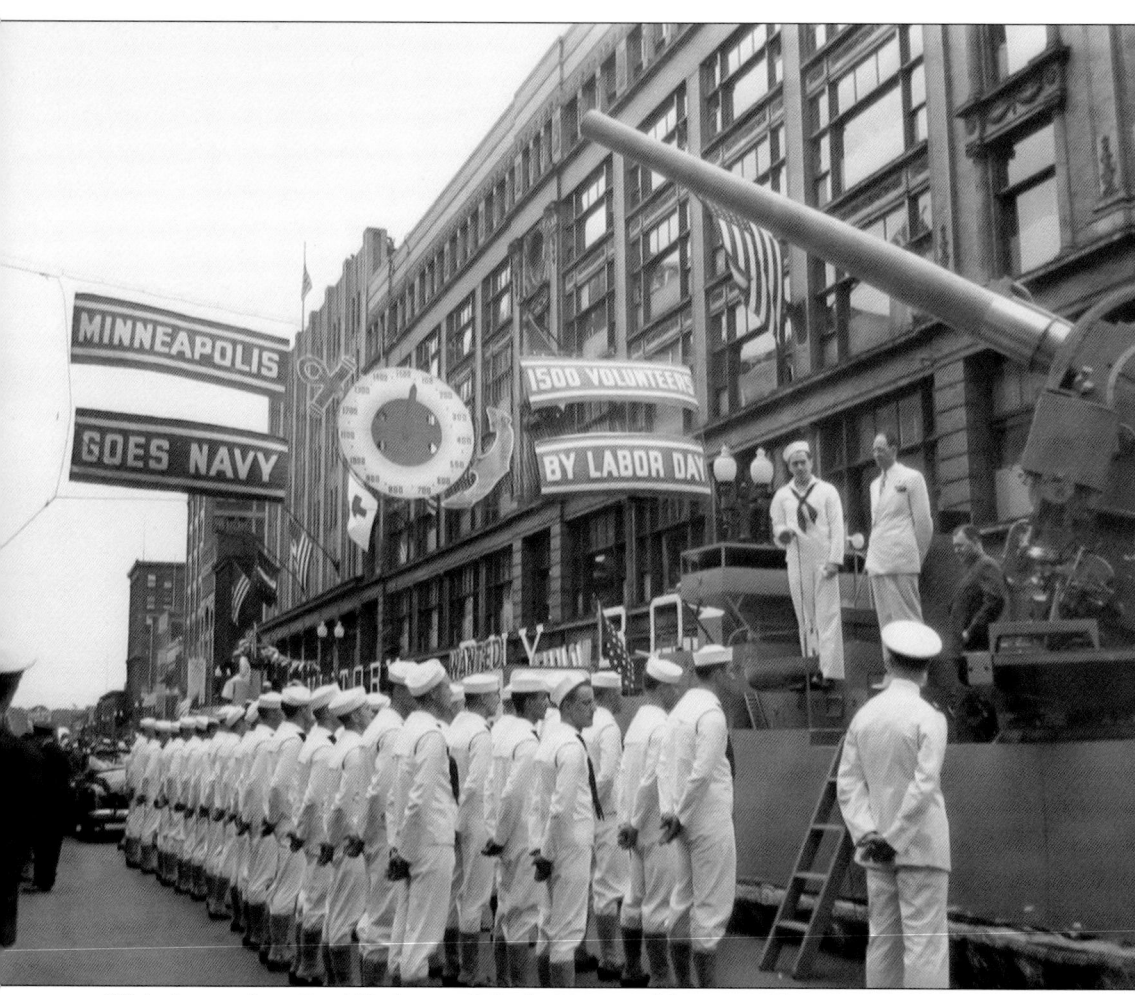

With the attack on Pearl Harbor in 1941, the US armed forces quickly ramped up their recruitment efforts. This Navy recruitment rally was held on Nicollet Avenue in front of Dayton's Department Store in 1942. That year, the Navy hoped to gain 1,500 new recruits from the Minneapolis area. (Courtesy of the Minnesota Historical Society.)

On May 9, 1942, a group of movie stars from Hollywood swept into town to stage a benefit for the service groups of the armed forces. Headlined by Bing Crosby, Bob Hope, and Cary Grant, the Saturday-night benefit broke box office records at the Minneapolis Auditorium. "Superlatives are a weak thing in describing a show of this kind," the *Minneapolis Tribune* gushed. "On the scores of names alone, it's THE BIGGEST THING OF ITS KIND EVER DONE HERE." (Courtesy of the Minnesota Historical Society.)

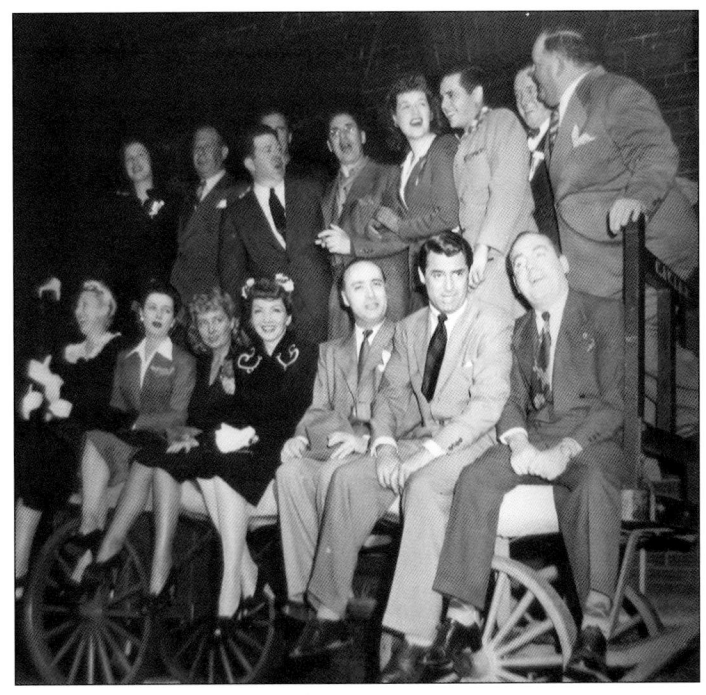

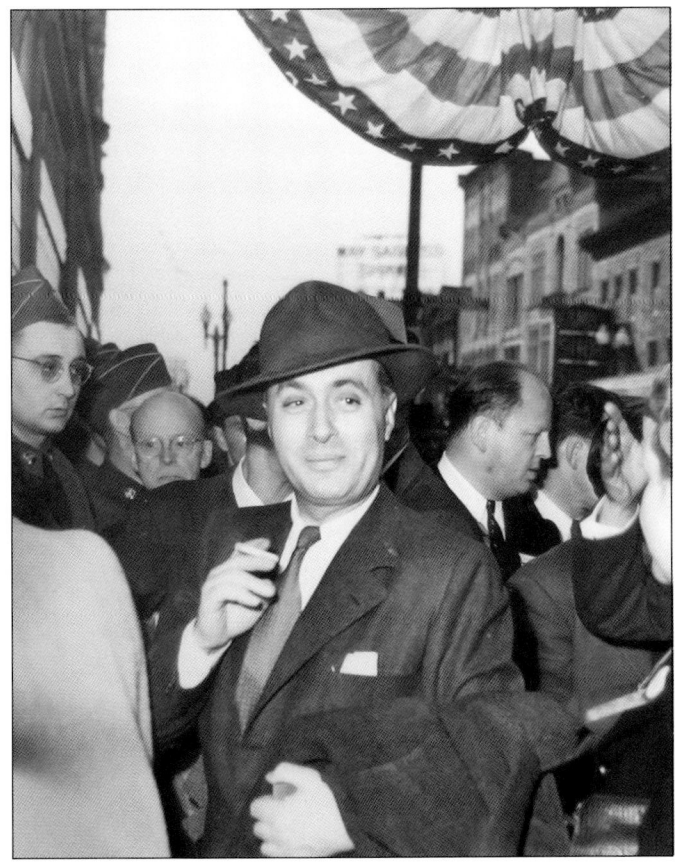

French-born actor Charles Boyer greeted his fans when he arrived at Minneapolis's Milwaukee Depot to participate in the Cavalcade of Stars at the Minneapolis Auditorium. Boyer had made a name for himself playing suave leading men with just a hint of mystery. In 1942, Minneapolis moviegoers could have seen Boyer in one of his greatest hits, *Hold Back the Dawn*, a romantic melodrama in which he starred opposite Olivia de Havilland and Paulette Goddard. (Courtesy of the Minnesota Historical Society.)

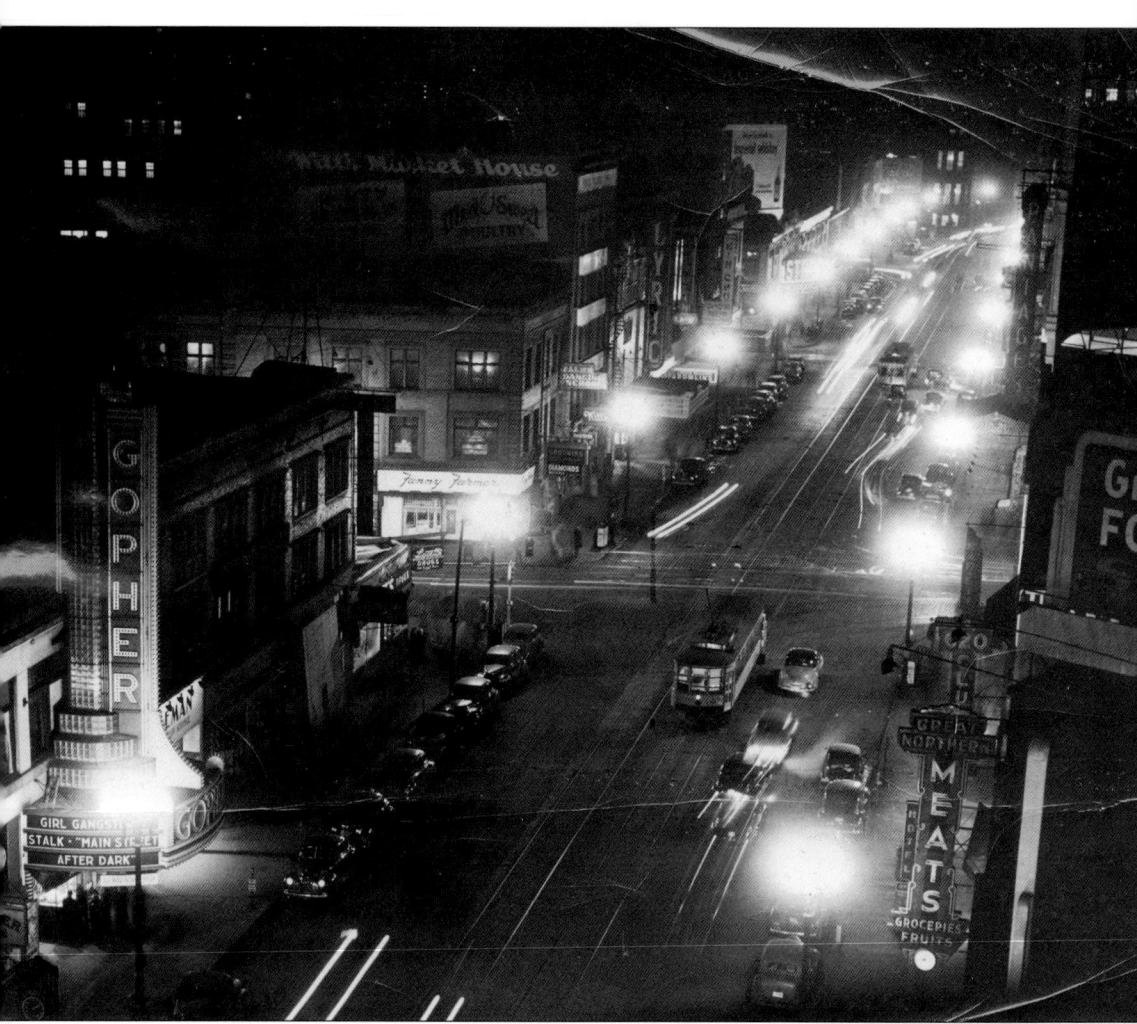

Most downtown lights were switched off during this 1945 brownout, a wartime effort designed to save electricity. Three years earlier, on September 11, 1942, downtown experienced a total blackout as a civil defense measure. The test of the civil defense system was intended to prepare Minneapolitans for a real blackout in the event of an enemy air raid. (Courtesy of Hennepin County Public Library Special Collections.)

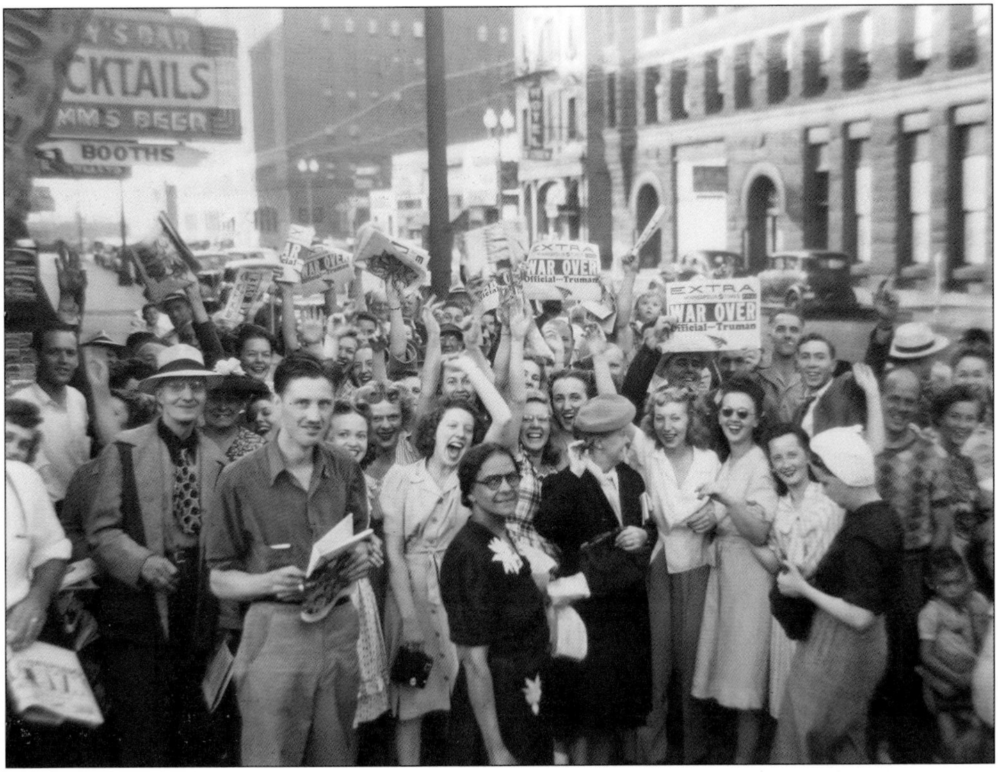

Minnesotans celebrated in the streets of downtown Minneapolis when they learned that the Japanese had surrendered on VJ Day, August 14, 1945. "Until the early morning hours, the loop was a defining bedlam of auto horns and shouting celebrants," the *Star Journal* reported. "There was bell ringing . . . there was dancing . . . and there was kissing, nice friendly kissing by service men and girls picked up atop a truck on Seventh Street." (Both, courtesy of Hennepin County Public Library Special Collections.)

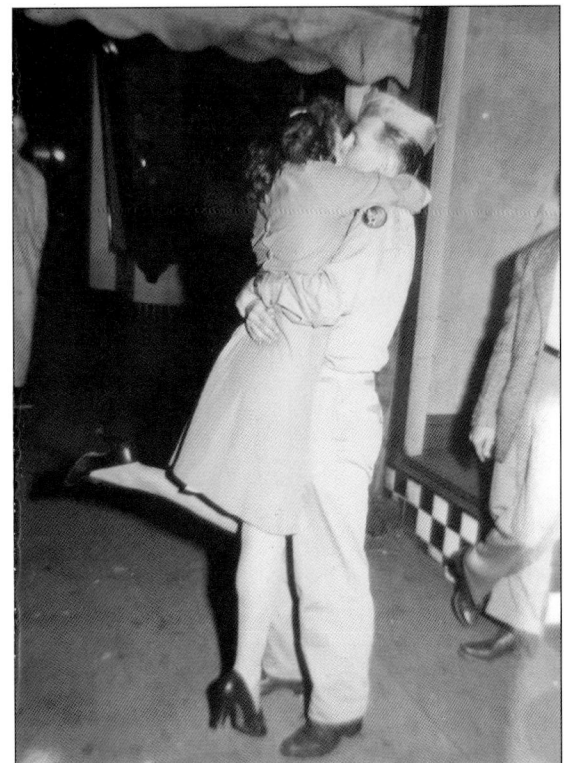

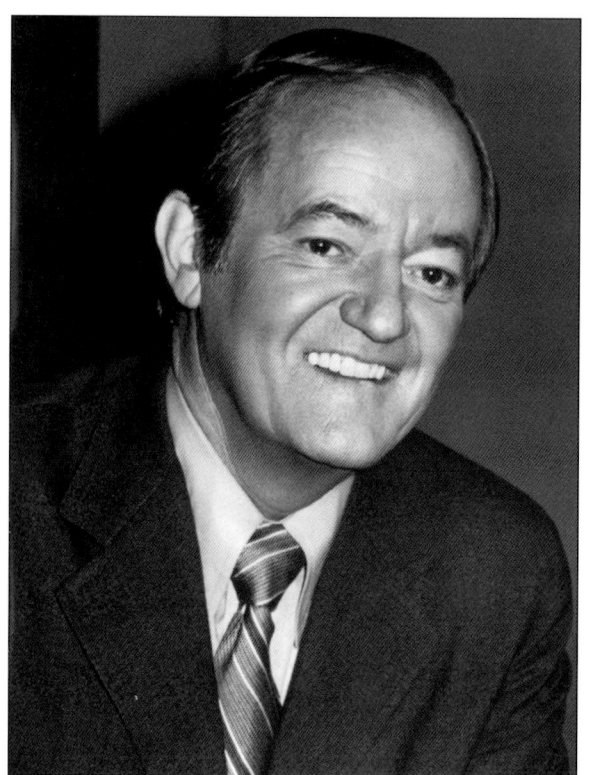

Hubert Humphrey, Minnesota's most prominent 20th-century political figure, was elected mayor of Minneapolis in 1945 at the age of 32. During his three years in office, Humphrey spearheaded efforts to combat ethnic and racial prejudice. In 1948, Humphrey was elected to the US Senate and embarked on a national political career that would take him almost to the presidency in 1968. (Courtesy of Hennepin County Public Library Special Collections.)

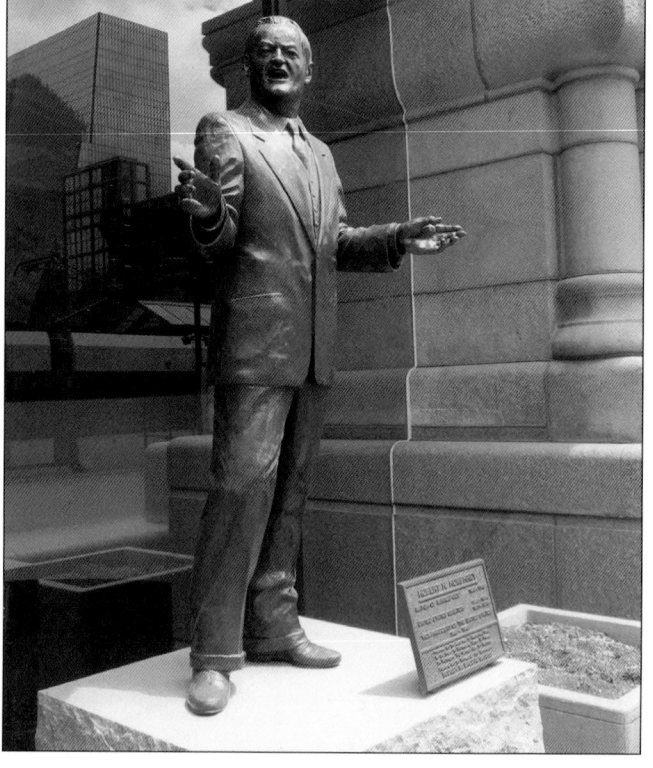

This bronze statue of Hubert Humphrey stands at the entrance to Minneapolis City Hall. It shows the former mayor and vice president with his arms outstretched, addressing an unseen audience. The statute, created by Minneapolis artist Roger Brodin, was installed at city hall in 1989. (Author's collection.)

Five

SUBURBAN CHALLENGE

In 1956, the country's first indoor climate-controlled shopping center took shape in a suburban cornfield south of the Twin Cities. Southdale Center would revolutionize American shopping habits and pose a serious challenge to downtown Minneapolis, the region's longtime commercial center.

City leaders took Southdale's threat seriously. While plans for the suburban shopping center were still on the drawing boards, they began work on a series of innovative urban development projects aimed at maintaining downtown's dominant role in the regional economy.

Downtown faced one threat from Southdale, but it faced another one closer to home in its decaying Gateway district. The Gateway had been the city's commercial hub during its early years in the mid-19th century. But after the Civil War, the retail district began moving south along Nicollet Avenue, away from the river, leaving behind a shabby skid row filled with bars, pawnshops, and flophouses.

In 1957, city leaders initiated an ambitious effort to clear and rebuild a large swath of the skid row district. While the 70-acre Gateway urban renewal project was criticized for demolishing early historical landmarks, including the highly prized Metropolitan Building, the redevelopment plan did succeed in eliminating much of downtown's urban blight.

While the bulldozers moved through Gateway, a dynamic local businessman named Leslie Park was promoting his own urban development scheme. Park came up with a plan to connect the downtown buildings at the second-story level with a series of covered walkways known as skyways. In 1959, Park built the first skyway connecting his newly developed Northstar Center with the Northwestern National Bank building across the street. Over the next 50 years, the skyway system would expand to cover more than 80 downtown blocks.

While the skyway system was expanding, city leaders were developing a plan to rebuild Nicollet Avenue, downtown's major retail street. The plan involved converting Nicollet to a transit way, embellished with artwork, flower beds, and bus shelters. The Nicollet Mall opened in 1967 to rave reviews by city leaders and downtown retailers. Along with the skyways, the Nicollet Mall helped downtown hold its own as suburban development gained momentum all around the Twin Cities.

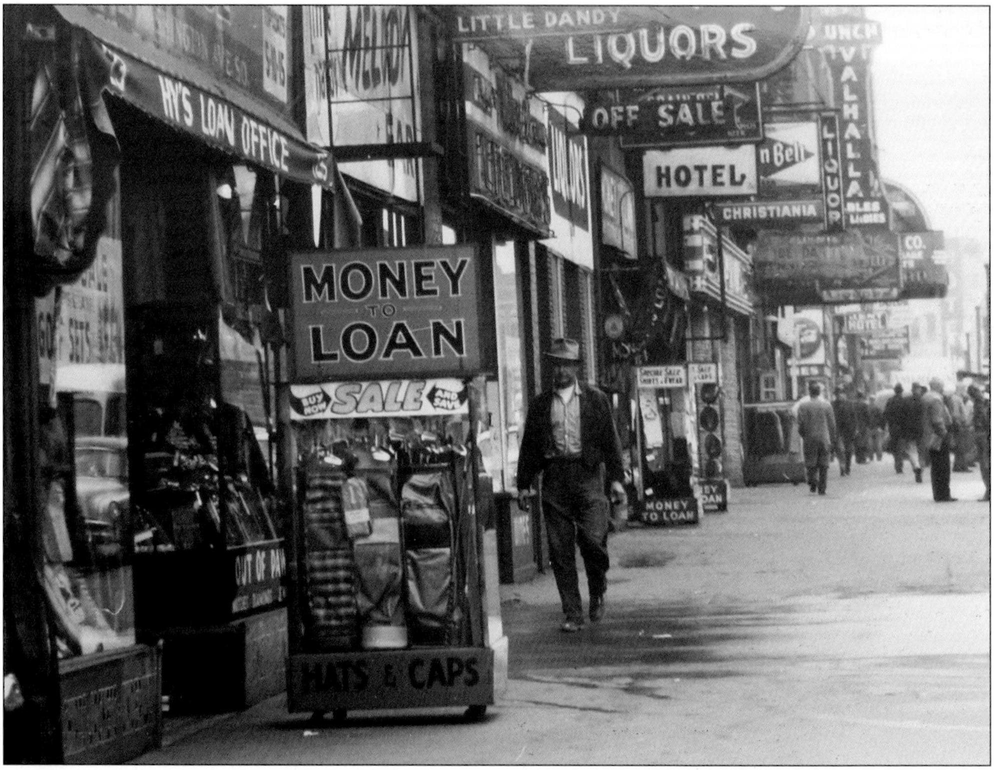

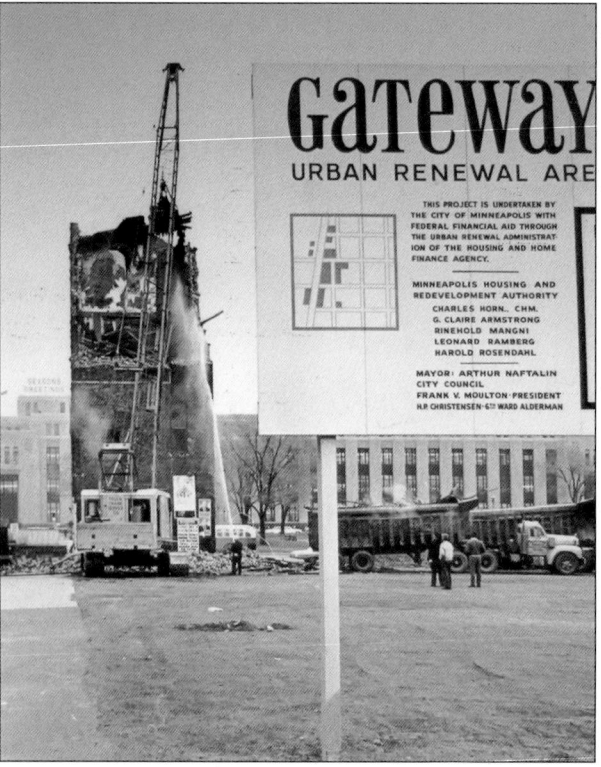

Through World War II and into the postwar era, the Gateway district around Washington Avenue continued to fester as the city's skid row. Local leaders who wanted to reposition Minneapolis as a modern communications and financial center saw the Gateway as an impediment to those efforts. Both inside and outside of city hall, support began to build for a major redevelopment of this blighted downtown district. (Courtesy of the Minnesota Historical Society.)

With the help of a federal planning grant, city officials developed an ambitious plan to redevelop nearly a third of the downtown in 1957. The Gateway urban renewal project would eventually cover a 70-block development encompassing the city's original riverfront commercial district. (Courtesy of Hennepin History Museum.)

The Gateway plan called for the demolition of the Metropolitan Building, known as the Guaranty Loan Building when it was constructed in 1890. With its Romanesque Revival style and ornate arched entrances, the Metropolitan was considered one of the city's most outstanding 19th-century buildings. Despite the best efforts of preservationists to save the building, it was taken down in 1961. (Courtesy of Minneapolis Community Planning and Economic Development.)

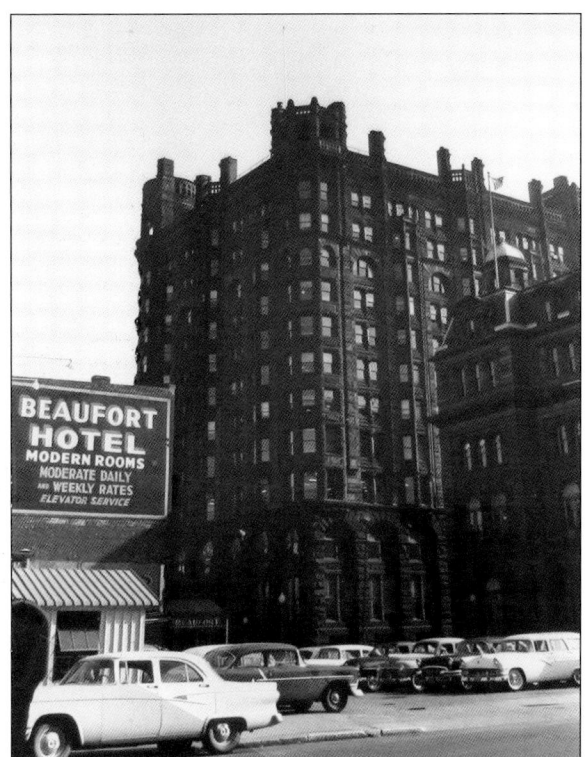

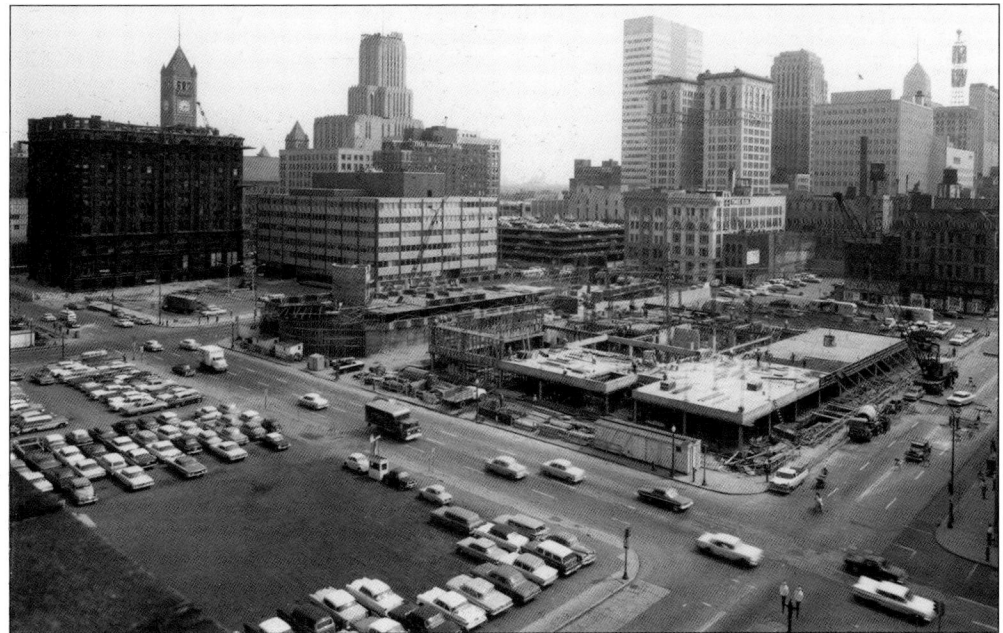

During the early years of the Gateway project, the city's Housing and Redevelopment Authority was able to clear much of the area, but it took a while for the redevelopment process to take hold. While several public buildings, including a new public library (shown here under construction), were built at the edge of the project, many blocks were used as parking lots for years before attracting new private development. (Courtesy of Hennepin County Public Library Special Collections.)

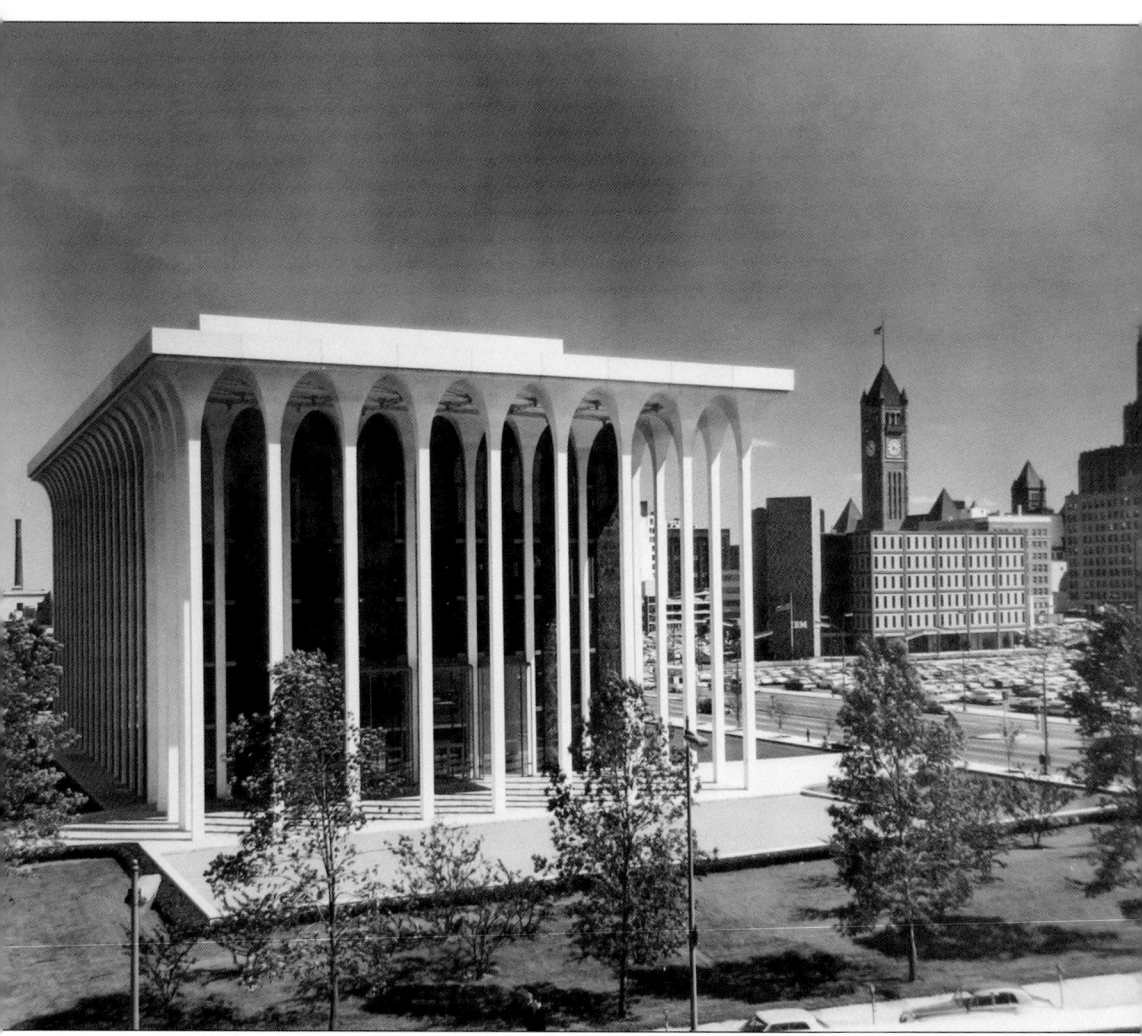

The Northwestern National Life Insurance Building, now known as Voya Financial, is one of the few downtown developments from Minneapolis's urban renewal era to survive into the 21st century. The building was designed by the Japanese architect Minouru Yamasaki, who also built the World Trade Center. The Voya's most dominant feature is its elegant portico that anchors the north end of the Nicollet Mall. (Courtesy of the Minnesota Historical Society.)

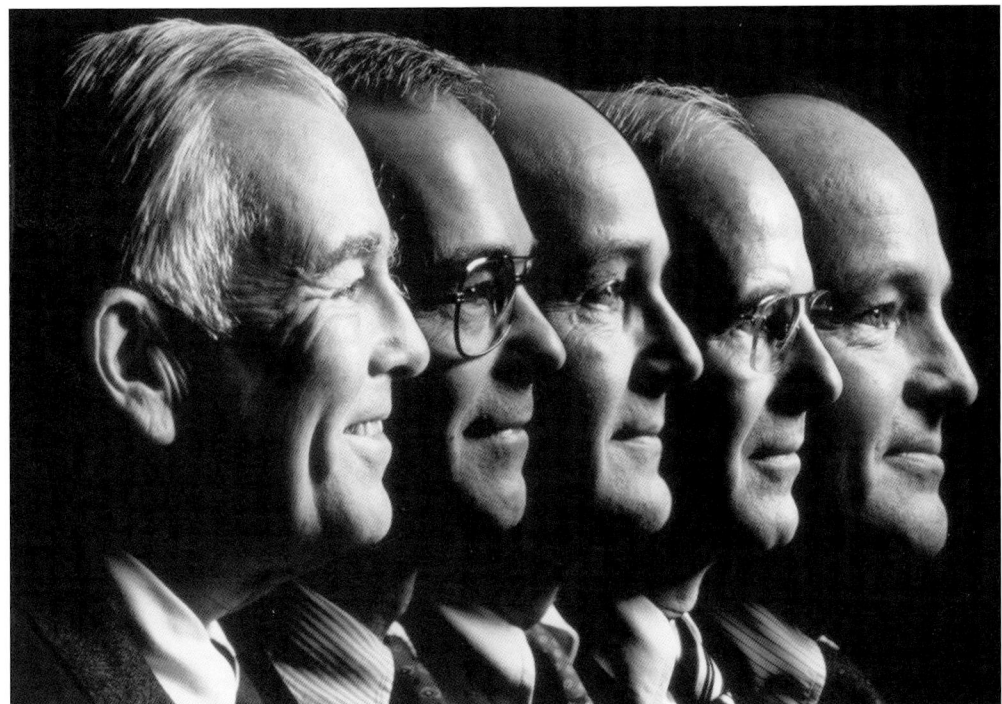

In 1950, the five Dayton brothers (from left to right, Don, Wally, Doug, Bruce, and Ken) took charge of the Dayton Company, the family business their grandfather started nearly 50 years earlier. The brothers were retailing innovators who built Southdale, the country's first climate-controlled shopping center in suburban Edina. The Daytons were able to balance their suburban interests with their efforts to maintain a strong environment for their downtown flagship store. (Courtesy of the Okabena Company.)

The Dayton Company's emphasis on high fashion was an important marketing tool for the local retailer. In 1961, the Minneapolis-based company brought its fashion expertise to a new line of business, a chain of discount stores with a red bull's-eye as its distinctive logo. Target would become a major retail chain with more than 1,000 stores nationwide. (Courtesy of Hennepin County Public Library Special Collections.)

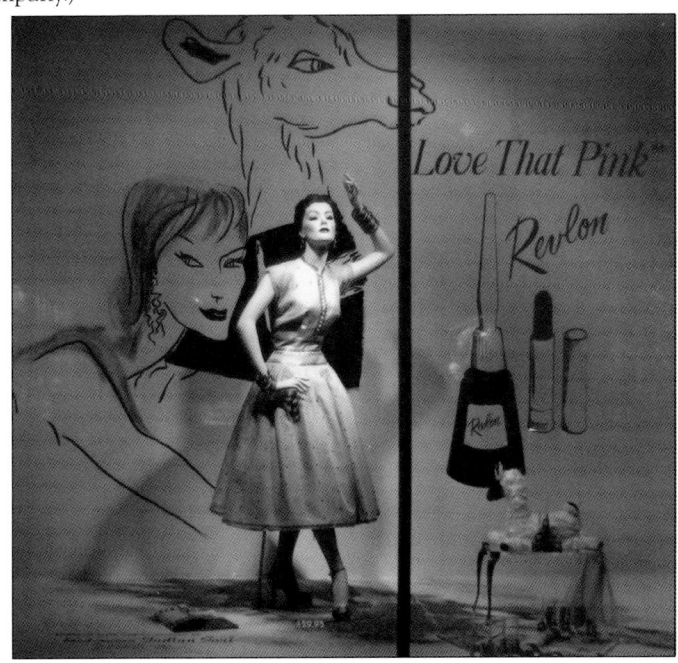

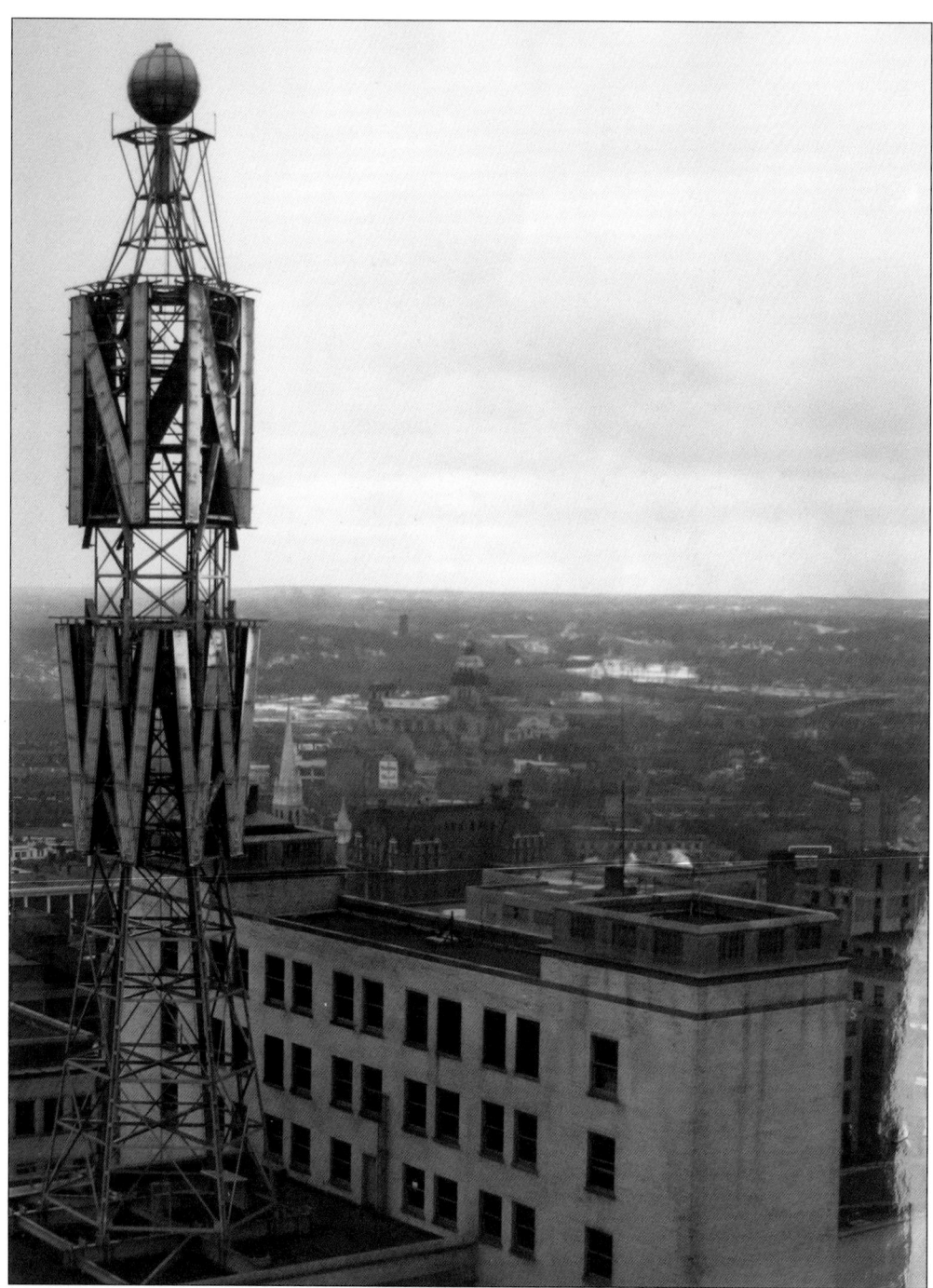

A downtown icon for more than 30 years, the Weather Ball was an illuminated sign on top of the Northwestern National Bank. The lighted ball provided a simple weather forecast: red meant warmer, white meant colder, and green meant no change. The Weather Ball disappeared from its 14-story perch during the 1982 Thanksgiving Day fire that destroyed the bank building. (Courtesy of the Minnesota Historical Society.)

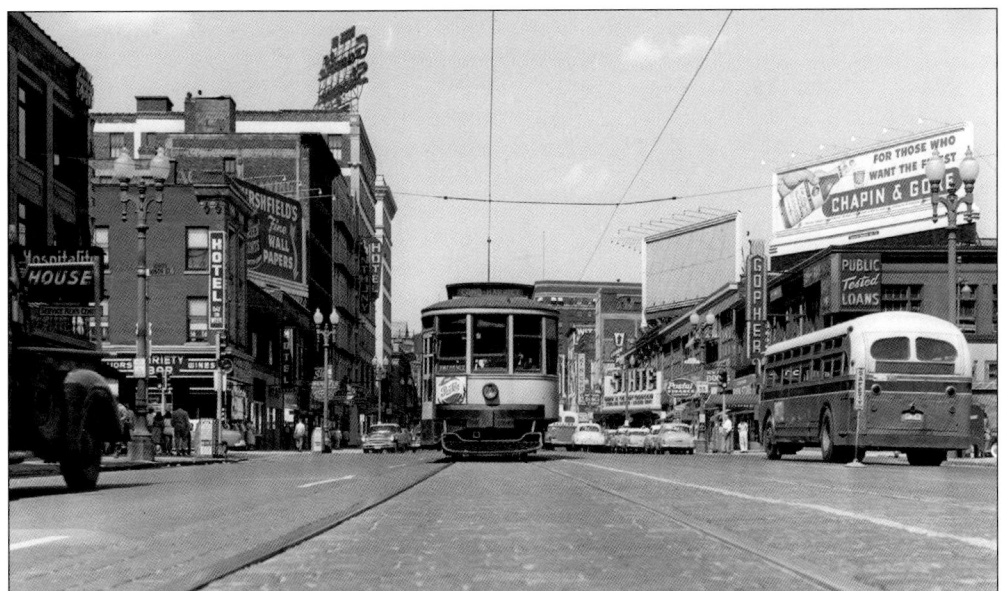

In 1954, the Twin City Rapid Transit Company (TCRT) decided to eliminate its streetcars and replace them with buses. TCRT's last street car made its final run on Saturday, June 19, 1954. A day earlier, local dignitaries celebrated the end of the streetcar era with a rolling luncheon served on eight of the remaining cars. "Minneapolis went off its trolley on Friday, and a good time was had by all," the *Minneapolis Tribune* reported. (Courtesy of Hennepin County Public Library Special Collections.)

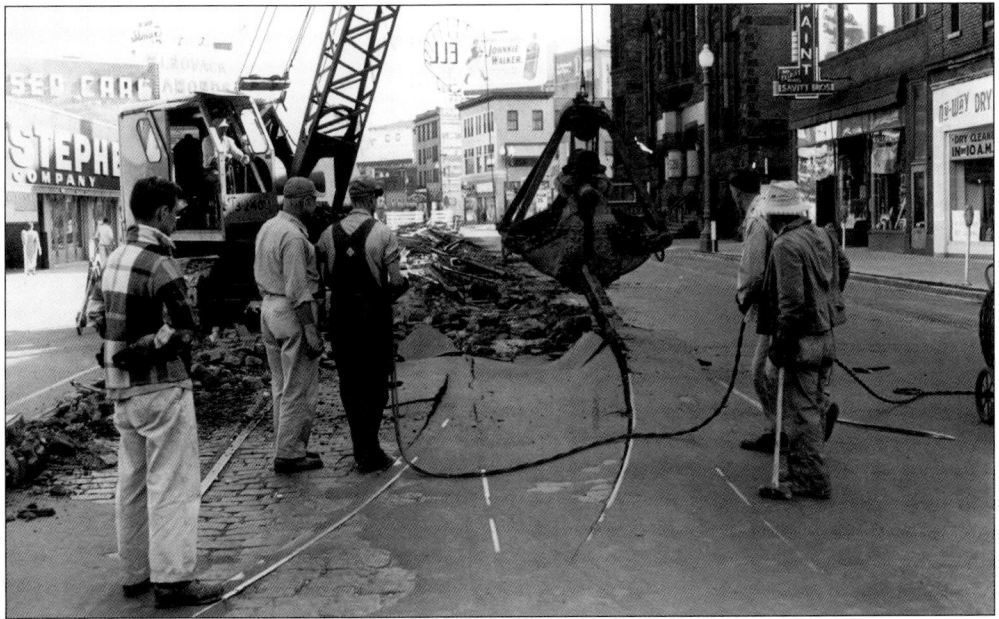

Once the trolleys were gone, construction crews began ripping out the tracks that crisscrossed downtown streets. Later, those tracks were at the center of a major corruption scandal. Public prosecutors learned that TCRT's head, Fred Ossanna, had been receiving kickbacks from a local scrap dealer in exchange for the scrap metal. Ossanna and the dealer both served jail time for their part in the scheme. (Courtesy of Hennepin County Public Library Special Collections.)

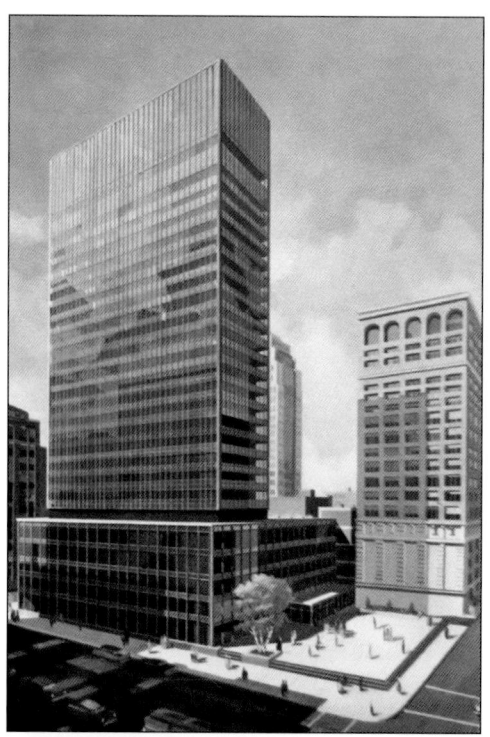

The First National Bank was downtown's first glass and steel skyscraper when it was built in 1960. The 28-story building reflected the influence of German-born architect Mies Van Rohe and the international style he championed. Architectural historian Larry Millet has written that the First National Bank "brought a sense of modernity to a skyline that in 1960 was still dominated by art deco towers." (Courtesy of the Minnesota Historical Society.)

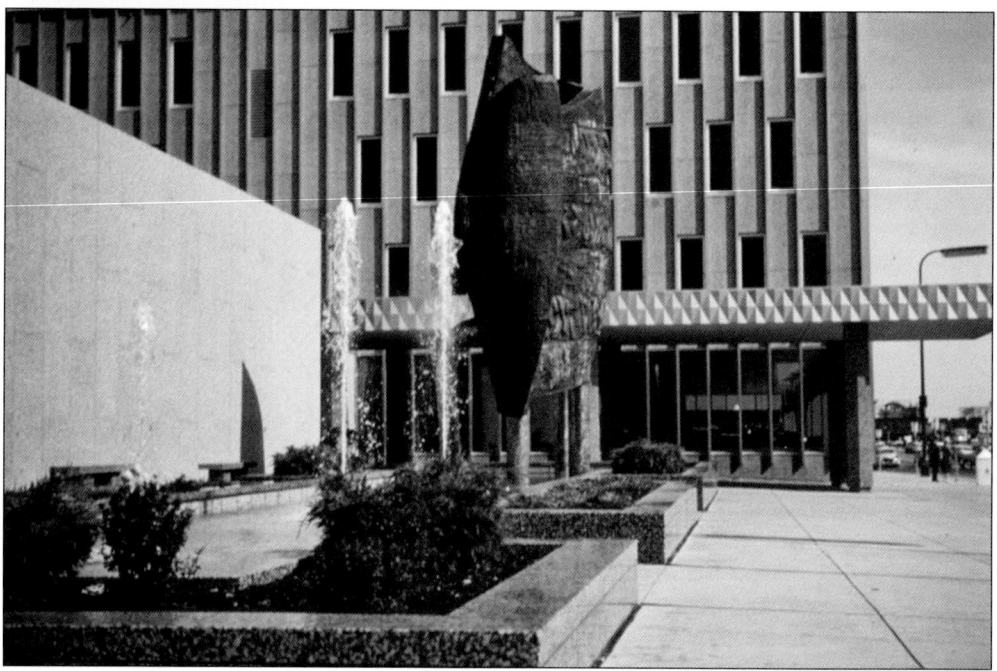

Minneapolis's second downtown library lasted 41 years, from 1961 to 2002. The sculpture at the library's entrance, known as *Scroll*, was created by John Rood, a well-known local artist. The Mid-century Modern building was one of downtown's least favorite architectural works and was not lamented when it was demolished to make room for an updated library building. (Courtesy of Hennepin County Public Library Special Collections.)

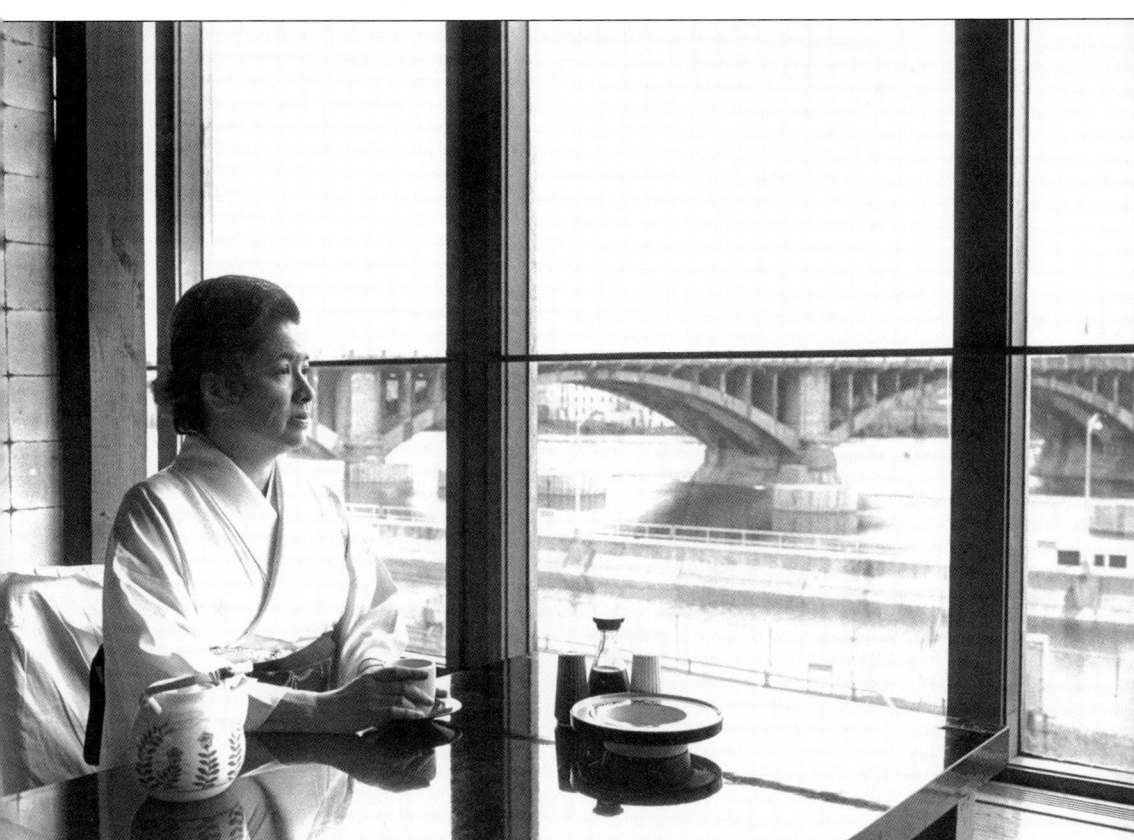

Reiko Weston launched a revival of the downtown riverfront when she built her popular Fuji Ya restaurant on the site of an abandoned flour mill in 1968. At the time, the riverfront was little more than an industrial wasteland. Fuji Ya occupied the riverfront site until it closed in 1990. The property was acquired by the Minneapolis Park Board. (Courtesy of Carol Hanson.)

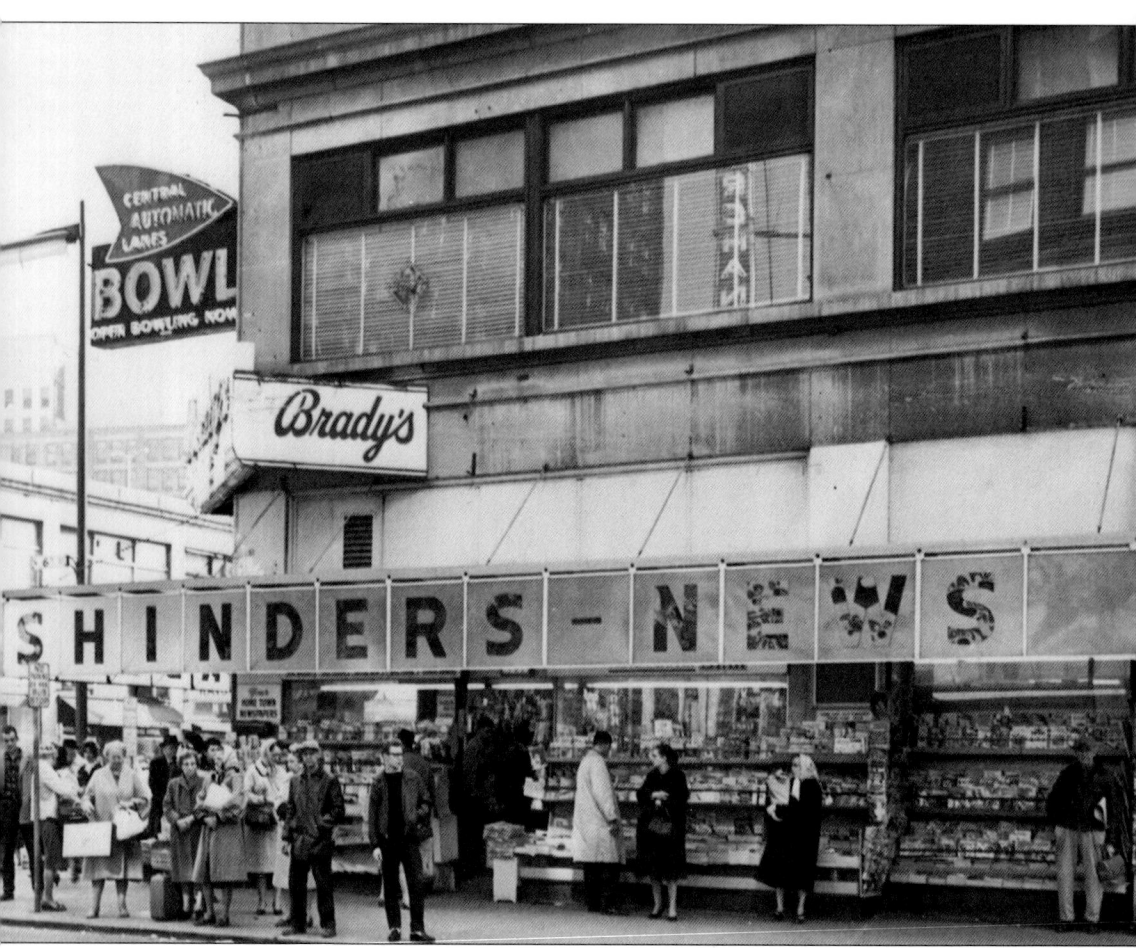

The origins of Shinders News extend back to 1916, when the three Shinders brothers began selling newspapers on the streets of downtown Minneapolis. Harry Shinders purchased a newsstand at Sixth Street and Hennepin Avenue in the 1920s. Later, his brother Al opened a store at the corner of Seventh Street and Hennepin Avenue that became the flagship for the family chain. Shinders was known for its wide selection of out-of-town newspapers. In 2007, the Hennepin Avenue store and the other Shinders locations closed. (Courtesy of Hennepin History Museum.)

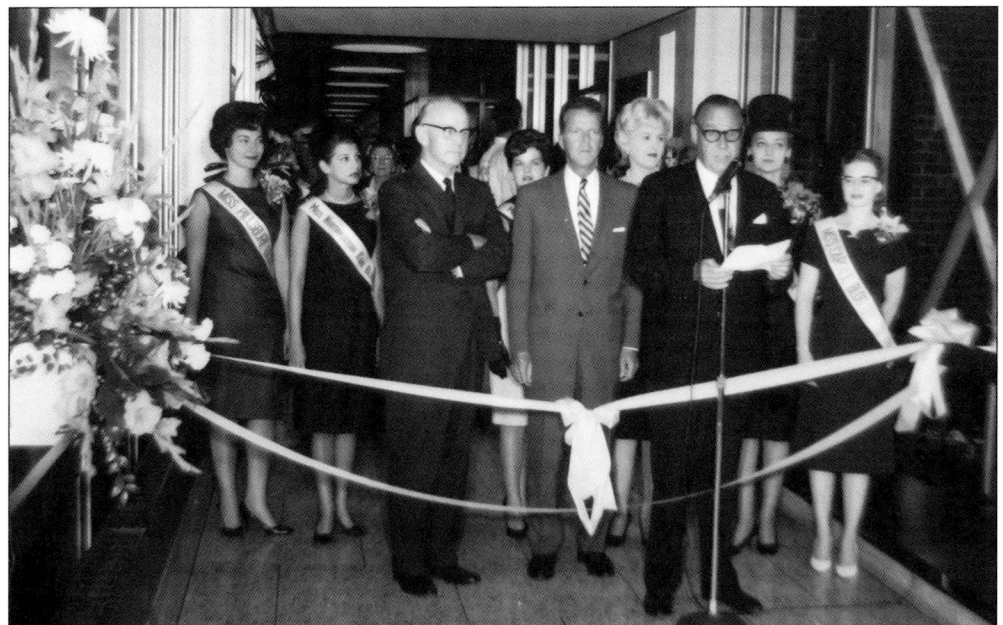

Leslie Park, shown here with his arms crossed, helped inaugurate a new downtown skyway in 1962. Park initiated the idea of covered walkways to help downtown withstand an economic threat from burgeoning suburban development all around the Twin Cities. Within 50 years, the skyways would connect more than 80 downtown blocks. (Courtesy of the Minnesota Historical Society.)

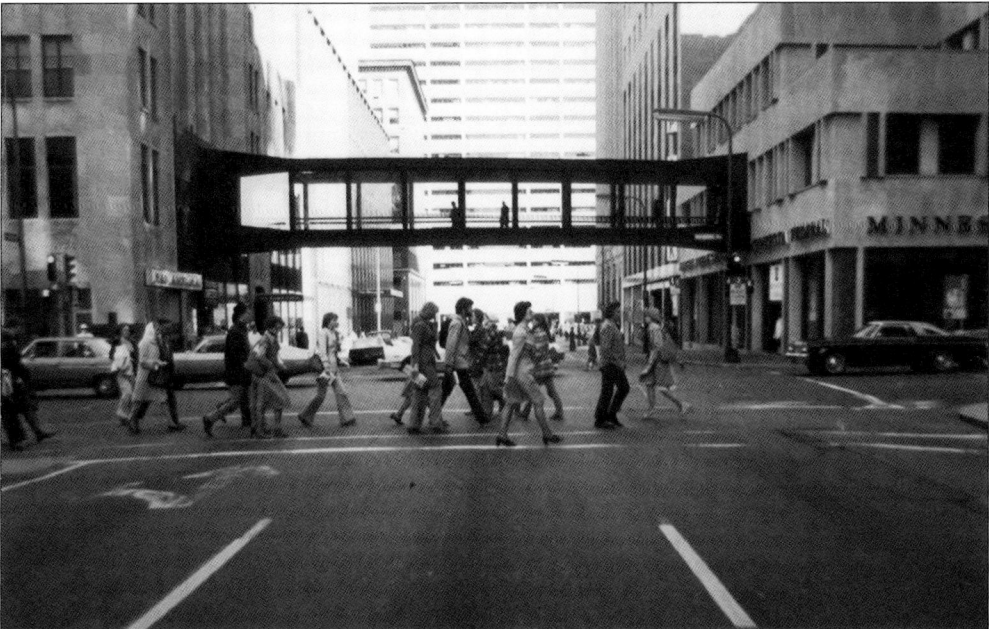

This skyway across Marquette Avenue connected the Northstar Center (right) with the Northwestern National Bank. The skyway was removed when the bank building was destroyed by a fire in 1982. A new connection was constructed across Marquette in 1989 when the Norwest Center was built on the site of the earlier Northwestern National Bank. (Courtesy of the Minnesota Historical Society.)

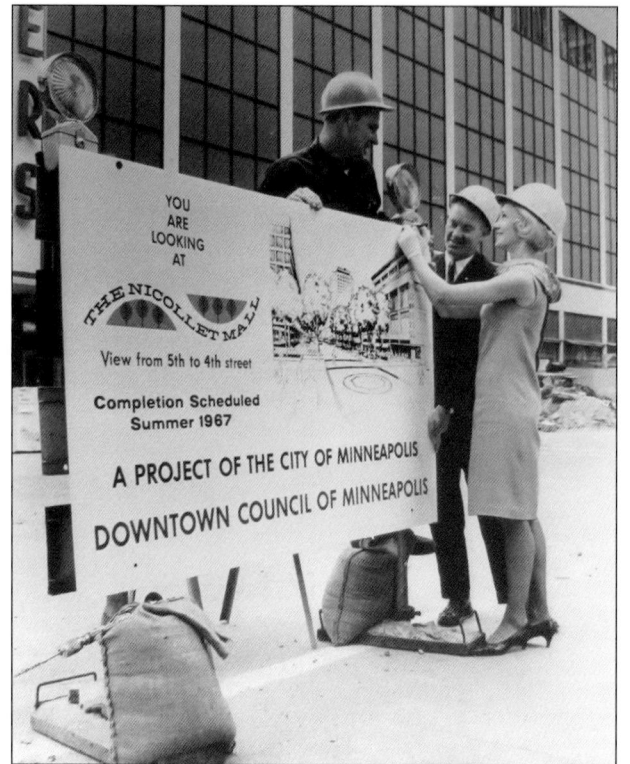

The Downtown Council was an early sponsor of the Nicollet Mall. The downtown business group was organized in 1955, just as construction of the suburban Southdale Center was getting under way. The council spearheaded efforts to reposition downtown Minneapolis as a major financial and communications center. (Courtesy of Hennepin History Museum.)

When it was built in 1967, the Nicollet Mall represented a defensive move by local civic leaders to protect downtown from the economic threat posed by the suburban postwar boom. Initially eight blocks in length and later extended four blocks on its south end, the mall was a curving transit way open to buses and pedestrians but off-limits to cars. (Courtesy of Meet Minneapolis Convention and Visitors.)

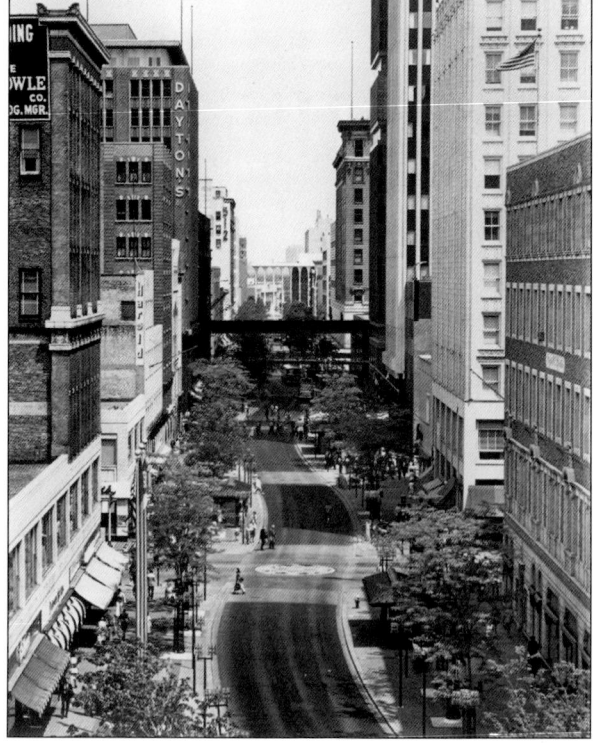

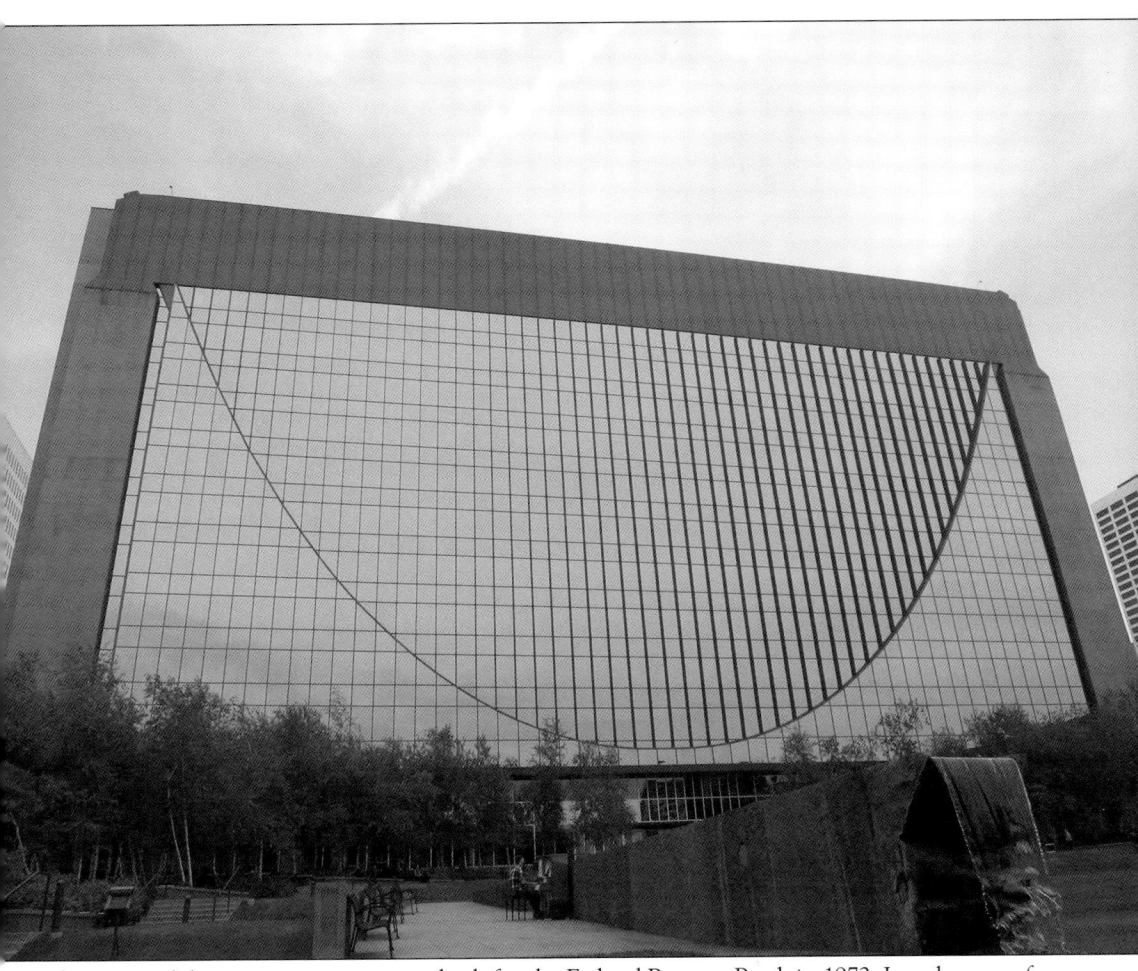

This unusual downtown structure was built for the Federal Reserve Bank in 1972. It makes use of a structural system that suspends the floors from steel cables at either end of the building, much like a suspension bridge. The Federal Reserve found that the architecturally unique building no longer met its needs after 25 years, and the bank moved to a new site on the downtown riverfront. The former bank is now an office building known as Marquette Plaza. (Author's collection.)

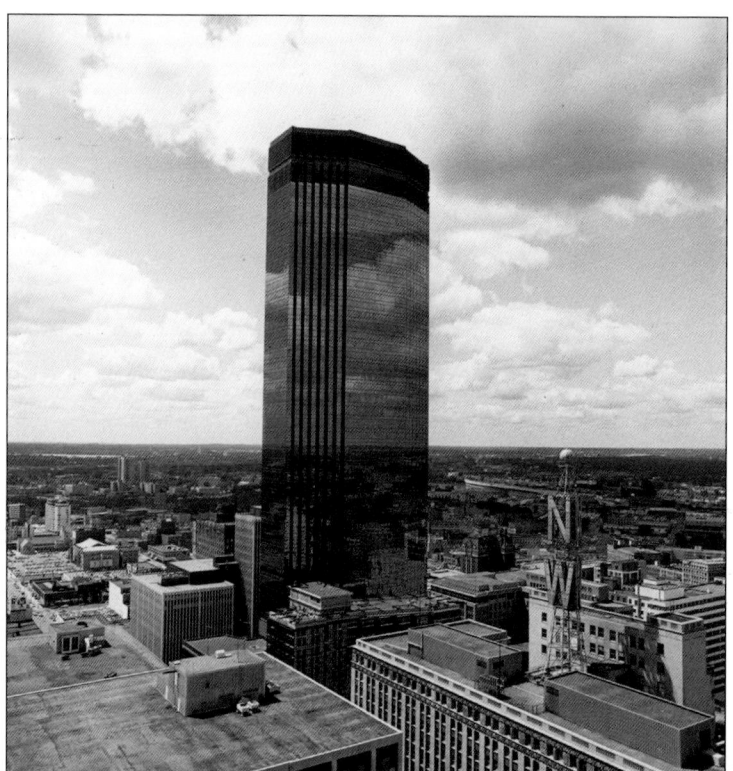

Considered one of Minnesota's most important architectural landmarks, the 57-story IDS Center towered over downtown Minneapolis when it opened in 1973. The skyscraper was designed by internationally acclaimed architect Phillip Johnson. One observer has described the IDS tower as "a very large building that carries itself with a ballerina's grace." (Courtesy of Hennepin County Public Library Special Collections.)

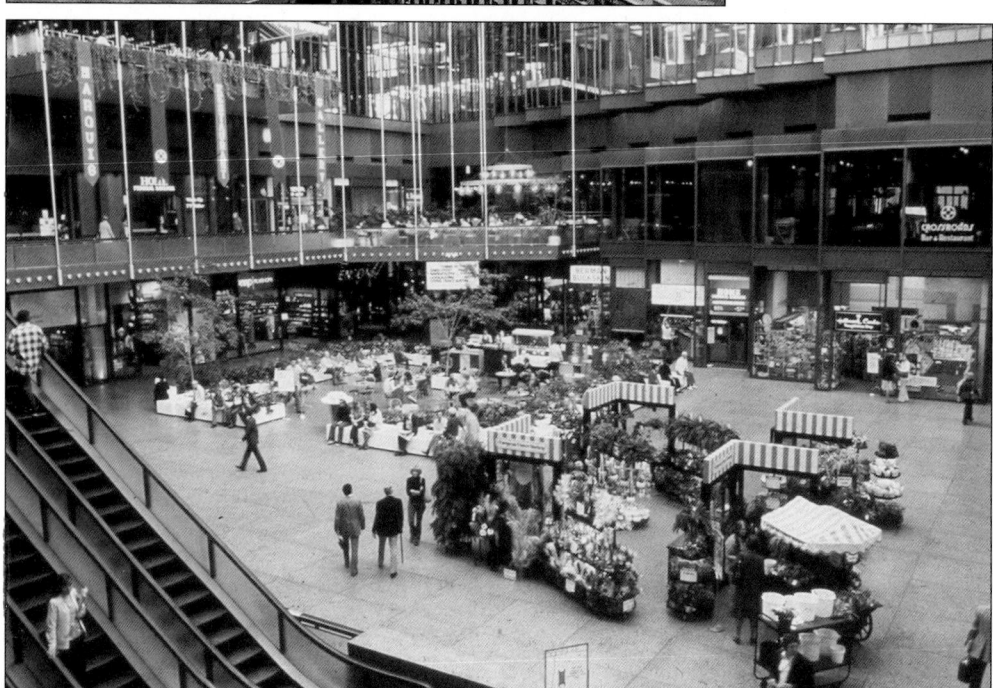

The IDS Crystal Court is covered with a series of glass panels that gives the space a light, airy feel. Located at the crossroads of downtown, Crystal Court serves as downtown Minneapolis's climate-controlled town square. (Courtesy of Meet Minneapolis Visitors and Convention Bureau.)

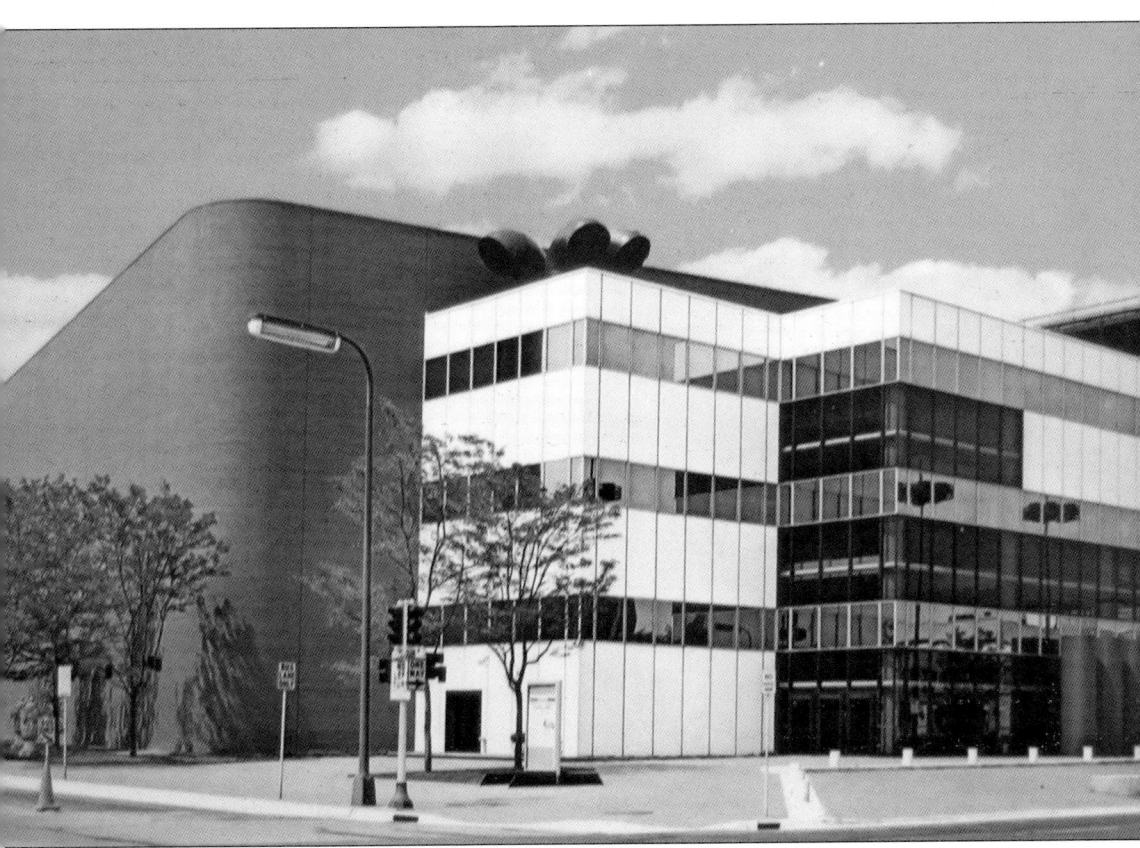

Orchestra Hall was built as the home for the Minnesota Orchestra in 1974. The building is known for its superb acoustics, achieved with the use of cube-shaped sound deflectors suspended from the ceiling. Orchestra Hall shares its Nicollet Avenue block with Peavey Plaza, a public open space scheduled for substantial renovation. Closed for several years, Orchestra Hall reopened in 2013 after undergoing a $50 million renovation. (Courtesy of Meet Minneapolis Visitors and Convention Bureau.)

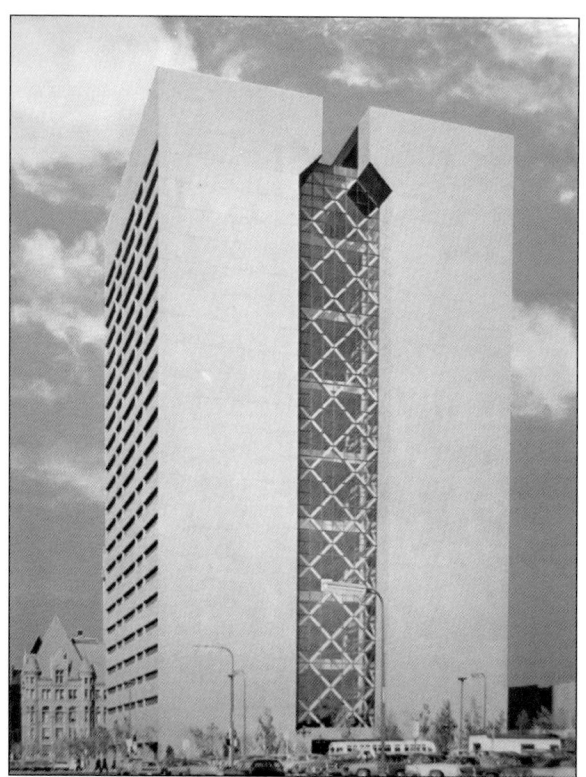

The Hennepin County Government Center was built in 1977 to house county offices that had outgrown their original space in the Minneapolis City Hall across the street. The building is best known for its atrium, which extends through its full 24 stories. Over the years, the county building has not won high marks for its bland 1970s-era design. (Left, Minnesota Historical Society; below, author's collection.)

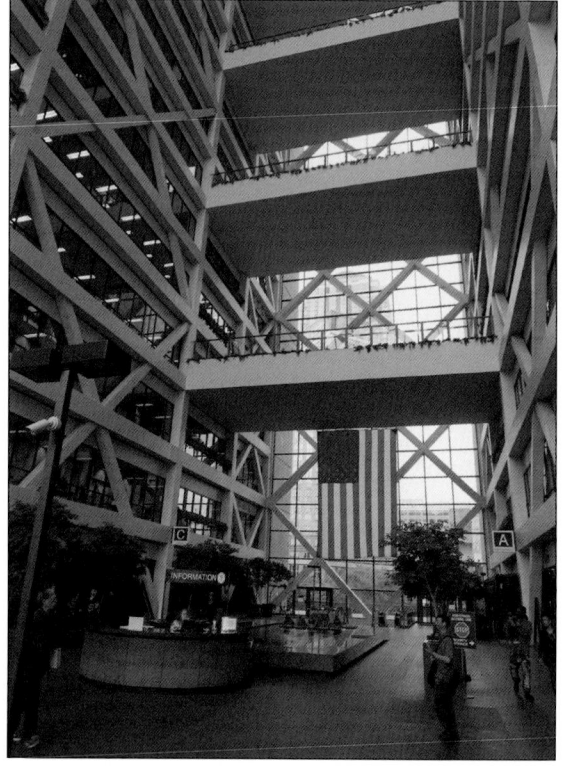

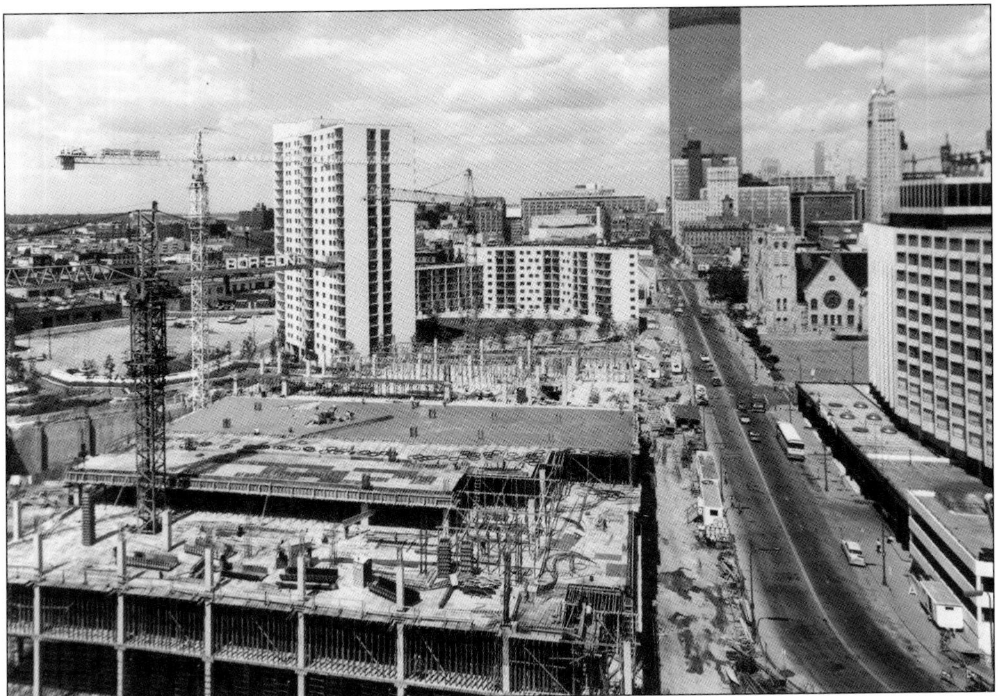

The two condominium buildings at the center of this photograph, 1225 LaSalle (left) and 1200 on the Mall, were built in the mid-1970s as part of the Loring Nicollet redevelopment project. This downtown project was the city's first effort to use tax increment financing to combat urban blight. The building under construction in the foreground is the Hyatt hotel. (Courtesy of Hennepin History Museum.)

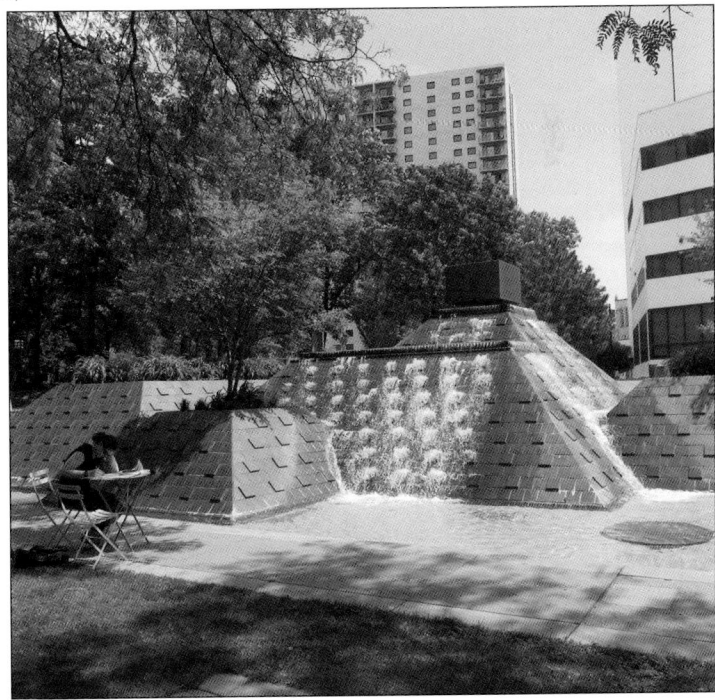

The Loring Greenway is a landscaped pedestrian pathway that connects the Nicollet Mall with Loring Park. Constructed as part of the Loring Nicollet project, the three-block walkway, lined with fountains and flower beds, helped spur the creation of a new high-density residential neighborhood at the south end of downtown. (Author's collection.)

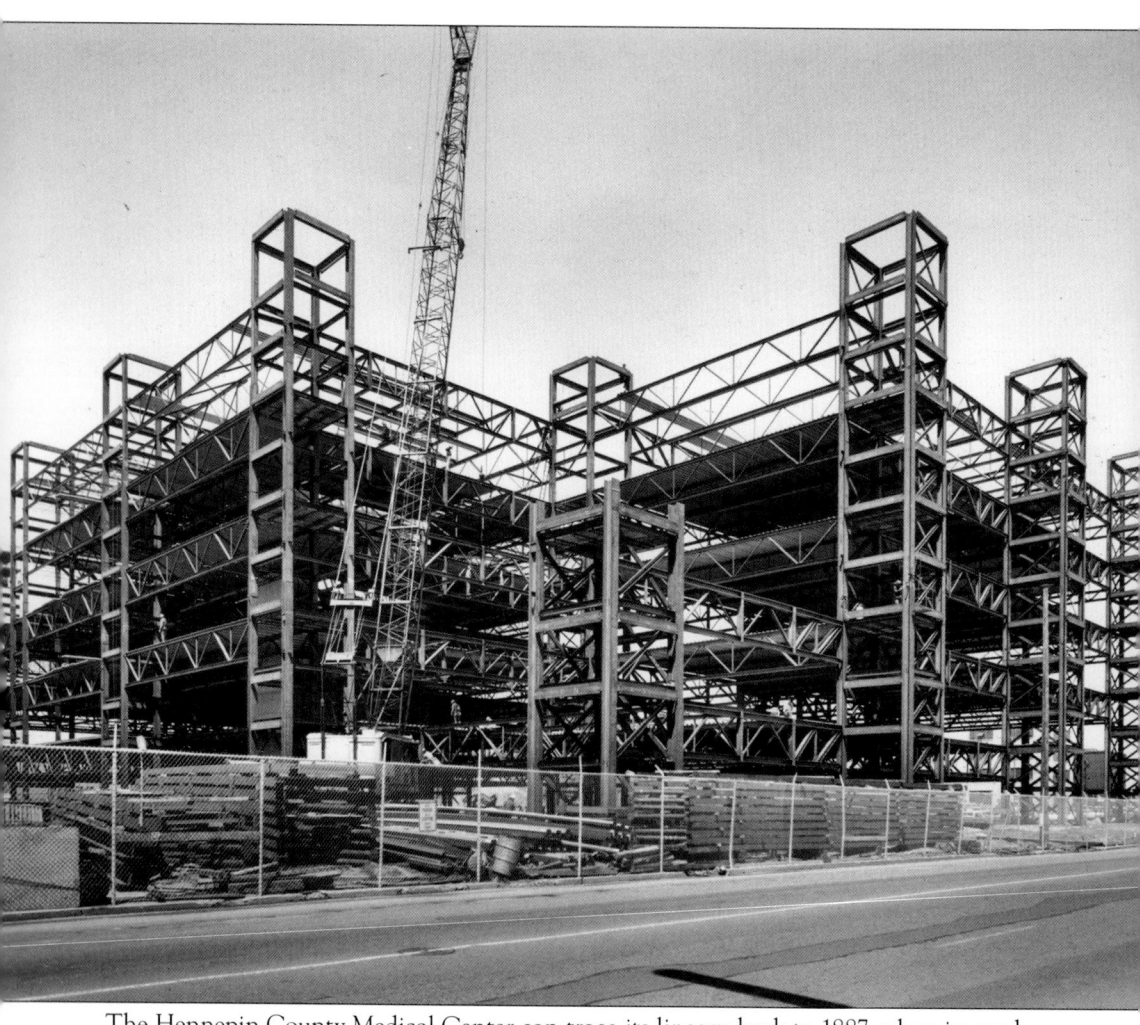

The Hennepin County Medical Center can trace its lineage back to 1887, when its predecessor was known as City Hospital. The new medical center, built in 1975, replaced a jumble of hospital buildings on the adjacent bock, some dating back to the turn of the 20th century. Originally a city-run facility, ownership and management of the hospital were transferred to Hennepin County in 1964. (Courtesy of Hennepin Medical History Museum.)

Six

MODERN TIMES

The 20th century's final decades saw a construction boom that remade the downtown skyline. That era's most notable building, Cesar Pelli's Wells Fargo Center, replaced the historic Northwestern National Bank destroyed during a Thanksgiving Day fire in 1982. Nearly 10 years later, another important historic site was nearly lost when a fire ripped through the Washburn A Mill in 1991. Luckily, several fire-damaged walls of the mill were retained and incorporated in a new riverfront-milling museum.

During these years, the city moved ahead with plans to convert the largely abandoned riverfront to a new cultural and recreational district. These efforts received an important boost when the Stone Arch Bridge became a biking and pedestrian pathway in 1994. Later, the east bank was reclaimed for housing when a series of abandoned mills were converted to riverfront condominiums.

Another decrepit downtown district was reclaimed when Minneapolis leaders realized that the aging and blighted movie theaters on Hennepin Avenue had the potential to further the city's urban revitalization goals. While several of the once elegant movie palaces had become sleazy X-rated theaters, their ornate furnishings, dating back to the golden age of cinema, were still in place.

The first of the Hennepin Avenue theaters, the State, was restored to its 1920s elegance in 1991. The State's success in drawing theatergoers back downtown led to the renovation of a second historic theater, the Orpheum, in 1993. These two historic preservation efforts, along with later theater renovations, recreated Hennepin Avenue's Great White Way.

The early years of the 21st century brought the tragic collapse of the I-35W bridge in 2007. The bridge was quickly rebuilt, greatly aiding the revival of the downtown riverfront. That revival was spurred by the construction of a new Guthrie Theater and the development of upscale condominium and rental housing overlooking St. Anthony Falls.

Two of Minnesota's big-league sports teams got new downtown homes in the 2000s. The Minnesota Twins came first with their Target Field in 2010, followed by the Vikings' US Bank Stadium in 2016. The new stadium was the catalyst for the redevelopment of a long-ignored downtown district now known as East Town.

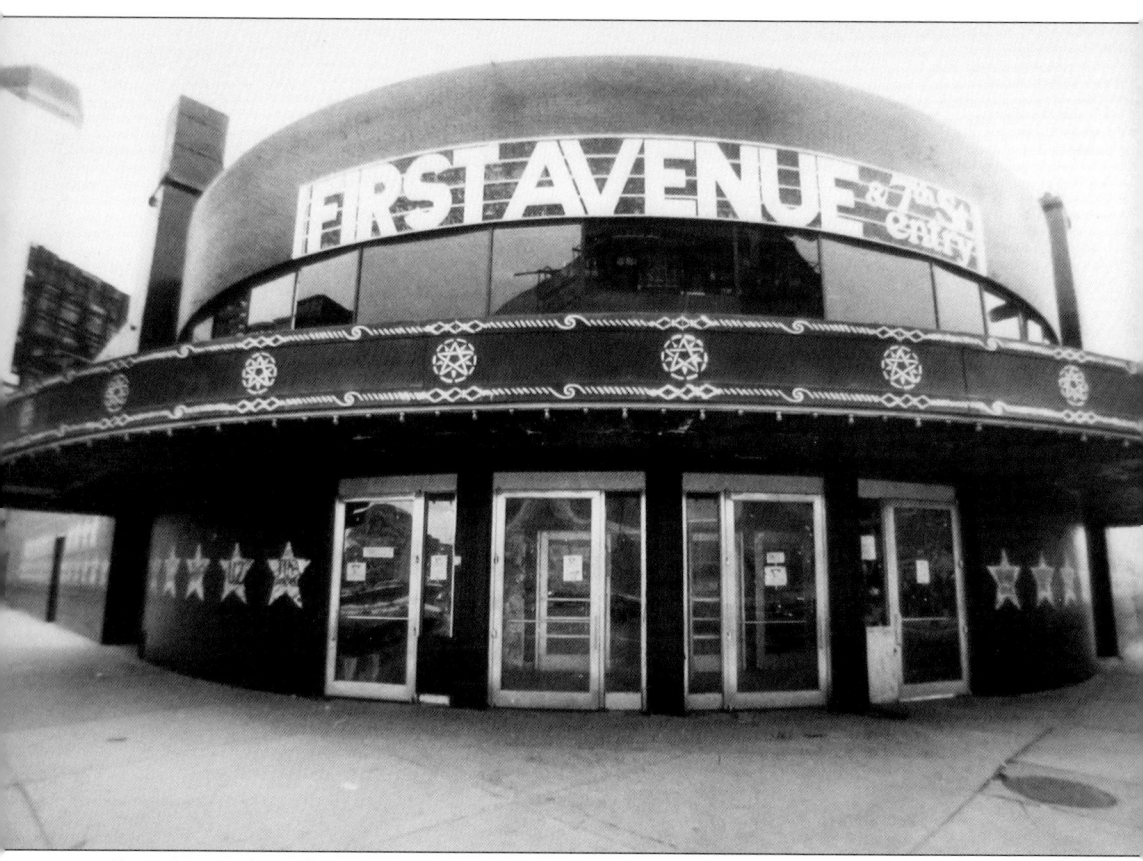

First Avenue brought international fame to the Minneapolis music scene when it was used as a setting for Prince's movie, *Purple Rain*. The nightclub began its life as an Art Deco Greyhound bus depot in 1936. After the depot closed, it became a music club named for the street that runs in front of the building. (Courtesy of Minnesota Historical Society.)

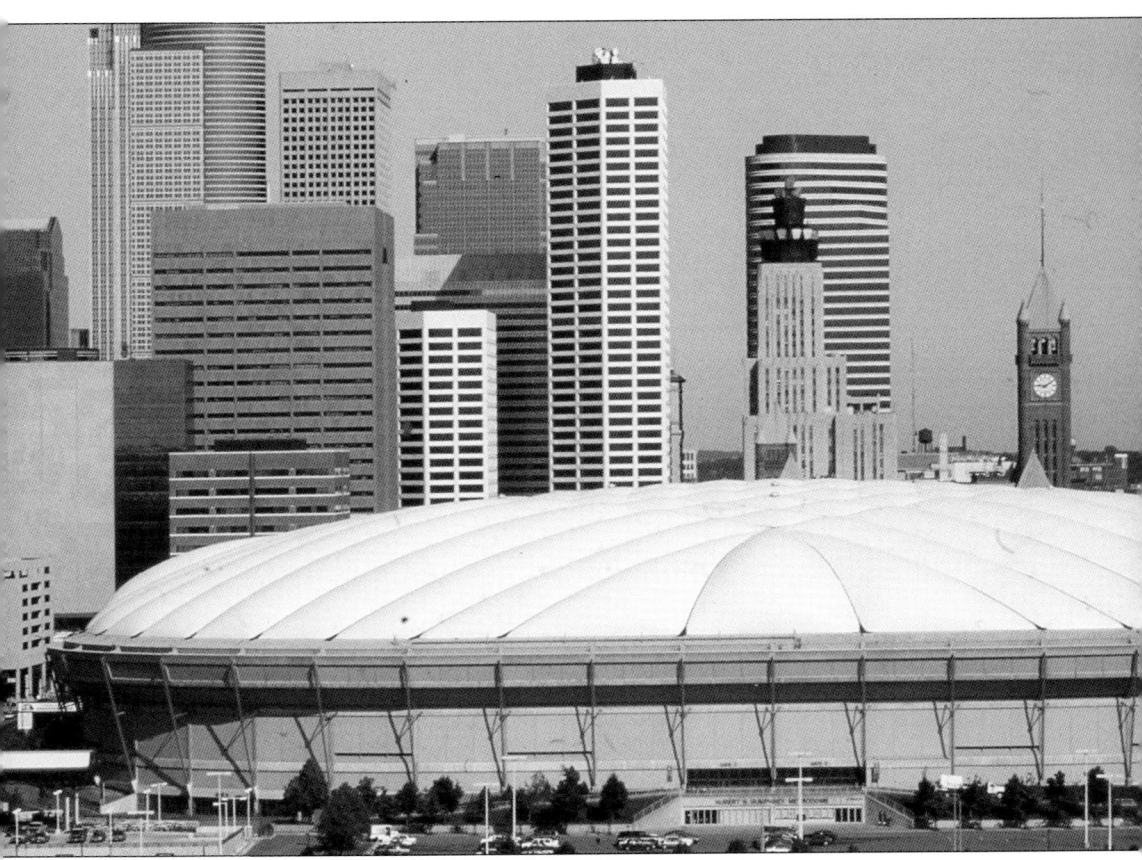

The Hubert H. Humphrey Metrodome brought big-league sports to downtown Minneapolis when it opened in 1982. The sports stadium was known for its fiberglass roof that was prone to collapse when subjected to heavy snowfall. The Metrodome replaced the Metropolitan Stadium that had been the home of the NFL's Vikings and MLB's Minnesota Twins. In 2014, the Metrodome was demolished to make room for the Vikings' new US Bank Stadium. (Courtesy of Meet Minneapolis Visitors and Convention Bureau.)

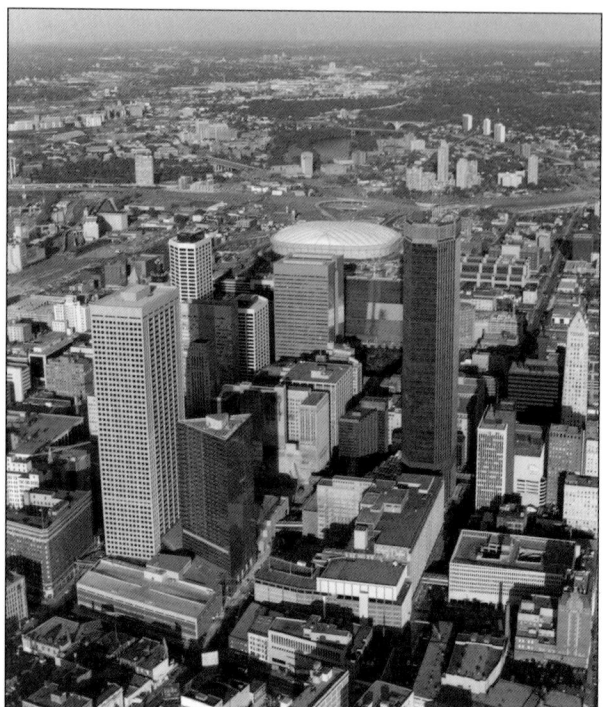

When it opened in 1982, City Center replaced a square block between Nicollet and Hennepin Avenues that was filled with small, obsolete commercial buildings. City Center's first tenant, Donaldson's Department Store, had relocated to the multiuse development just before its original Nicollet Avenue building was destroyed by the Thanksgiving Day fire in 1982. (Courtesy of Hennepin History Museum.)

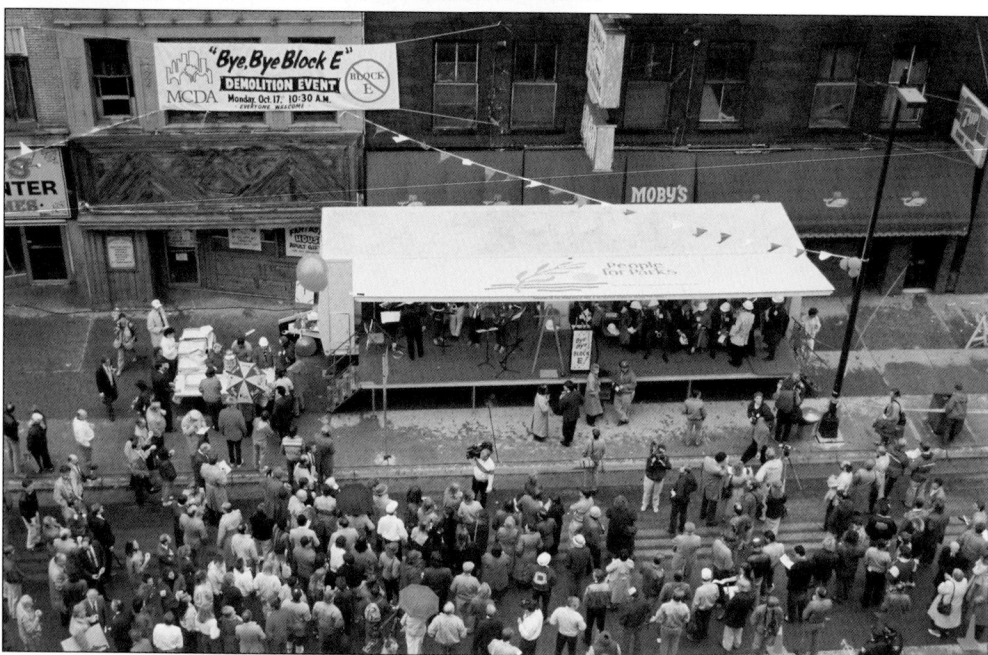

On October 17, 1988, city officials organized a block party to celebrate the demolition of downtown's notorious Block E, a strip of seedy bars and restaurants on Hennepin Avenue. A new Block E, designed as an entertainment and retail center, opened in 2001, but it was not successful and kept losing tenants. In 2015, the development, renamed Mayo Clinic Square, was converted to a sports medicine center and practice facility for the city's two professional basketball teams. (Courtesy of Minneapolis Community Planning and Economic Development.)

Shown here under construction, this downtown skyscraper was originally known as the Norwest Center when it opened in 1989. Now known as the Wells Fargo Center, the building evokes the Art Deco style of the Manhattan office towers from the 1920s and 1930s. The financial center was designed by internationally renowned architect Cesar Pelli. (Courtesy of Minneapolis Community Planning and Economic Development.)

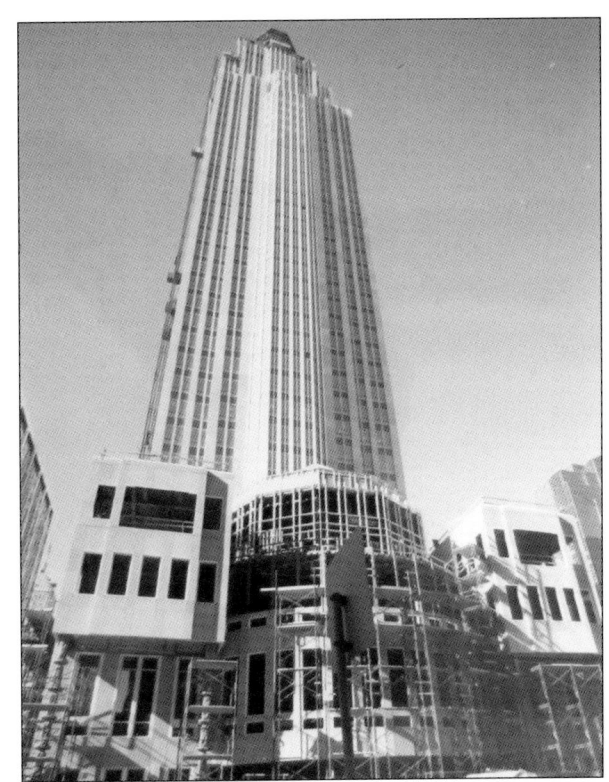

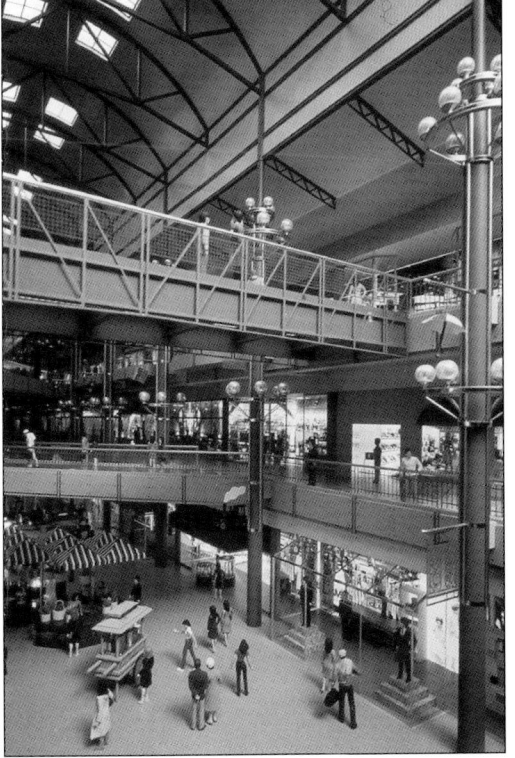

Gaviidae Common took its name from the Latin term for the loon, the Minnesota state bird. During its early years, this suburban-style shopping center, spanning two adjacent blocks, brought upscale retailers to Nicollet Avenue. By 2016, however, the exclusive shops at Gaviidae had disappeared and been replaced by offices and stores catering to the day-to-day needs of downtown's growing residential population. (Courtesy of Meet Minneapolis Visitors and Convention Bureau.)

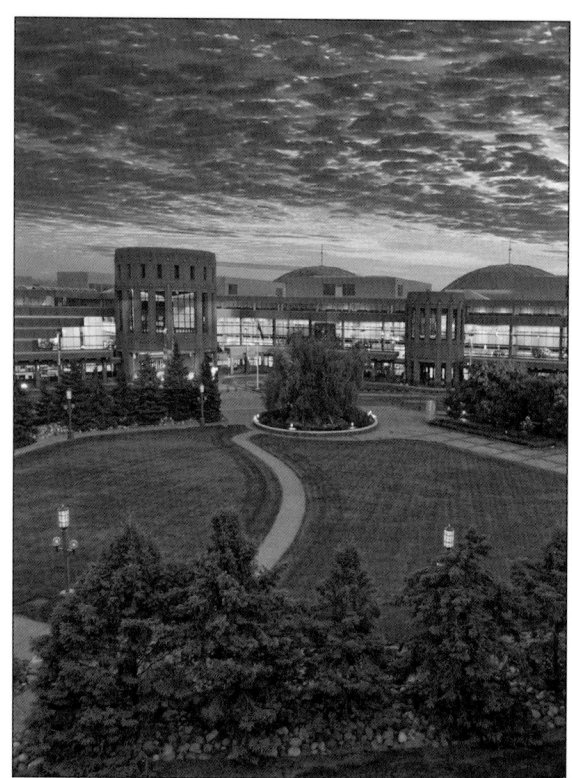

The Minneapolis Convention Center, built in 1991, replaced the 1927 auditorium on the same site. Later remodeled and expanded, the convention center's most notable architectural features are its two front towers and four low domes. Nearly 500,000 square feet of exhibition space and skyway connections to downtown hotels make the center an attractive site for large national conventions. (Both, courtesy of Meet Minneapolis Visitors and Convention Bureau.)

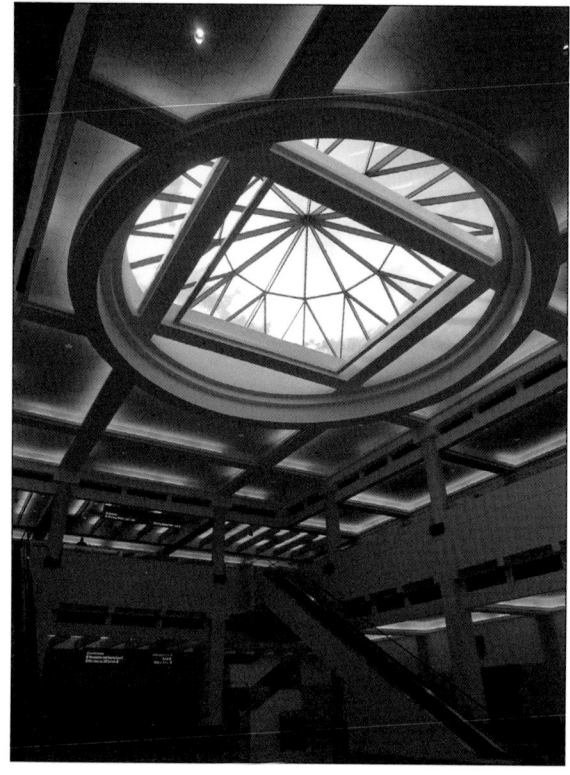

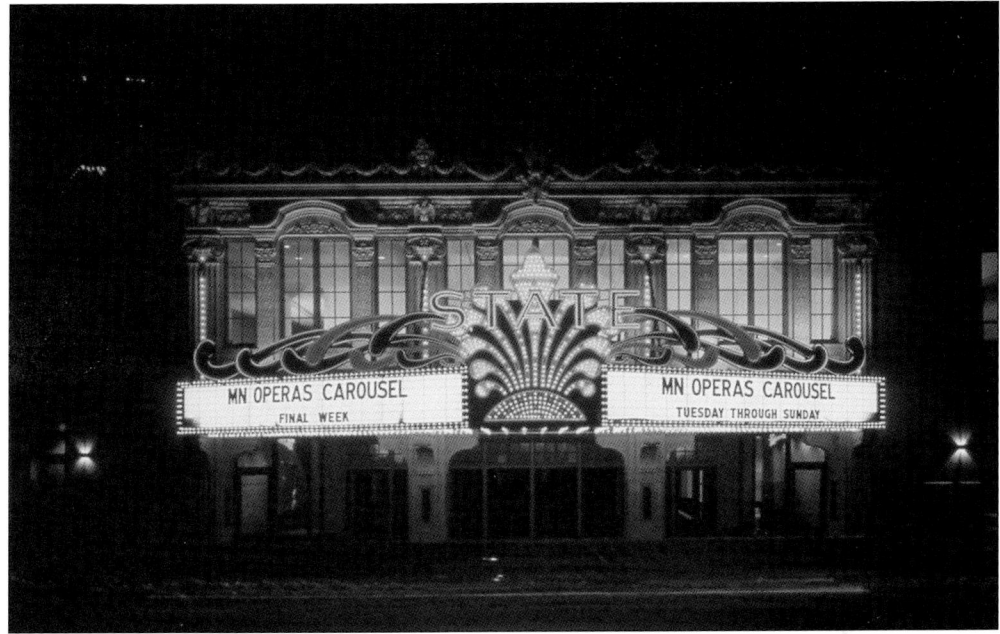

The State Theater, once the crown jewel of Minneapolis's Great White Way, fell on hard times after World War II. The State had been an X-rated theater and a church before it was purchased by the City of Minneapolis's development arm in 1989. Restored to its 1920s elegance, the newly named Historic State Theatre opened to rave reviews in 1991 with a performance of the musical *Carousel*. (Both, courtesy of Meet Minneapolis Visitors and Convention Bureau.)

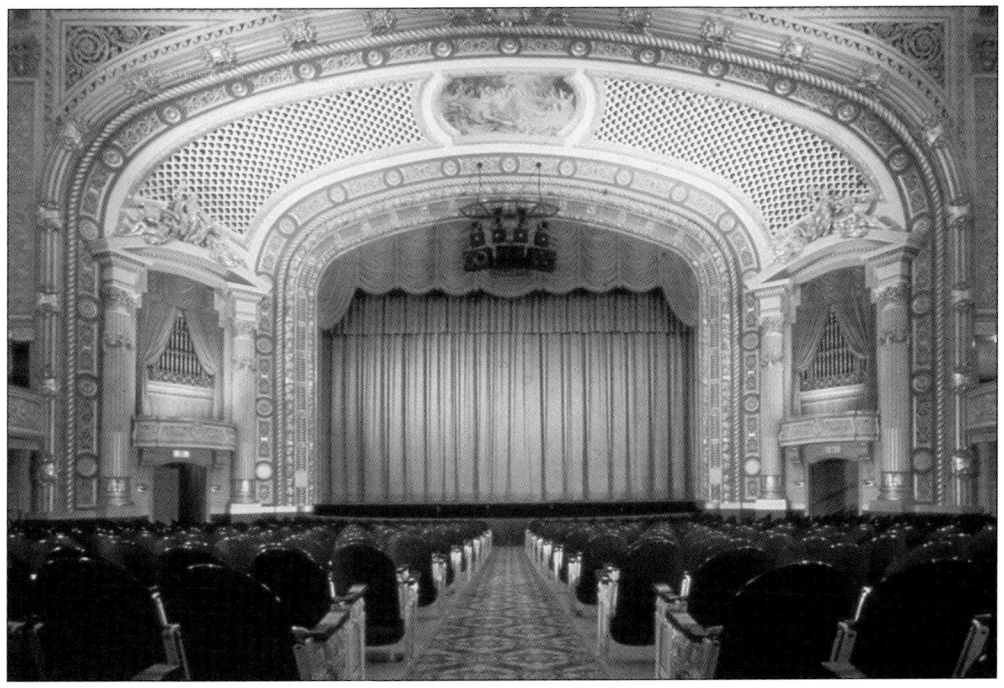

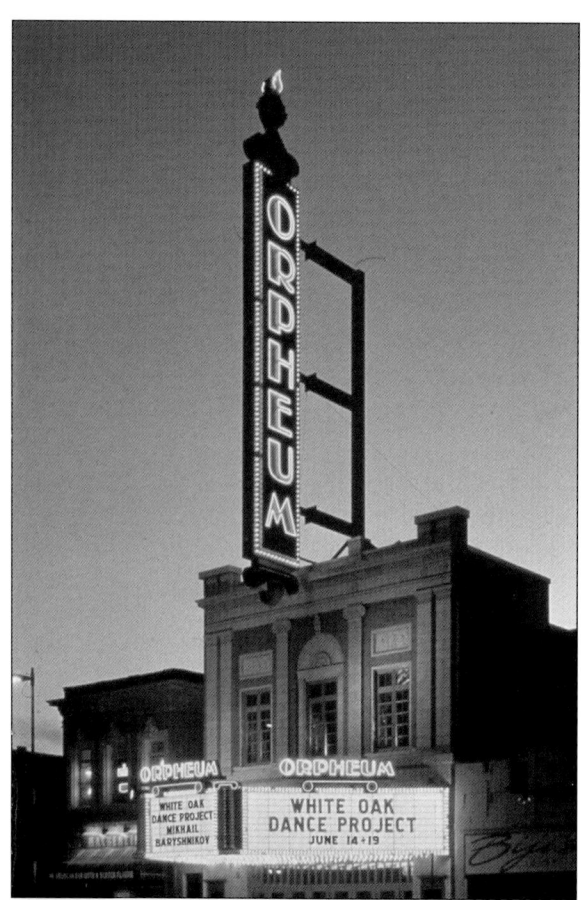

With more than 1,260 seats, the Orpheum Theater was once called "the biggest vaudeville theater west of New York." Dating to 1921, the Orpheum was the second Hennepin Avenue theater restored by the City of Minneapolis in the 1990s. As the largest theater venue on Hennepin, the Orpheum now brings hit Broadway musicals to Minneapolis. (Both, courtesy of Meet Minneapolis Visitors and Convention Bureau.)

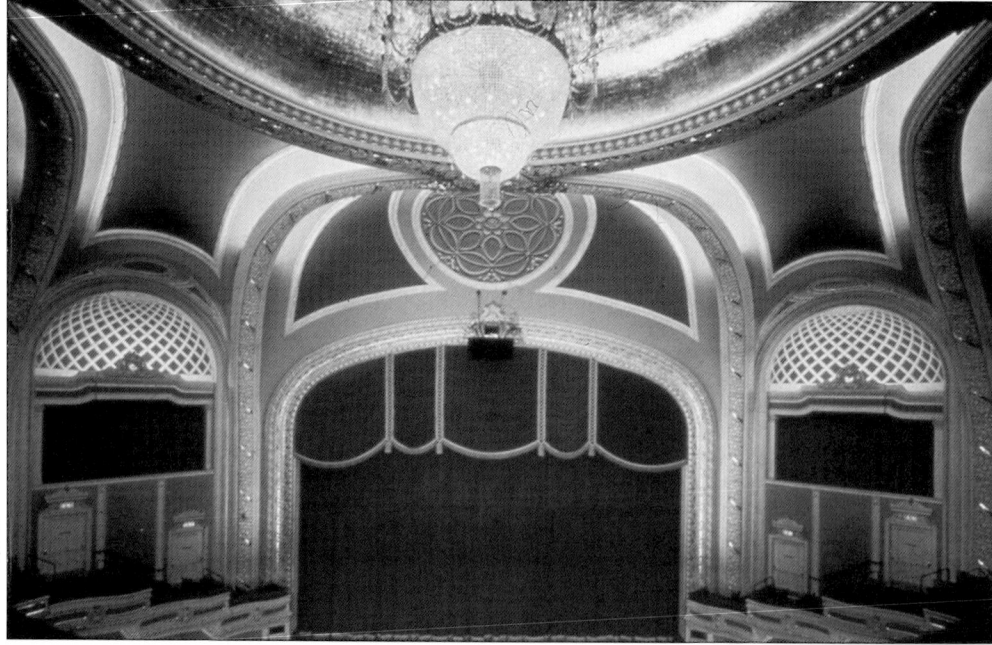

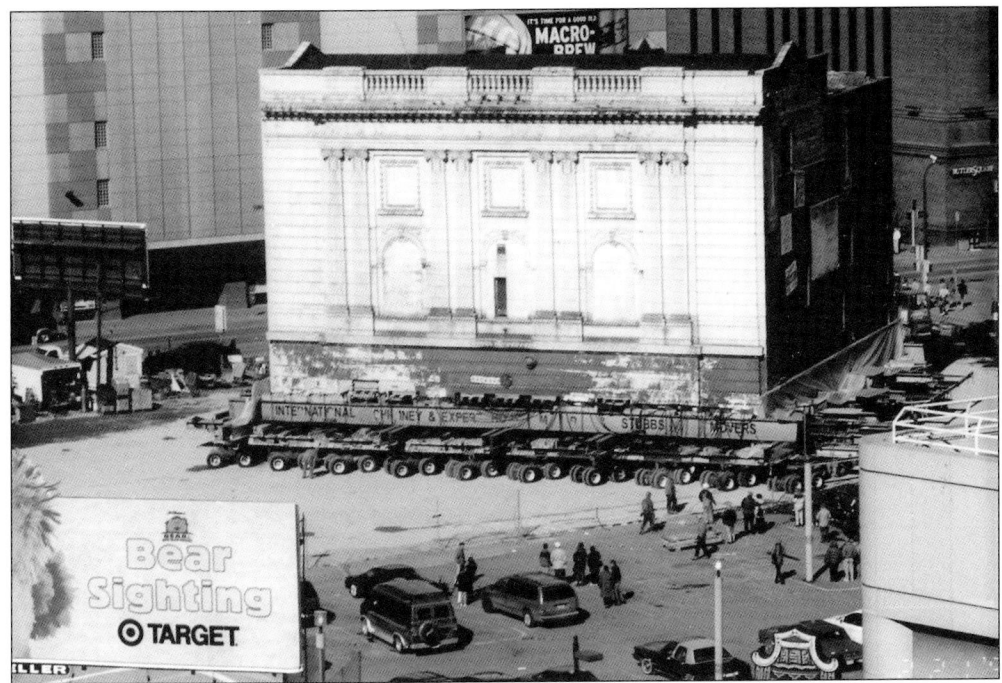

Originally known as the Shubert when it was built in 1910, this downtown theater underwent several transformations during its 100-year history. In the early 1990s, the theater was about to be demolished when local historic preservationists persuaded city officials to move the downtown landmark to a new location on Hennepin Avenue. It took 12 days to complete the three-block move down Hennepin in 1999. The rebuilt theater is now known as the Cowles Center for Dance and the Performing Arts. (Above, courtesy of Stubbs Movers; below, author's collection.)

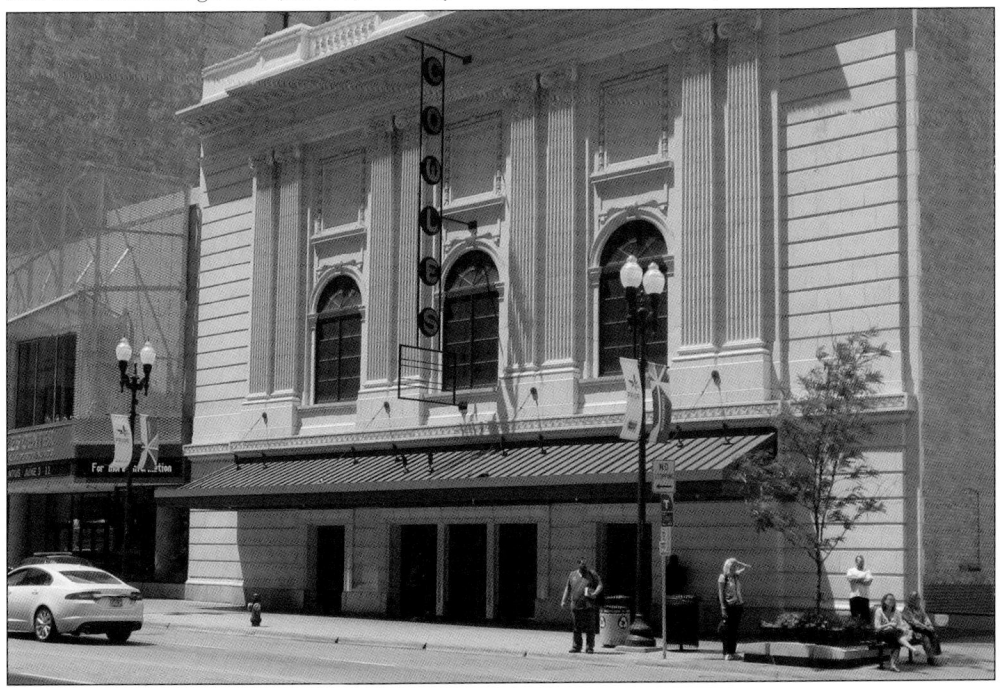

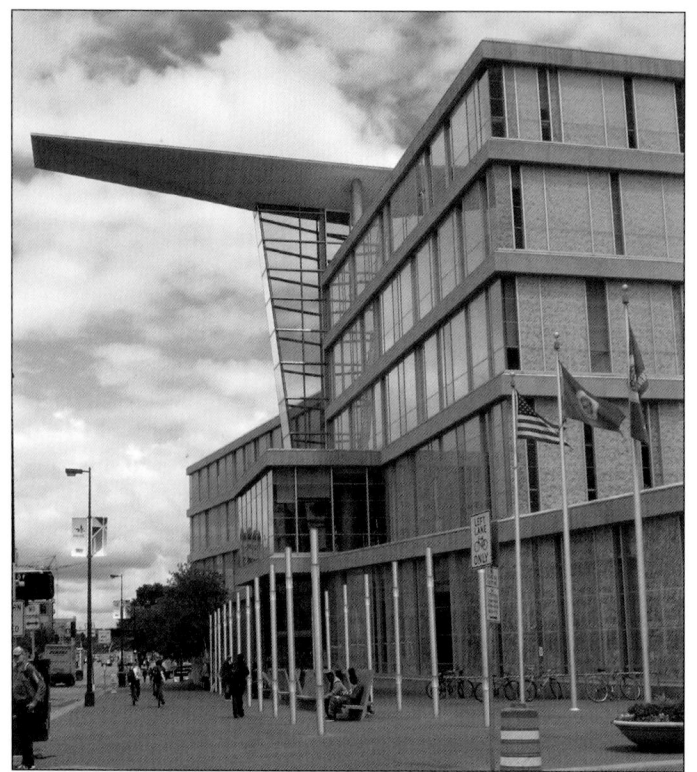

The Minneapolis Central Library, completed in 2006, was designed by Cesar Pelli. It replaced the 1961 library building on the same site. The central atrium brings natural light into the library's working areas. Minerva, the goddess of wisdom, presides over the library's main floor. The bronze statue was originally installed in a niche over the first Minneapolis Public Library in 1890. (Both, author's collection.)

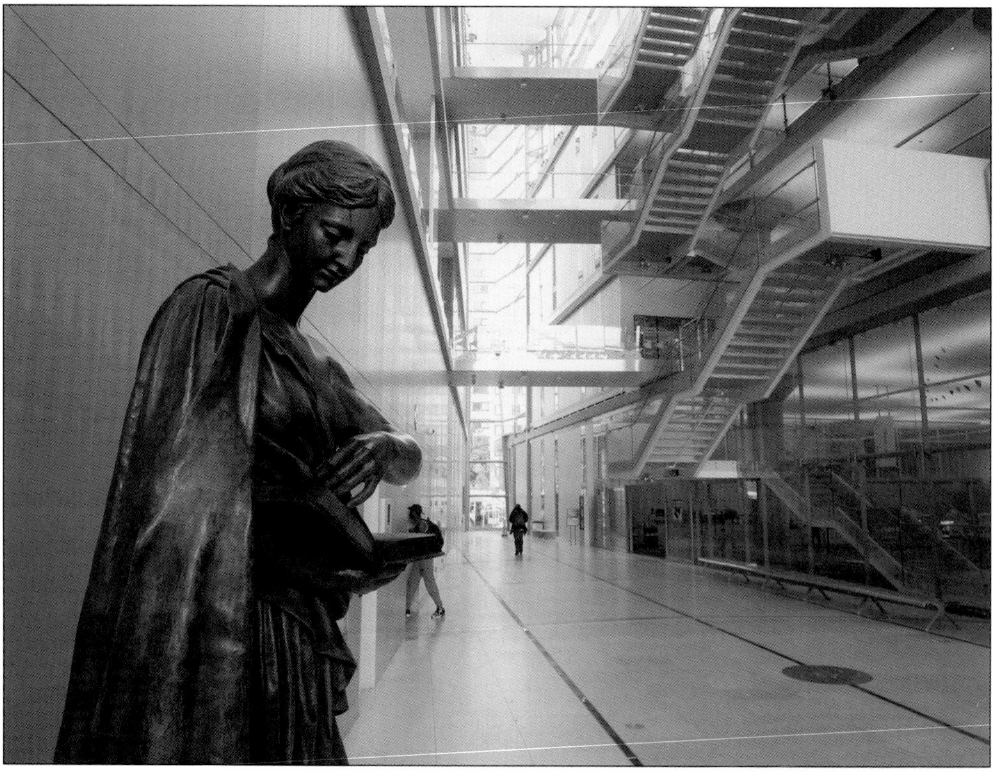

With its distinctive red bull's-eye logo, the Target store brought discount retailing to downtown when it opened in 2001. While still in the planning stage, Target became embroiled in a controversy over the use of public financing for the commercial development that would eventually house its two-story store at Ninth Street and Nicollet Avenue. (Author's collection.)

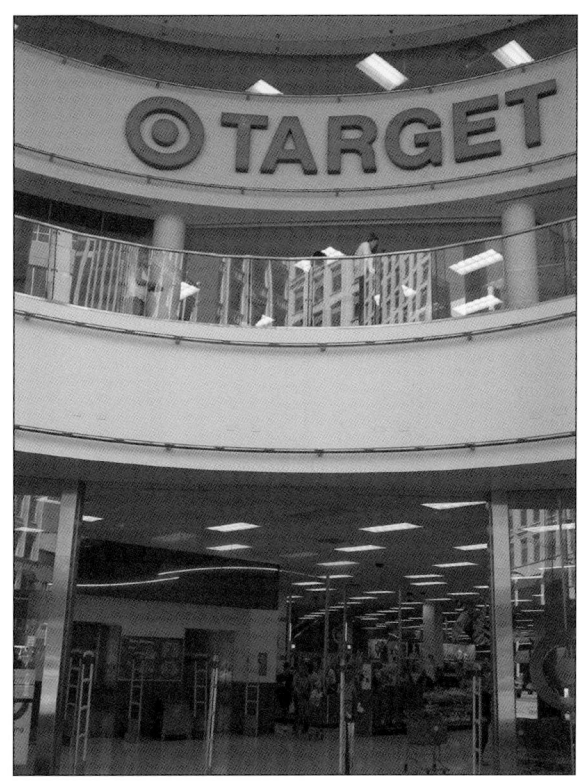

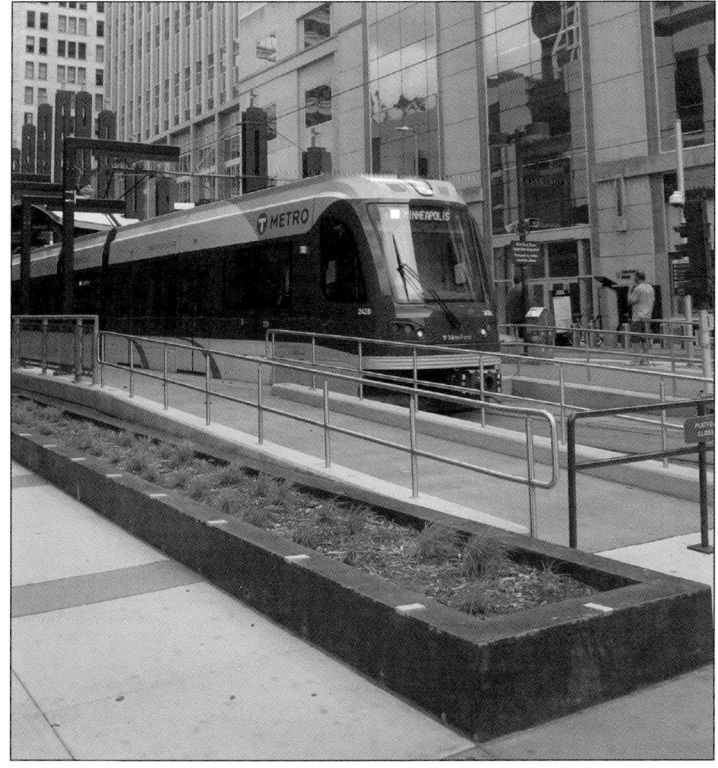

Light rail transit (LRT) reached downtown in 2004 when the Hiawatha Line, now known as the Blue Line, began operation. The 23-mile transit line connects downtown with the Minneapolis–St. Paul Airport and the Mall of America. A second LRT project, the Green Line, was started in 2014, providing a link between the Twin Cities' two downtowns. (Author's collection.)

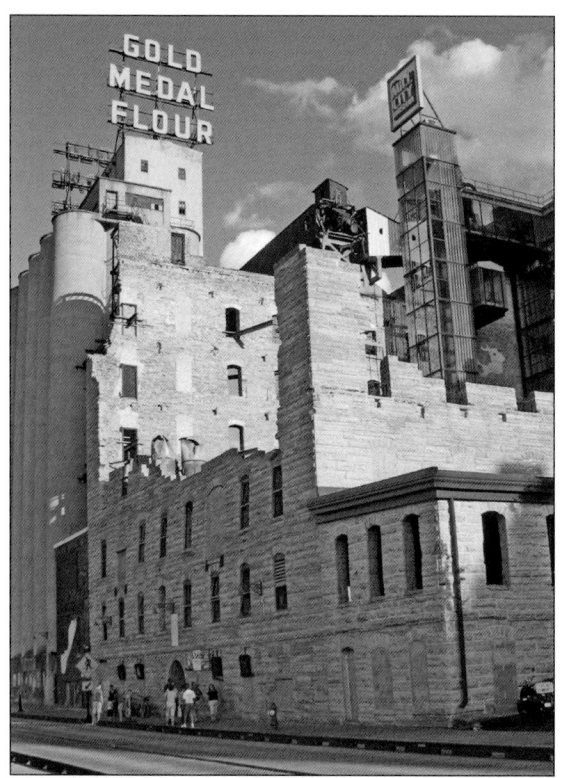

One of the city's most unique structures, the Mill City Museum incorporates the ruins of the historic Washburn Crosby Mill in a modern interpretive center. The museum, which opened in 2003, recalls Minneapolis's early riverfront history, with a special emphasis on flour milling and other local industries powered by St. Anthony Falls. (Courtesy of the Mill City Museum.)

In 2006, the Guthrie Theater completed a new $125 million performance center, which replaced its original theater on Vineland Place. The imposing riverfront building, made of glass with a dark-blue skin, was designed by French architect Jean Nouvel. (Courtesy of Meet Minneapolis Visitors and Convention Bureau.)

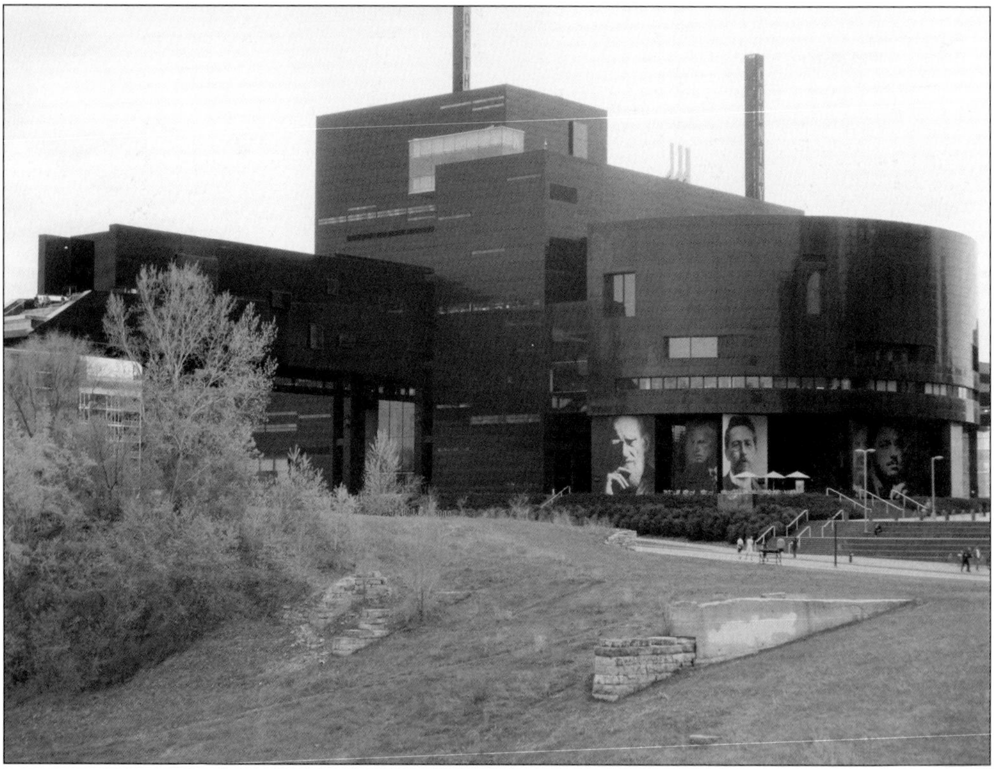

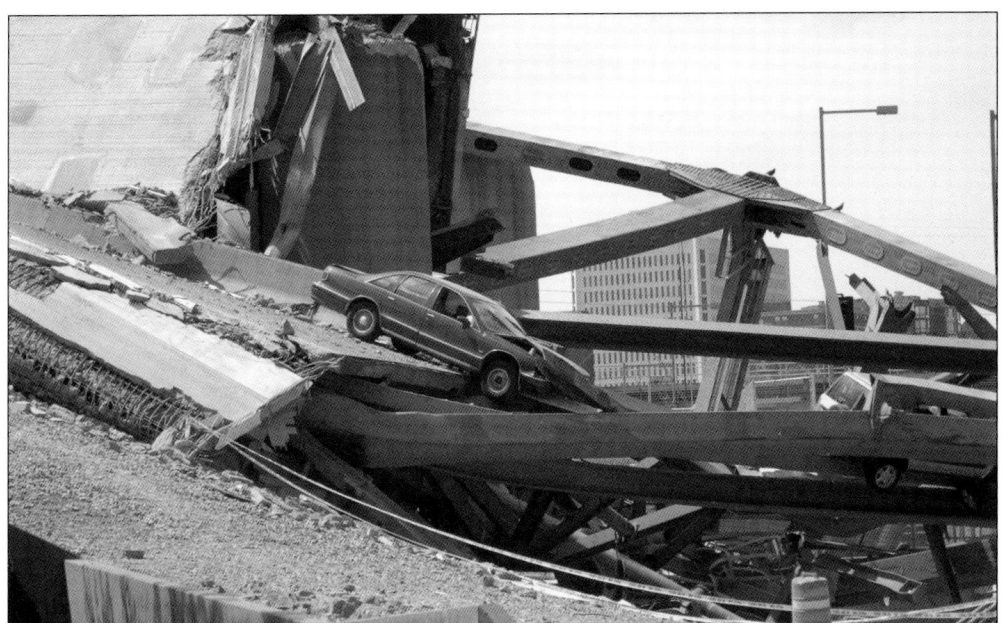

On the evening of August 1, 2007, the I-35W Mississippi River bridge collapsed, killing 13 people and injuring 120 others. At the time of the collapse, the I-35W bridge was one of the most heavily traveled river crossings in Minnesota, carrying 140,000 vehicles daily. The National Transportation Safety Board later determined that the disaster was probably caused by design flaws and heavy traffic on the bridge during the evening rush hour. (Courtesy of the Minnesota Historical Society.)

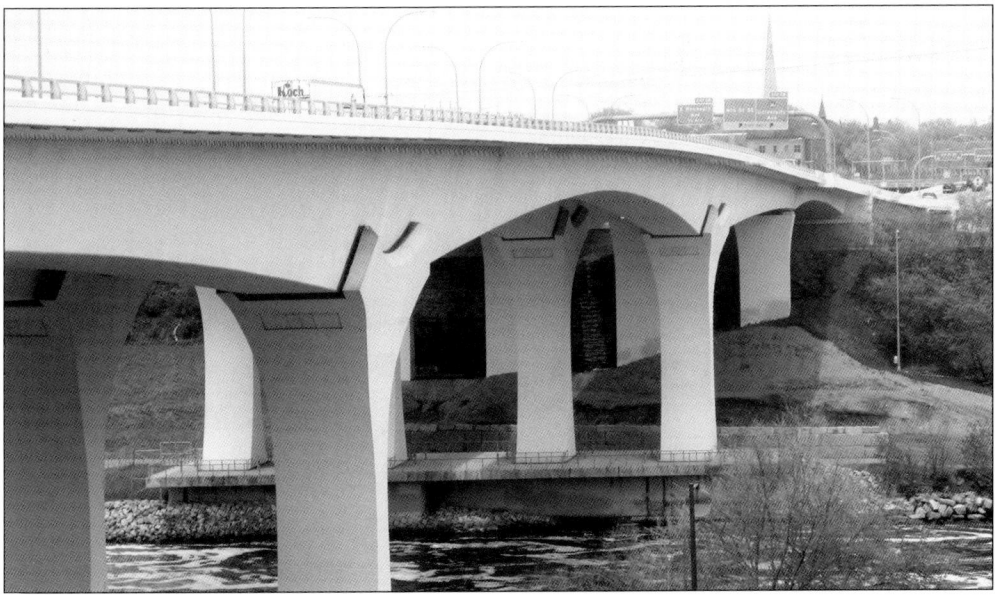

Soon after the I-35W bridge collapsed, highway officials began making plans for its replacement. The new I-35W St. Anthony Falls Bridge opened in September 2009, well ahead of schedule. The new 10-lane bridge was built with high-strength concrete and a series of sensors that measure bridge conditions, such as deck movement, stress, and temperature. (Courtesy of Meet Minneapolis Convention and Visitors Bureau.)

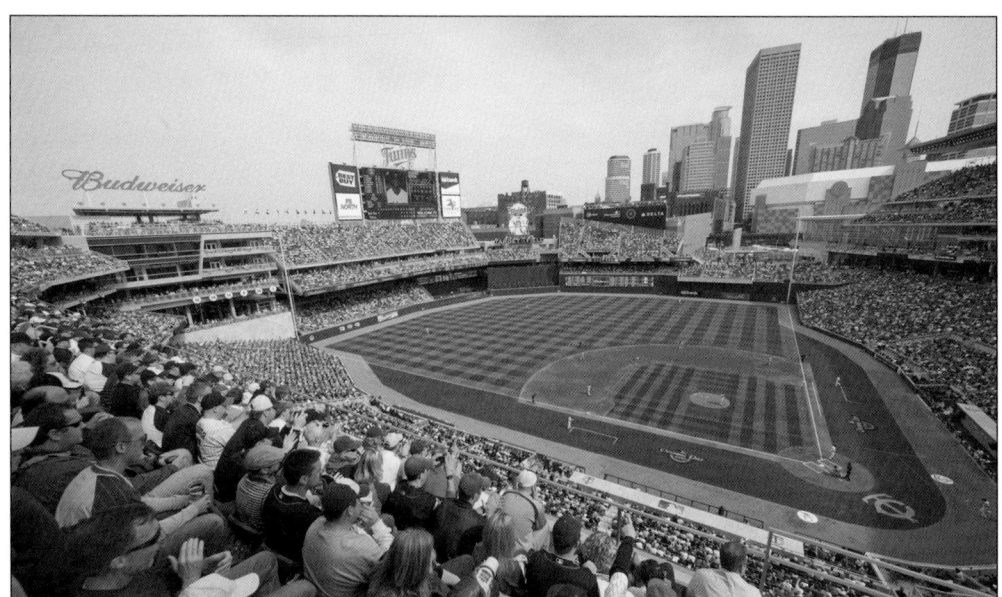

Target Field, home of the Minnesota Twins Baseball Club, opened in 2010. The low-profile stadium was designed to blend in with its warehouse district neighborhood. Unlike the climate-controlled Metrodome (the Twins' previous home), the roofless Target Field provides an open-air experience for fans. Heated seats and a canopy over the top deck help fans withstand the wintry blasts that can sweep through the ballpark at either end of the baseball season. (Courtesy of the Minnesota Twins Baseball Club.)

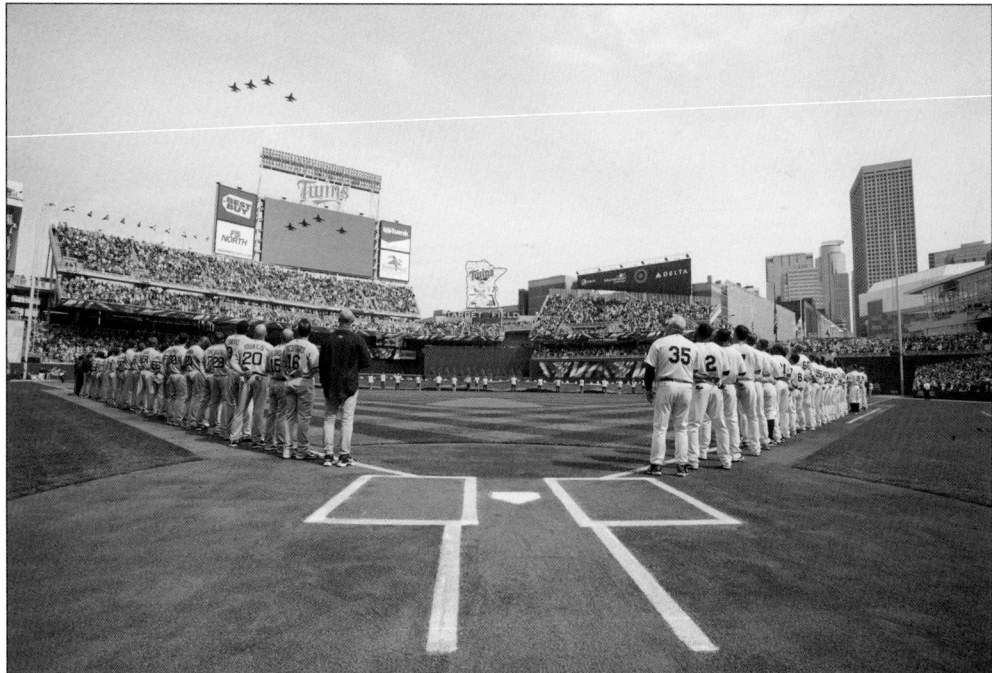

The Twins played their first regular season game in their new home on April 12, 2010. Balmy spring weather with temperatures in the 60s greeted opening-day fans who watched the Twins defeat the Boston Red Sox 5-2. (Courtesy of the Minnesota Twins Baseball Club.)

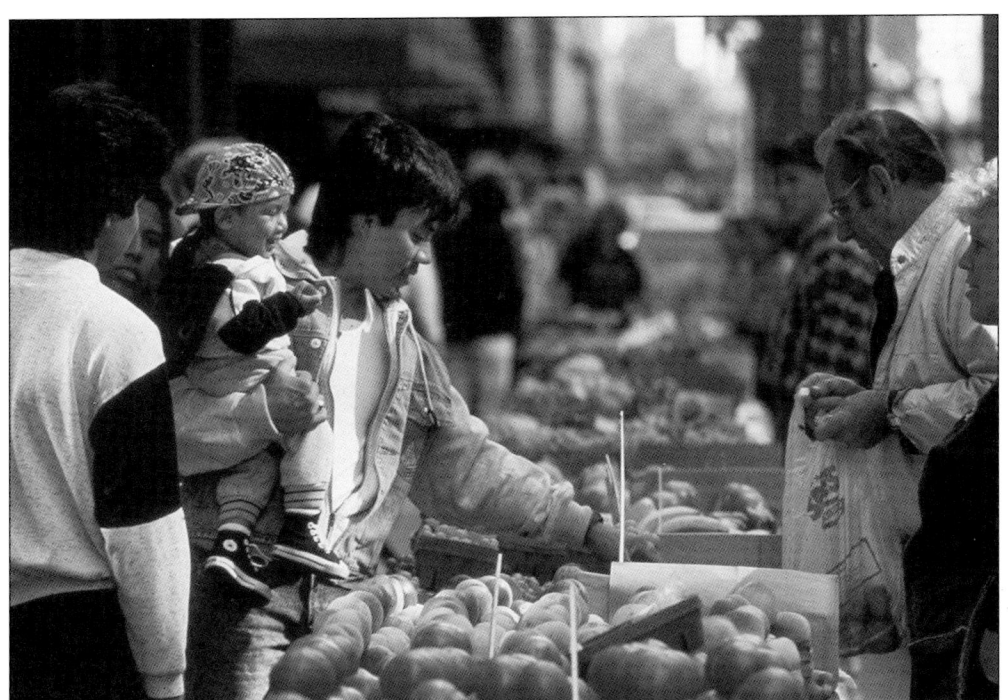

The downtown farmers' market brings fresh produce to downtown shoppers, workers, and residents every Thursday during the spring, summer, and fall growing seasons. In 2016, the market moved from its usual Nicollet Mall location to a temporary site on the Hennepin County Government Center's south plaza while the mall was being rebuilt. (Both, courtesy of Meet Minneapolis Visitors and Convention Bureau.)

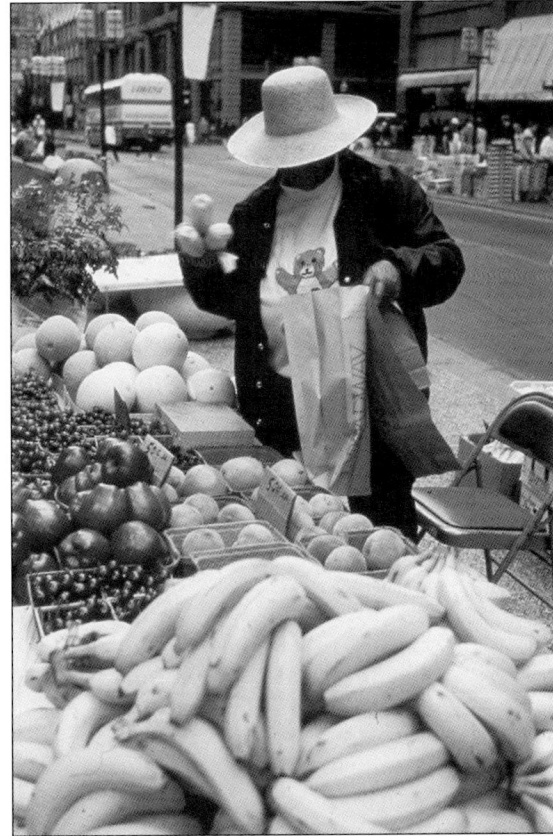

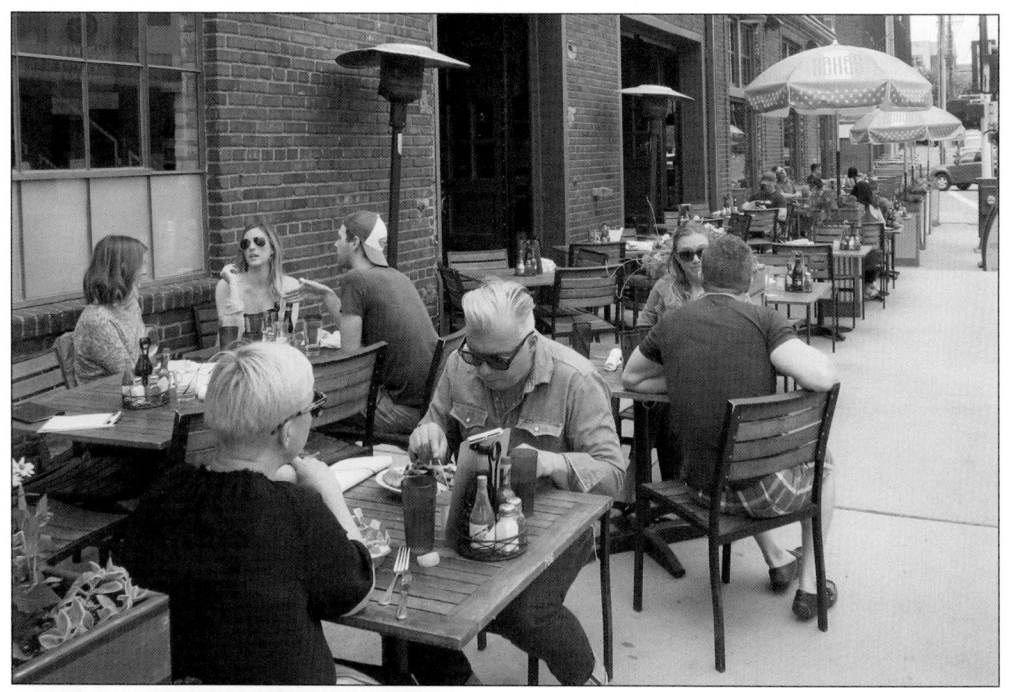

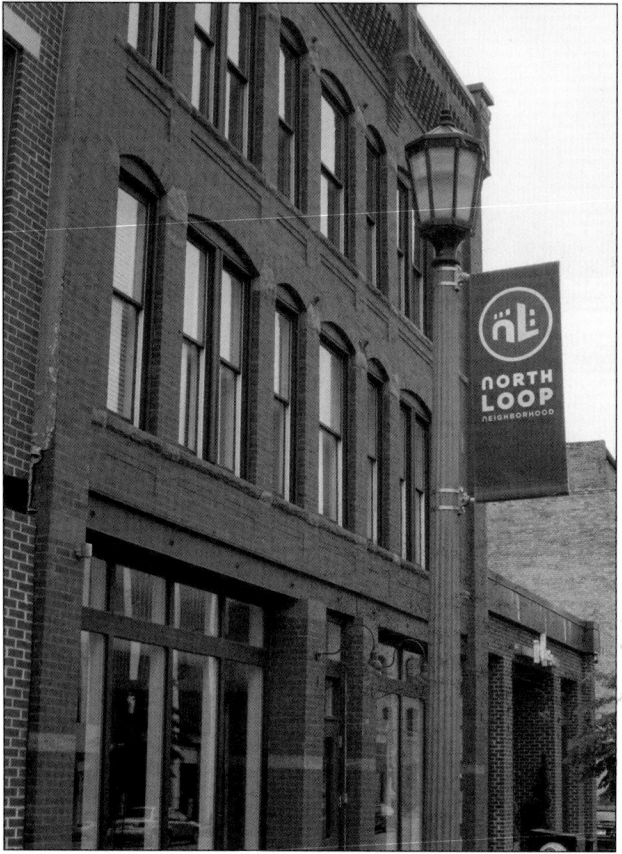

Once a quiet warehouse district, the North Loop has emerged as a thriving downtown neighborhood that attracts new residents seeking an urban living experience. The neighborhood has a mix of reconverted warehouses and ultramodern 21st-century apartment buildings and condos. Now the city's fastest-growing neighborhood, North Loop had more than 5,000 residents in 2016. (Both, author's collection.)

The fictional Mary Richards started each episode of *The Mary Tyler Moore Show* by throwing her hat in the air on the Nicollet Mall. The show, which ran on network television from 1970 to 1977, was set in Minneapolis. Now, Mary and her famous hat toss have been frozen in time with a life-size bronze statue. Mary is temporarily staying indoors at the Minneapolis Visitors Center while the Nicollet Mall is being rebuilt. She will move back outdoors on the mall when the transit way reopens in 2017. (Courtesy of Meet Minneapolis Convention and Visitors Bureau.)

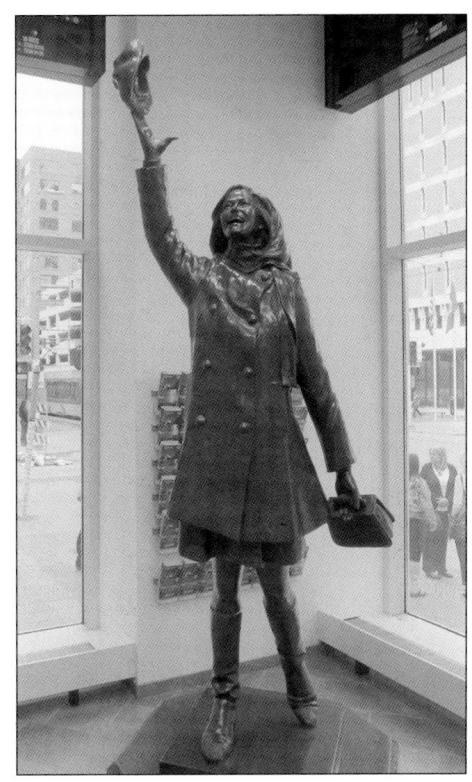

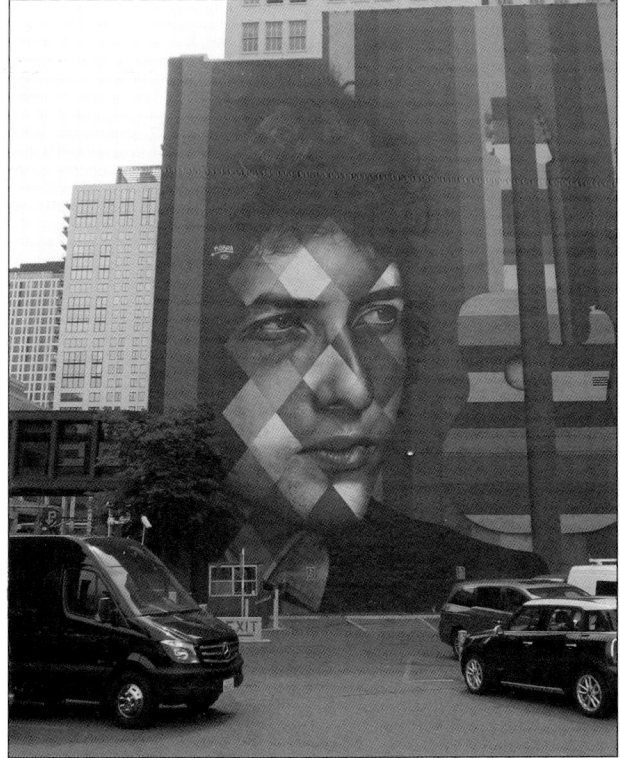

Hibbing native Bob Dylan was not always sure he wanted to acknowledge his Minnesota roots, at least early in his career, but his native state has always claimed him for one of its own. For a time in the 1950s, while he was still known as Bobby Zimmerman, Dylan appeared in coffeehouses around the University of Minnesota, just a few miles from this mural on Hennepin Avenue. (Author's collection.)

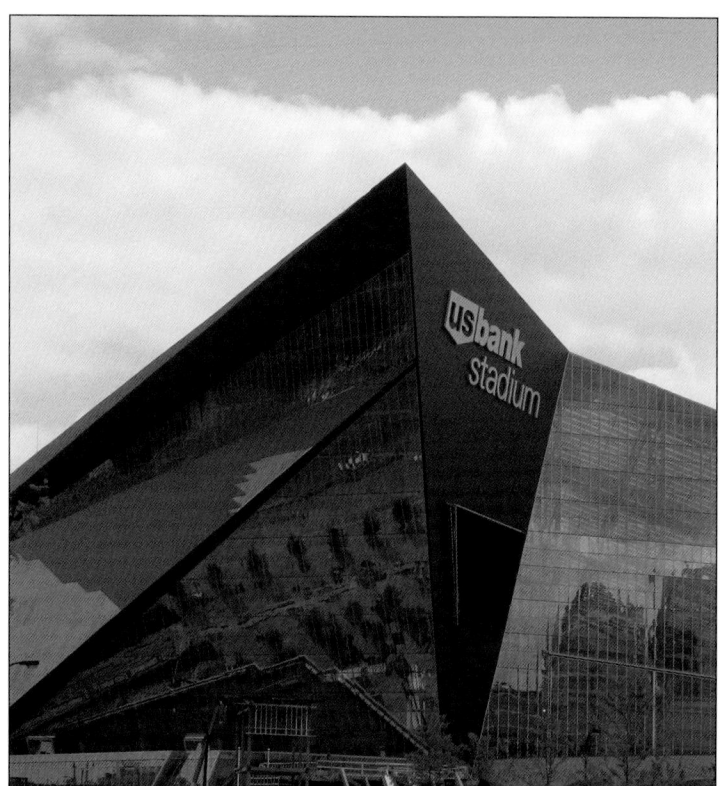

The newest addition to the Minneapolis skyline, the US Bank Stadium is now the home of the Minnesota Vikings. The stadium's dramatically sloping roof gives it the appearance of a giant spaceship about to take flight. Movable glass wall panels provide an outdoor experience for the fans when the weather cooperates. US Bank Stadium will host the 2018 Super Bowl. (Author's collection.)

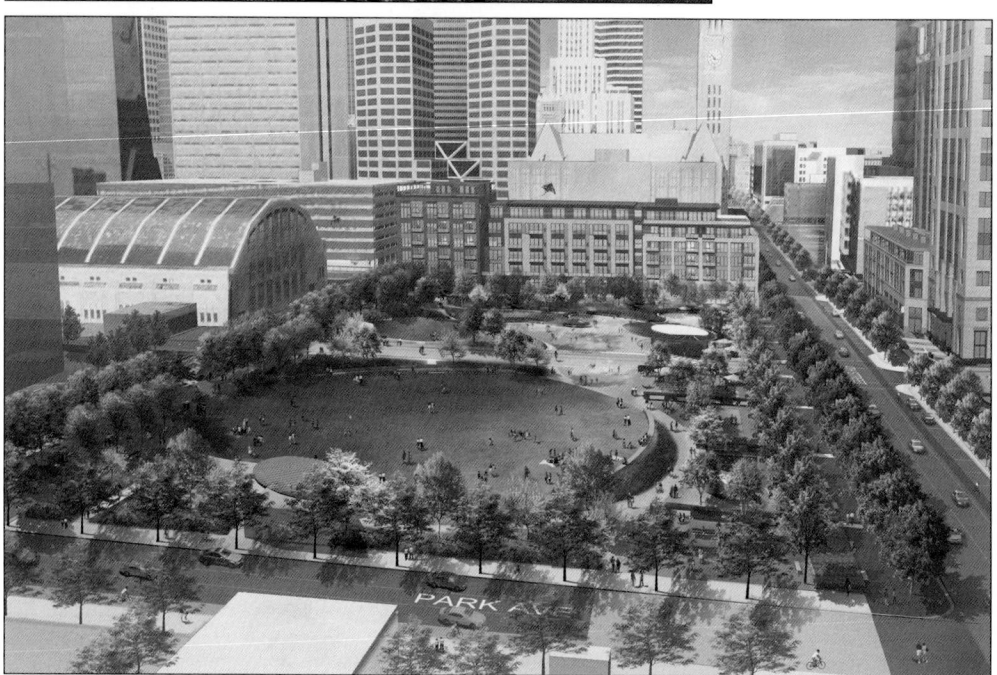

Opened in 2016, East Commons Park is downtown's newest green space. The park occupies a two-block site facing the new US Bank Stadium. The park was designed to accommodate game-day fans and serve downtown workers and residents year-round. (Courtesy of Hargreaves Associates.)

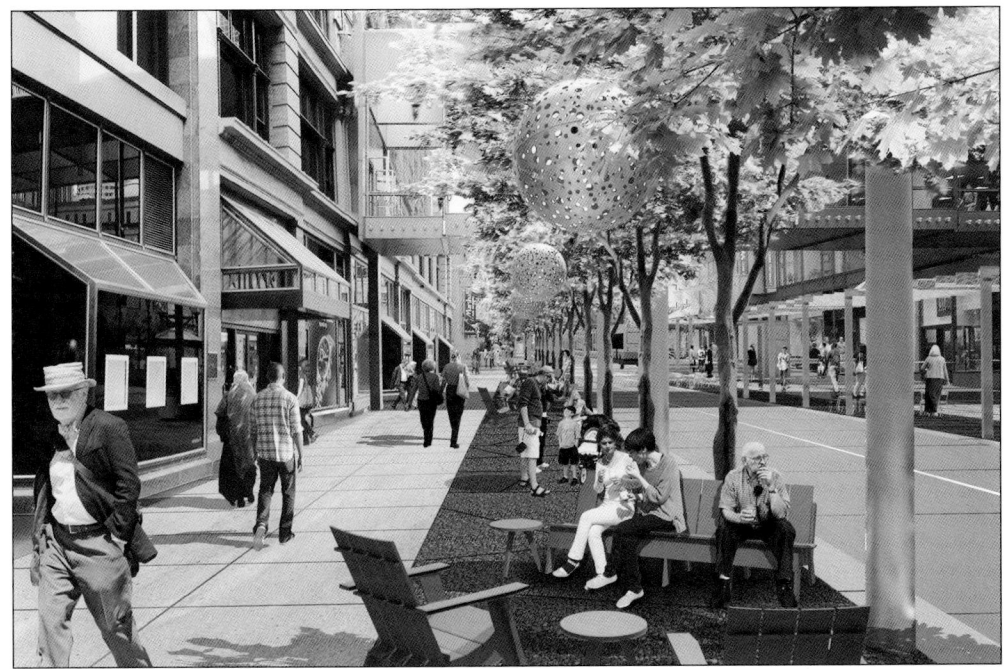

The rebuilt Nicollet Mall, under construction in 2016, aims to provide a greener, more pedestrian setting for the 12-block transit way. The $50 million project was designed by James Corner Field Operations, the urban design group best known for the High Line, New York's linear park built on the site of a former railroad line. The new Nicollet Mall is scheduled to reopen in 2017, the 50th anniversary of the original mall, built in 1967. (Both, courtesy of James Corner Field Operations.)

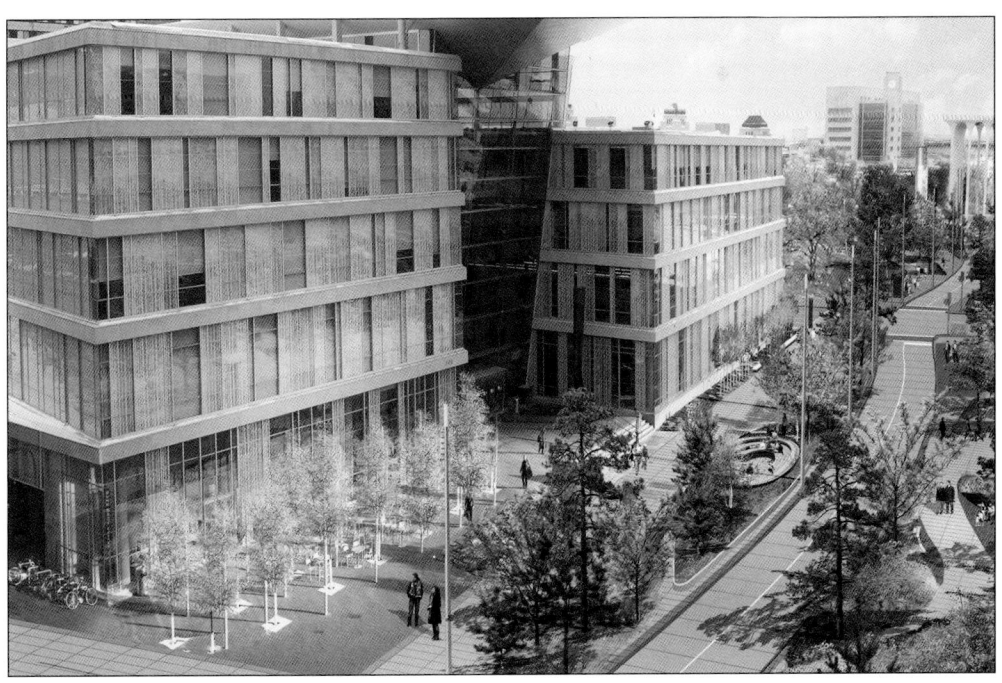

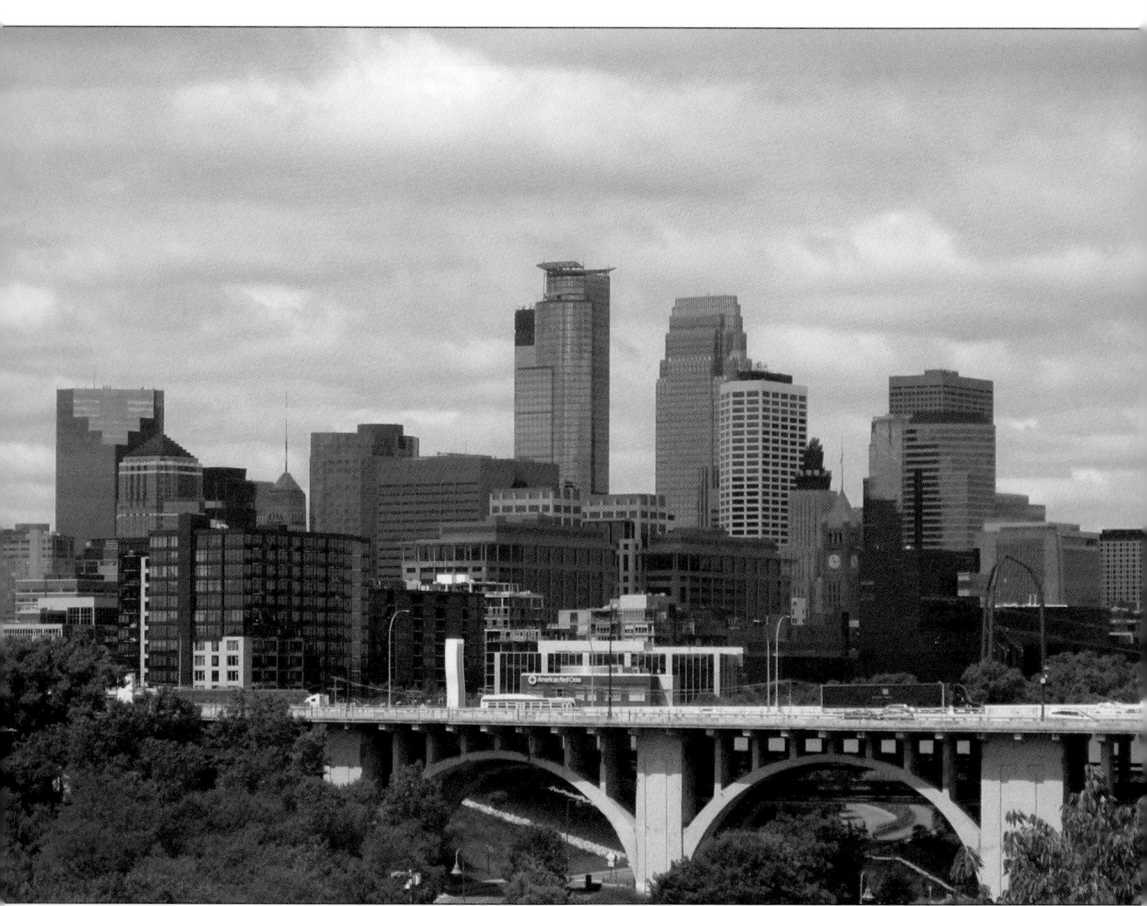
During the last half century, downtown Minneapolis has overcome the economic and cultural challenges facing many of this country's central cities. Now home to nearly 40,000 residents, downtown has emerged as one of the country's most vibrant and forward-looking urban centers. (Author's collection.)

Bibliography

Diers, John W. and Aaron Isaacs. *Twin Cities by Trolley: The Streetcar Era in Minneapolis and St. Paul*. Minneapolis, MN: University of Minnesota Press, 2007.

Hofsommer, Don L. *Minneapolis and the Age of Railways*. Minneapolis, MN: University of Minnesota Press, 2005.

Kane, Lucile. *The Falls of St. Anthony: The Waterfall That Built Minneapolis*. St. Paul, MN: Minnesota Historical Society Press, 1987.

Kenney, Dave. *Twin Cities Picture Show: A Century of Moviegoing*. St. Paul, MN: Minnesota Historical Society Press, 2007.

Millett, Larry. *AIA Guide to the Twin Cities*. St. Paul, MN: Minnesota Historical Society Press, 2007.

————. *Lost Twin Cities*. St. Paul, MN: Minnesota Historical Society Press, 1992.

Nathanson, Iric. *Minneapolis in the Twentieth Century: The Growth of an American City*. St. Paul, MN: Minnesota Historical Society Press, 2010.

————. *The Minneapolis Riverfront*. Charleston, SC: Arcadia Publishing, 2014.

Pennefeather, Shannon. *Mill City: A Visual History of the Minneapolis Mill District*. St. Paul, MN: Minnesota Historical Society Press, 2003.

Smith, David C. *City of Parks: The Story of Minneapolis Parks*. Minneapolis, MN: The Foundation for Minneapolis Parks, 2008.

Discover Thousands of Local History Books
Featuring Millions of Vintage Images

Arcadia Publishing, the leading local history publisher in the United States, is committed to making history accessible and meaningful through publishing books that celebrate and preserve the heritage of America's people and places.

Find more books like this at
www.arcadiapublishing.com

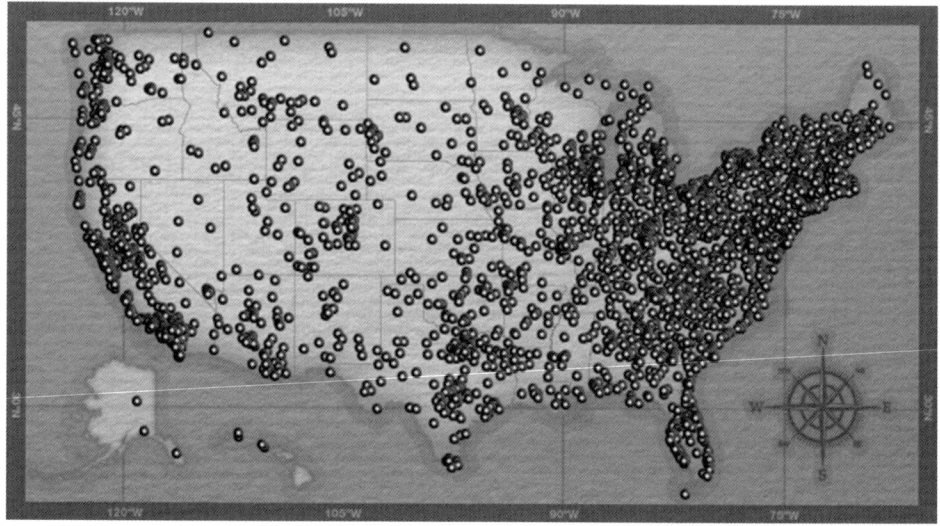

Search for your hometown history, your old stomping grounds, and even your favorite sports team.

Consistent with our mission to preserve history on a local level, this book was printed in South Carolina on American-made paper and manufactured entirely in the United States. Products carrying the accredited Forest Stewardship Council (FSC) label are printed on 100 percent FSC-certified paper.

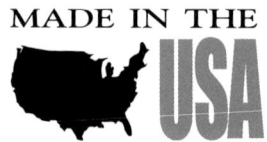

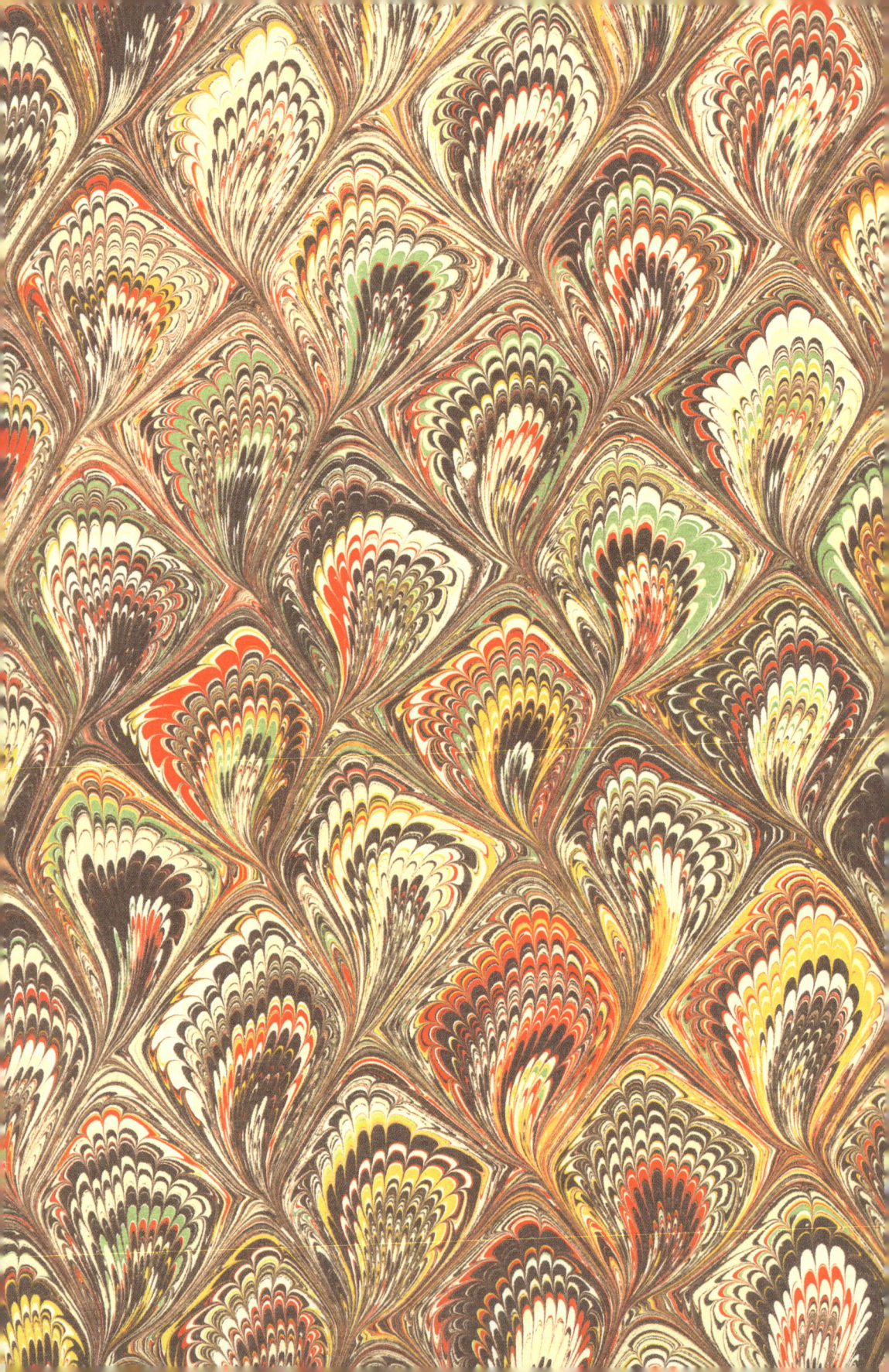